# PLINY
## the
## Younger

*Selected Letters*

### Jo-Ann Shelton

Bolchazy-Carducci Publishers, Inc.
Wauconda, Illinois USA

*Editor:* Laurel Draper
*Contributing Editor:* Bridget Dean
*Design & Layout:* Adam Phillip Velez
*Maps:* Mapping Specialists
*Cover Image:* Fresco painting from Pompeii, Italy © Shutterstock

**Pliny the Younger**
**Selected Letters**

Jo-Ann Shelton

**Bolchazy-Carducci Publishers, Inc.**
1000 Brown Street
Wauconda, Illinois 60084
www.bolchazy.com

Printed in the United States of America
**2024**
by Publishers' Graphics

ISBN 978-0-86516-840-4

Library of Congress Cataloging-in-Publication Data

Names: Pliny, the Younger, author. | Shelton, Jo-Ann, editor.
Title: Selected lett ers / Pliny the Younger ; Jo-Ann Shelton.
Description: Mundelein, Illinois, USA : Bolchazy-Carducci Publishers, Inc.,
    2016. | Includes bibliographical references, appendix, and indexes.
Identifi ers: LCCN 2015050532 (print) | LCCN 2015051395 (ebook) | ISBN
    9780865168404 (pbk. : alk. paper) | ISBN 9781610412018 (ePub and PDF)
Subjects: LCSH: Pliny, the Younger--Correspondence. | Pliny, the Younger.
Classifi cation: LCC PA6638 .A4 2016b (print) | LCC PA6638 (ebook) | DDC
    876/.01--dc23
LC record available at htt ps://lccn.loc.gov/2015050532

*To my Latin teachers, especially*

Elizabeth (Betty) A. Nicks
Cecil J. Burrows
George J. Reeve

*who inspired in me a love of the Latin language and
an abiding interest in the people who spoke it.*

# Contents

# Maps and Illustrations

## Maps

## Illustrations

# Acknowledgments

Many people assisted me in the creation of this book.

I am especially indebted to Charles Hedrick of the University of California at Santa Cruz who carefully scrutinized my manuscript and generously offered many invaluable suggestions for improving it. I was fortunate to have been the recipient of his wisdom, knowledge, and advice. He is, of course, in no way responsible for any errors or infelicities that may remain.

Several colleagues and friends also deserve my thanks for their help: Hal Drake, Dorota Dutsch, Frances Hahn, Anna Roberts, and Nathanael Troupe of the University of California at Santa Barbara, and John Rundin and David Traill of the University of California at Davis.

I am grateful to the staff of Bolchazy-Carducci, particularly Bridget Dean and Laurel Draper, who guided me so patiently in the production of this book. It has been a pleasure to work with them.

I was first introduced to Pliny's letters when I was about 14 years old. They continue to fascinate me. My interest in Latin literature was nurtured by my Latin teachers at all levels of schooling. I hope that, in turn, I have encouraged my students and, with this book, another generation of students, to find enjoyment in reading Latin authors.

Last, but certainly never least, my husband, Daniel Higgins, deserves my gratitude and love for his unwavering support.

# Abbreviations

| | | | |
|---|---|---|---|
| abl. | ablative | indef. | indefinite |
| acc. | accusative | indic. | indicative |
| adj. | adjective | interr. | interrogative |
| adv. | adverb | m. | masculine |
| c. | circa | n. | neuter |
| concess. | concessive | pers. | person, personal |
| conj. | conjunction | pl. | plural |
| dat. | dative | poss. | possessive |
| defect. | defective | prep. | preposition |
| demon. | demonstrative | pron. | pronoun |
| dep. | deponent | reflex. | reflexive |
| exclam. | exclamation, exclamatory | relat. | relative |
| | | semi-dep. | semi-deponent |
| f. | feminine | sing. | singular |
| gen. | genitive | subj. | subjunctive |
| impers. | impersonal | temp. | temporal |
| indecl. | indeclinable | | |

# Introduction

## The Life of Pliny

The man whom we know in English as Pliny the Younger was born in 61 or 62 CE. His affluent family owned several large agricultural properties in the Comum (modern Como) area of northern Italy (see Map 1). These properties were the source of the family's considerable wealth. Pliny was fondly attached to the Comum area for both sentimental and financial reasons and, throughout his life, remained proud to be identified as a northern Italian. He was, in addition, a generous benefactor to his hometown, donating funds for a school, library, public bath, and the care of children (see Letter 4.13). Roman benefactors expected their generosity to be memorialized by a grateful community. Pliny's gifts were therefore recorded and publicized by an inscription that was undoubtedly placed in a prominent location in Comum (CIL v. 5262). During the Middle Ages, the inscription was moved (for unknown reasons) to the church of St. Ambrose in Milan. Only a fragment now remains, but the text was preserved in a fifteenth-century manuscript. This preservation has been significant because, aside from the writings of Pliny himself, this inscription and three smaller fragments (CIL v. 5263, CIL v. 5667, and CIL xi. 5272) are our only sources of information about Pliny and his career. (The texts of these inscriptions are available in the Appendix of Inscriptions.)

Pliny did not begin life with the name "Pliny" (Plinius). His father's name was Lucius Caecilius, and this was undoubtedly also the name that Pliny received as an infant. Caecilius was the name of his father's family. Men who were Roman citizens had at least two names (**nomina**). The first was a **praenomen**, such as Lucius or Gaius, which corresponded to our "first" or "personal" name. The second was a **nomen gentilicium** (or **gentile**), such as Caecilius, which identified the clan or extended family group (**gens**) to which a person belonged. Many men also had a third (and even fourth) name, a **cognomen**, which identified different branches of a clan.

Women who were Roman citizens traditionally received only one **nomen**, the feminine form of their father's **nomen gentilicium**. Some women, however, also received a **cognomen**. We think that Pliny's mother's name was Plinia, which was the feminine form of the name Plinius. (See Genealogy Chart 1.) Both his paternal family and his maternal family belonged to the municipal gentry of Comum and were treated with deference by residents of lower status. From childhood, Pliny enjoyed a life of privilege but was expected to use his talents and resources to enhance the reputation of his family.

Pliny never mentions having siblings. His father died when he was a child, and his maternal uncle, Gaius Plinius Secundus, assumed an important role in raising him. Eventually his uncle adopted him and, at this point, our Pliny changed his name. It was customary for an adoptee to take the name of his adopter but to retain a reference to the family name of his natural father. Thus Lucius Caecilius became Gaius Plinius Caecilius Secundus. In English, the terms Pliny the Elder and Pliny the Younger are used to differentiate the two Plinys, uncle and nephew. In addition to receiving a new name, Pliny became heir to his uncle's substantial wealth, much of it in the form of real estate, not only in the Comum area but also throughout Italy.

Pliny may have received his primary-level education in Comum, but, as he recounts in Letter 4.13, his hometown lacked a school for more advanced studies. He was sent to Rome for what we would consider his secondary and college-level education. Among his teachers in Rome was the famous Roman rhetorician Quintilian. The focus of Pliny's education was the training required to enable him to have a successful career in law, politics, and government. No one in Pliny's northern Italian family had been a member of the Roman Senate or gained a position as a high-ranking official of the Roman state. Pliny was determined to do so. His achievement of these goals offers evidence that he was ambitious, talented, and diligent. It was impossible, however, for a man to advance far in Roman politics without the assistance of well-connected people. Pliny's uncle, who had had a distinguished career in the imperial administration, helped him, and several influential family friends who were senators advised and advocated for the younger Pliny.

In his early twenties, he began his pursuit of a seat in the Roman Senate by serving as an attorney and establishing a reputation for skillfully handling legal cases. At the same time, he received appointments to several

minor public offices, including a term, in about 81 CE, as a **tribunus militum** (military tribune). (For this and other titles, see the Vocabulary at the
end of the book.) He spent this term in the Roman province of Syria, where
his duties included auditing the financial accounts of his army unit (see
Letter 3.11). We have a record of the offices that Pliny held because of the
four ancient inscriptions mentioned above. Unfortunately the inscriptions
do not provide any dates for Pliny's terms of service. In 89 or 90 CE, he was
selected to be a **quaestor**, a public office (or magistracy) that had a term
of only one year, but which guaranteed lifelong membership in the Senate.
Pliny had been nominated for the office of **quaestor** by the emperor Domitian, an indication that he had won the emperor's favor. He continued his
climb up the political ladder with his selection as a **tribunus plebis** (tribune
of the plebs) in 91 or 92, and then, in 93 CE, as a **praetor**. Both these offices
also had one-year terms. Domitian played a role in Pliny's advancement to
the praetorship, and, after his term as a **praetor**, Pliny was appointed by
the emperor to a three-year term as a **praefectus aerari militaris** (prefect
of the military treasury).

Some of Domitian's contemporaries denounced him as a ruthless tyrant. Because Pliny was the recipient of the emperor's patronage, some
scholars have raised questions about his character. Domitian had become
emperor in 81 CE, about the same time that the young Pliny was beginning his work as a lawyer and politician. His career flourished during the
reign of Domitian. Other men, too, similarly enjoyed success in their senatorial careers. Not all senators, however, thrived under Domitian. After
Domitian's death, Pliny described the emperor who had favored him as
a monster (see Letter 4.11) and recorded stories of his persecution of his
enemies (see Letters 3.11 and 7.19). The senator and historian Tacitus, who
also outlived Domitian and wrote about him after his death, portrayed him
as a cruel ruler who did not hesitate to silence his opponents by execution or exile. His opponents, in contrast, were depicted as high-minded
men who resisted Domitian's schemes to deprive senators of their rights
and privileges, and who risked their lives to defend their beliefs. It is difficult now, two thousand years later, to ascertain the veracity or the bias
of these ancient accounts, or to grasp the motivations of either Domitian
or his opponents. Some modern historians have challenged the ancient
accounts. Citing information from Suetonius, a historian contemporary
with Tacitus and Pliny, they argue that Domitian was a capable and conscientious ruler who strengthened a flagging Roman economy, fortified the
defense of the borders of the Empire, tried to suppress corrupt behavior

among public officials, and was popular with the common people and the army. However, Tacitus's account gives scant attention to Domitian's accomplishments and instead emphasizes the antagonism between the emperor and some (though not all) members of the Senate. These senators believed that Domitian was an autocrat who refused to share with them the responsibility of shaping state policy. From the point of view of these senators, Domitian was denying them the role that senators had traditionally held. From Domitian's point of view, these senators were obstructing his attempts to establish an effective form of governing an empire. Each side became exasperated by the other's unwillingness to cooperate. When a conspiracy to overthrow him was discovered in 87 CE, Domitian thenceforth interpreted the words and activities of his opponents as treason and punished them severely. In 93 CE, several people whom Pliny claimed as friends were convicted. Some were executed, some sent into exile. (See Letters 3.11 and 7.19.) Because of the threats of punishment, the number of senators who openly expressed their hostility was relatively small.

Domitian was assassinated in 96 CE. We do not know who planned the assassination or how it might have been connected to senatorial hostility toward Domitian. The assassination was carried out not by senators but by members of the emperor's staff. Immediately after Domitian's death, however, members of the Senate rejoiced in his death and proclaimed one of their own, Nerva, as the new emperor.

Pliny's ability to gain and maintain the favor of Domitian might suggest that he had acted in a cowardly and sycophantic manner when others were putting their careers and lives in danger by criticizing the emperor. In fact, however, most of Pliny's senatorial peers had acted just as he had, vying for and serving in public offices while being very careful not to offend Domitian. Tacitus, for example, the historian whose devastatingly negative account of Domitian's reign has shaped modern opinions of that period, prospered as much as Pliny and was selected as praetor in 88 CE, the year after the conspiracy that had stiffened Domitian's resolve to destroy his enemies. Politically ambitious men like Pliny and Tacitus adopted a prudent policy of acquiescence. Most senators were unwilling to jeopardize their public and personal survival by expressing any hostility toward the emperor or any sympathy for his critics. After his assassination, however, they were quick to condemn Domitian and to try to justify their own behavior during his regime. They strove to convince one another that they had indeed made efforts to restrain Domitian and to support his more vocal opponents, but their efforts had simply gone unnoticed. For example, nowhere in his writings (composed after the assassination) does Pliny mention the prefecture of the military treasury to which Domitian appointed him in 94 CE, just a year after the executions of his friends. This information has been preserved for us only in the inscriptions discussed above. Pliny apparently wanted people to forget that he had enjoyed Domitian's favor. In fact, despite the evidence that he had prospered under Domitian, Pliny later claimed that he had supported the emperor's opponents, that his own life had been in danger in the 90s, and that he had been forced to curtail his career plans. (See the introduction to Letter 3.11.) It is important, however, to remember that he was not alone in his attempts to put a positive, and imaginative, spin on his actions. Many of his senatorial colleagues played the same game.

Although there was some turmoil in the Senate in the aftermath of Domitian's assassination, Pliny seems to have emerged unscathed. He continued to enjoy professional advancement under Domitian's successors. Nerva's tenure as emperor was short; he died of natural causes in 98 CE. Before his death, he had appointed Pliny to a three-year term as **praefectus aerari Saturni** (prefect of the treasury of Saturn). In 100 CE, under the emperor Trajan, Pliny was selected to the office of **consul suffectus** (suffect consul) for the months of September to December. During this brief term, he delivered in the Senate a speech, the *Panegyricus*, in which he praised Trajan effusively for developing a style of governing that was a complete contrast to Domitian's repressive autocracy. Indeed in the speech, which he later expanded and published, Pliny portrays Trajan as the model of an excellent emperor. (The *Panegyricus* and the *Letters* are the only writings of Pliny that are now extant.) In truth, however, even under Trajan the role of the Senate in matters of state was much more limited than it had been in the time of Cicero, over 150 years earlier. The Senate's loss of power had, in fact, begun under the first emperor, Augustus. Several of Domitian's predecessors, moreover, had also been harsh in their treatment of critics. Trajan, for his part, did not allow the senators to regain the power held by their ancestors. However, he carefully cultivated a more cordial and respectful relationship with the senators than Domitian had, and for this reason, he was revered.

About 103 CE, Pliny was granted a position as **augur**, and, about 104 or 105, he was appointed **curator alvei Tiberis** (curator of the Tiber River), a position of considerable responsibility because of the frequent flooding of the river. He also served on the prestigious emperor's council (**consilium principis**), a select group of senators with whom the emperor occasionally consulted. During this time, Pliny continued his work as a lawyer and was active particularly in the standing court that dealt with litigation about property and wills. He was also involved in several high-profile cases in the Senate, which served as a court of law to try senators indicted on criminal charges. At some time between 109 and 111 CE (the exact date cannot be determined), Trajan appointed Pliny to be governor of the province of Bithynia-Pontus, in the area of what is now northern Turkey. (See Map 3.) His official title was **legatus pro praetore consulari potestate** (legate of praetorian rank with consular power). The title **legatus** indicated that he was the emperor's direct representative in the province.

Trajan probably chose Pliny as his representative because of his expertise in some pertinent areas. For example, Pliny had served as prefect of two treasuries (see above), proved himself skillful in fiscal management, and handled court cases about property. In addition, he had been involved in several senatorial investigations of governors who had been charged with misconduct in the provinces, including two men who had been governors of Bithynia-Pontus.

Bithynia-Pontus was a prosperous province, but one plagued by financial corruption among civic officials. Pliny's assignment was to travel through the province, scrutinize the financial records of each city, uncover misadministration of funds, and reorganize public finance systems. He was also empowered to maintain public order and to hear and decide on legal cases that required a judgment by a Roman official rather than a local magistrate. During the period of about two years that Pliny served in Bithynia-Pontus, he encountered a wide range of problems, and he corresponded regularly with Trajan, reporting on events in the province and requesting advice. The letters between Pliny and Trajan form the contents of Book 10. They provide an excellent source of information about the administration of Roman provinces in the early imperial period. They demonstrate, moreover, that the emperor and his staff kept remarkably close oversight of what was happening in even the very distant regions of Rome's far-flung empire.

The correspondence ends abruptly. It is assumed that Pliny died while serving in the province.

Pliny was married three times. We don't know if the first marriage was ended by death or divorce. His second wife, about whom we know very little, died in 97 CE. His third wife, Calpurnia, was, like Pliny, a native of the Comum area. (See Genealogy Chart 1.) There is no indication that they had children. (See Letters 4.19, 6.4, 7.5, and 8.10.) She had accompanied him to Bithynia-Pontus but returned to Italy to comfort her aunt when her grandfather died. The last letters in Pliny's correspondence (10.120 and 121, not included in this volume) are a report by Pliny that he had given his wife a special travel pass to expedite her journey back to Italy, and a reply by Trajan assuring Pliny that he acted correctly in issuing the pass.

# The Letters of Pliny

The extant collection of Pliny the Younger's letters contains 368 letters, written between about 97 and about 113 CE and arranged into ten books. Books 1 to 9 consist of letters to friends, relatives, and acquaintances on a wide range of topics. Unfortunately Pliny did not include any of the replies that he may have received. Book 10 is a different kind of collection, both because of its content and because it includes the replies that Pliny received. Published probably after Pliny's death, Book 10 consists of correspondence between Pliny and the emperor Trajan. Most of the letters were composed during the period of about two years that Pliny served as governor of the province of Bithynia-Pontus. As he traveled through the province, investigating fiscal mismanagement, adjudicating legal cases, and listening to local concerns, he wrote frequently to Trajan, to keep the emperor informed of events and to solicit his advice. Pliny's questions and Trajan's responses are a major source of information about how Roman provinces were governed in the early imperial period. Much of the correspondence indicates that both the emperor and his legate strove to address the needs of the province conscientiously and fairly. Nonetheless, the letters sometimes reveal an apprehension among Roman officials about the possibility of insurrection and the need to be firm in preventing disorder. (See Letters 10.33, 34, 96, and 97.)

The letters of Books 1 to 9 were published while Pliny was alive, and he served as his own editor. They consist of letters that the upper-class Pliny wrote to people mainly in his own social circle. Most of the addressees are men, but seven are women. Because Pliny included only his own letters, his is the only "voice" present in the nine books. The letters of Books 1 to 9 offer a wealth of information about many different aspects of life in Italy during the early imperial period. More specifically, the letters document the activities, interests, and concerns of a wealthy landowner from northern Italy who had achieved the privileged position of Roman senator. They inform us about his relationships with his wife and family, his cultivation of friendships, his engagement in senatorial matters, his work in the judiciary, his investments in real estate, his ideas about slave ownership, his support for education and literary endeavors, and his participation in the deep-rooted patronage system, as both a benefactor and a beneficiary.

Letter writing was an important activity in the ancient world because there were no telephones or electronic devices with which people could communicate. In a period without motorized vehicles, moreover, a distance of just five or six miles could prevent people from meeting in person to talk. In addition, men of the senatorial class traveled frequently, both within Italy, on private or public matters, and throughout the Roman empire, on government business. Aside from messages passed on orally, letters were the only method of keeping in touch. During his lifetime, Pliny must have written (or dictated to a slave) hundreds and hundreds of letters to friends, family members, clients, business associates, property managers, fellow senators, and government officials. For a man of Pliny's status, letter writing was an essential activity, not only for conveying information, but also for establishing a social network and for gaining and maintaining political alliances. There was no state postal service except for government and military business, and therefore Pliny would have used private messengers to deliver the letters of Books 1 to 9.

Pliny is often compared to Cicero (Marcus Tullius Cicero), who lived from 106 to 43 BCE. Both men were born to nonsenatorial families, in towns outside of Rome, but succeeded in rising to the pinnacle of Roman magistracies, the consulship. Both men were actively engaged in public affairs as senators and public officials. Cicero flourished at a time when senators and magistrates still wielded enormous power, but he witnessed the decline of the state toward an autocracy. Pliny lived when the autocracy—the rule of emperors—had become established, and when senators and magistrates held much less power than their republican predecessors. (The efforts of some imperial-period senators to regain power, and their punishment by Domitian, are discussed in "The Life of Pliny" in the introduction.) Both Cicero and Pliny earned respect as orators, speaking in the courts and in the Senate. And for both there are extant collections of letters that provide information about events of the late republican period (Cicero) and the early imperial period (Pliny). There are, however, significant differences between the two collections of letters. For Cicero, we have almost nine hundred letters extant, including about ninety that were written by other people. Most importantly, the letters of Cicero were edited and published after his death. The fact that Pliny edited his own letters in Books 1 to 9 and arranged for their publication prompts questions about their nature. Most people assume that the extant letters of Cicero are copies of the very letters that Cicero sent to his addressees, and that few changes were made by the editor and publisher after Cicero's death. In the case of Pliny, however, we cannot determine whether or why or to what extent he may have made changes before publication.

In the first letter of Book 1 (Letter 1.1), Pliny announces to a friend that he has collected some of the letters that he has previously written and that he has published them. Presumably he had kept copies of the letters he sent. He also explains that he has not arranged them in the order in which he wrote them. Although we are confident that the letters were written after the assassination of the emperor Domitian in 96 CE, it has been impossible, because Pliny provides no dates, for modern scholars to establish a secure chronology for the composition of the letters or for the events mentioned in them. Of crucial importance to understanding the nature of his published correspondence is another statement in Letter 1.1: that Pliny plans to publish even more letters, either ones that he has previously written or ones that he will write in the future. The last part of this statement raises some important issues. Pliny's initial publication (perhaps Books 1 to 3) contains old letters, but the additional books contain letters that he wrote when he was fully aware that he would be publishing them, that is, putting them out for the world to read. To what extent did Pliny edit the letters before publishing them, even those in Books 1 to 3? Did he revise some passages? Delete some? Add some? And did he perhaps create some letters specifically for publication? Did he, in other words, compose a letter and send it to the addressee for the express purpose of then being able to put it in the published collection? Because Books 1 to 9 were self-published (Book 10 was published probably after Pliny's death), he was able to ensure not only that his letters would reach the public but also that the public received only the information about him that he wanted to be released.

Modern scholars have found it difficult to define the nature of Pliny's published correspondence. There is general agreement that the letters of Books 1 to 9 were sent to the addressees. However, there is debate about whether we should call them "genuine" letters if we think that they were edited before publication, and especially if we think that some of them may have been composed specifically for release to the public. An issue related to that of defining the nature of the letters is the question of why Pliny chose to self-publish them. Like many of his senatorial colleagues, Pliny hoped that he would earn a place in history and be immortalized as a man who had made positive contributions to his state. Several of his letters indicate that he hoped that his fellow senator, the historian Tacitus, would include him in the book he was writing about the events of the period in which they both lived. (See Letters 6.16 and 20.) However, because only a small portion of Tacitus's *Histories* is extant, we do not know whether he ever mentioned Pliny. Perhaps fearing that historians would neglect to record his achievements, or worse, that they would not depict them in the most flattering light, Pliny published his letters as a kind of autobiography. Self-editing and self-publication enabled him to reveal only what he wanted to reveal, to focus on events from his perspective, and thereby to manipulate public memory of his role in those events. In doing so, Pliny created a persona that he could present not only to his contemporaries in Rome but also to future generations in far distant locations. (Could he ever have imagined, however, that people living two thousand years later, on continents unknown to him, would be reading his descriptions of his activities?) One prominent aspect of Pliny's self-portrayal has been pointed to in "The Life of Pliny" in the introduction: He was eager, after the assassination of Domitian, to depict himself as having been a staunch supporter of the emperor's critics. Nowhere in the letters does he acknowledge that he owed his career advancement to the favor of Domitian and that he must have, during the reign of Domitian, behaved as a trusted supporter of the emperor. In several letters, in fact, he portrays himself as having assisted Domitian's enemies, without, however, specifying the extent or nature of the assistance. (See Letters 3.11 and 7.19.) Scholars have consequently wondered whether Pliny exaggerated or even invented the claims he makes in his letters about his involvement with Domitian's enemies in order to create a portrait of himself as a man of courage. Nonetheless it is likely that, in the aftermath of Domitian's assassination, other senators also scrambled to justify their activities while Domitian was alive and similarly told heroic stories of their behavior. Perhaps we should not be too harsh on Pliny.

Pliny wanted the self-portrait that he produced in the letters of Books 1 to 9 to show him as a good friend to Domitian's critics. There are, however, also many letters in which he shows himself to be a good friend to other people as well, providing legal, financial, political, or social advice, helping them with property investments, recommending them for positions, and consoling them on losses of loved ones. He appears as a respected orator, attorney, and statesman; a patron to younger men, supporting both their political and literary aspirations; a promoter of education; and a benefactor to his hometown and to other communities where he owned estates.

He also depicts himself as a husband who loves his wife and as a man who applauds happy marriages. Inscriptions corroborate Pliny's accounts of his willingness to contribute to community projects. As to the other elements of his self-portrait, we cannot determine whether Pliny is providing an accurate account of his character or whether he has distorted the image by including only letters that reflect positively on him. Was he truly and always a loyal friend, a generous patron, a dedicated public official, and a loving husband? Since we lack opinions from his contemporaries, we cannot know. It is useful, however, to keep in mind that the image that Pliny projects in his letters is the image that he wanted us to see. And what he wanted us to see is that he was a man of integrity, benevolence, good manners, and goodwill. He may not always have lived up to the image he created for himself (few people do), but his goal in carefully selecting his letters for publication seems to have been to be remembered by posterity as much for his kindness as for his career, as much for his compassion as for his public achievements. With reference to his goodwill, it is noteworthy that Pliny very rarely writes negatively about anyone. Indeed the only sustained targets of his condemnation are the emperor Domitian and a man named Regulus, an informer who betrayed his fellow senators to Domitian. Perhaps the most reliable insights into Pliny's character may be gained from the letters of Book 10, written while he was governor of the province of Bithynia-Pontus. Since we assume that they were published after his death, and not edited by him, they provide credible accounts of how he dealt with matters in his province. In his correspondence with Trajan, Pliny reveals that he was an industrious administrator, determined to fulfill the responsibilities assigned to him. Not all governors were so dutiful or so honorable. Some saw their overseas postings as an opportunity to enrich themselves at the expense of the residents of the province and to deal harshly with anyone who tried to curb their avarice. Indeed Pliny had participated in the senatorial investigations of at least two such governors. (Letters 2.11 and 12, and Letters 3.4 and 9, not in this collection, provide accounts of these investigations.) Pliny, in contrast, appears to have been a conscientious governor who strove to handle with fairness and sensitivity the issues brought to his attention. He was required to uphold the laws of Rome and the wishes of the emperor, but it is clear from the letters that he also kept in mind the interests, concerns, and customs of the people of the province. In many respects, the image of Pliny that emerges from the letters of Book 10 mirrors the image that Pliny strove to produce in the letters of Books 1 to 9.

# Chronology

All dates are CE

| | |
|---|---|
| c. 61 or 62 | birth of Pliny the Younger |
| 68 | death of Nero, the last of the Julio-Claudian emperors |
| 68–69 | civil war and the Year of Four Emperors |
| 69 | Vespasian becomes emperor. |
| 79 | Death of Vespasian. His son, Titus, becomes emperor. |
| | Eruption of Mount Vesuvius. Death of Pliny the Elder. |
| 81 | Death of Titus. His brother, Domitian, becomes emperor. |
| c. 81 | Pliny the Younger serves as **tribunus militum** in Syria. |
| c. 89 or 90 | Pliny is selected as **quaestor**; becomes a member of the Senate. |
| c. 91 or 92 | Pliny is selected as **tribunus plebis**. |
| 93 | Pliny is selected as **praetor**. Domitian imposes capital punishment on his opponents, among whom are friends of Pliny. |
| 94–96 | Pliny serves as **praefectus aerari militaris**. |
| 96 | Assassination of Domitian. Nerva becomes emperor. |
| 97 | Death of Pliny's second wife. |
| | Domitian's opponents, exiled in 93, return to Rome. |
| 98–100 | Pliny serves as **praefectus aerari Saturni**. |
| 98 | Death of Nerva. Trajan becomes emperor. |
| 100 | Pliny is selected as **consul suffectus** for the months of September to December. Pliny delivers his speech, *Panegyricus,* in the Senate. |

| c. 100 or 101 | Pliny marries his third wife, Calpurnia. |
| c. 103 | Pliny is appointed **augur**. |
| c. 104 or 105 | Pliny is appointed **curator alvei Tiberis**. |
| c. 109, 110, or 111 | Pliny is appointed **legatus pro praetore consulari potestate** for the province of Bithynia-Pontus. |
| c. 111, 112, or 113 | Presumed death of Pliny, perhaps in Bithynia-Pontus. |

# Note to Readers

I created this commentary to serve the needs of intermediate Latin students, whom I define as students who have completed at least one year of college Latin. I hope it will both help them expand their knowledge of Latin and also introduce them to the pleasure of reading letters that document the political and social life of the early imperial period of Rome. My intention has been to provide students with enough notes on grammar and syntax so that they do not need to spend a lot of time searching through grammar books, and so that instructors do not need to use large amounts of class time reviewing basic material. I have also included (as Index 1) a list of the grammatical and syntactical features that are identified in the notes. Students can use this index to locate the occurrences of and discussions about these features in the letters that appear in this book. Nonetheless, students should keep a grammar book ready at hand to review information and to read about constructions with which they may not be familiar. In identifying grammatical and syntactical features, I have, for the most part, used terms that are found in *Allen and Greenough's New Latin Grammar*. In some instances, students may have learned different terminology in their beginning Latin textbooks. It should be noted that I have chosen to use the term *indirect command* for the construction that Allen and Greenough refer to as *substantive clause of purpose*, and that other books variously refer to as *final noun clause, jussive noun clause, substantive clause of purpose*, or *noun clause of purpose*. My decision to use the term *indirect command* is based solely on my belief that it is the simplest to remember.

Line numbers are given in the margins to the left of the Latin text to facilitate classroom discussion and study. The Arabic numerals within the Latin text are section numbers. The commentary makes frequent reference to these section numbers; the numbers in the margins to the left of the commentary correspond to the section numbers in the Latin text.

I have kept the letters in the order in which they appear in the manuscripts. However, instructors may prefer to have students read them in an order based on thematic content. Realizing that instructors may wish to make their own arrangement of reading assignments, I have provided commentaries that are consistent in terms of comprehensiveness, that is, the number of notes does not decrease from the beginning to the end of the volume. Students who begin with letters at the end of the volume will receive the same amount of help as those who start at the beginning.

Instructors who prefer a thematic order may find the following categories useful.

| | |
|---|---|
| 1.1 | Pliny's plans to publish his letters |
| 1.11 | letter writing and friendship |
| 1.6, 1.15, 6.34, 9.6, 9.36 | leisure activities and literary endeavors |
| 1.21, 3.14, 8.16 | slave ownership |
| 3.11, 3.16, 4.11, 7.19 | opposition to imperial rule, Arria and her family, the cruelty of Domitian's punishment of a Vestal Virgin |
| 4.6 | agriculture and land ownership |
| 4.13 | Pliny's generosity and support for education |
| 4.19, 6.4, 7.5, 8.10 | Pliny's wife Calpurnia |
| 5.16, 6.34, 8.5 | the death of loved ones/Roman ideals of marriage |
| 6.16, 6.20 | the eruption of Mount Vesuvius |
| 9.12 | advice to a father |
| 10.17, 10.33 and 34, 10.96 and 97 | Pliny as governor of Bithynia-Pontus |

# Suggestions for Further Reading

Carlon, Jacqueline. *Selected Letters from Pliny the Younger's* Epistulae. Oxford: Oxford University Press, 2016.

Gibson, Roy K., and Ruth Morello. *Reading the* Letters *of Pliny the Younger: An Introduction.* Cambridge: Cambridge University Press, 2012.

Gibson, Roy K., and Christopher Whitton. *Oxford Readings in Pliny the Younger.* Oxford: Oxford University Press, 2016. This volume provides a collection of essays by several scholars who examine various aspects of Pliny's life and work.

Hoffer, Stanley. *The Anxieties of Pliny the Younger.* Oxford: Oxford University Press, 1999.

Morello, Ruth, and Roy K. Gibson, eds. "Re-Imagining Pliny the Younger." Special issue, *Arethusa* 36.2 (2003). This volume contains essays by eight scholars who discuss Pliny's literary style.

Morello, Ruth, and A. D. Morrison, eds. *Ancient Letters: Classical and Late Antique Epistolography.* Oxford: Oxford University Press, 2007. Essays in this volume address the issue of why and how people in the ancient world wrote letters. Of particular interest to students of Pliny are "What is a Letter?" by Gibson and Morrison, "Confidence, *Invidia* and Pliny's Epistolary Curriculum" by Morello, and "The Letter's the Thing" by Fitzgerald.

Shelton, Jo-Ann. *The Women of Pliny's Letters.* London; New York: Routledge, 2013.

Sherwin-White, A. N. *The Letters of Pliny: A Historical and Social Commentary.* Oxford: Oxford University Press, 1962. Readers are encouraged to consult this book, which is an excellent resource for information about the historical, political, and social environment in which Pliny lived and wrote.

# ITALY AND SICILY

0 50 100 Miles
0 50 100 Kilometers

Comum

Mediolanum
(Milan)

Verona

Padus (Po) R.

Rubicon
River

Florentia

Pisae

Arno R.

ETRURIA
(TUSCANY)

Tiberis R.

Roma

Ostia

LATIUM

CAMPANIA

Neapolis

Pompeii

CORSICA

*Mare*
*Adriaticum*

ILLYRICUM
DALMATIA

SARDINIA

*Mare*
*Tyrrhenum*

Aetna (Etna)

SICILIA

Syracusae

AFRICA

*Mare*
*Mediterraneum*

# CENTRAL ITALY

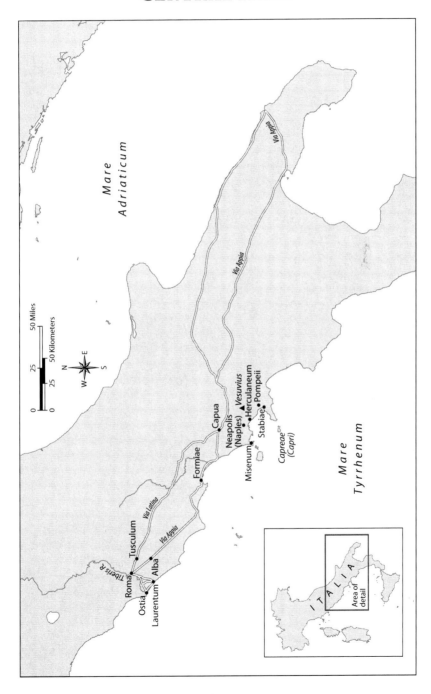

# GREECE AND ASIA MINOR

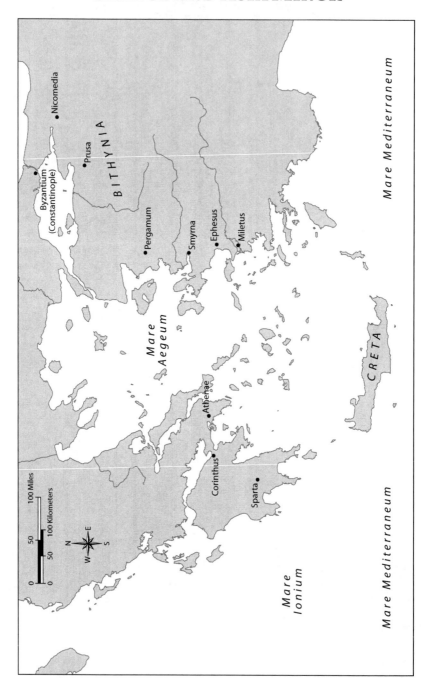

# The Letters
# of Pliny

# 1. Letter 1.1

I n Letter 1.1, Pliny explains to his addressee, Septicius, his plans for publishing some of the letters he has written. He claims that he is following his friend's advice because Septicius had frequently urged him to publish letters that were particularly well composed. He reveals that he will not be arranging the letters in the order in which they were written, but rather in the order in which he is able to retrieve them. He also states that he reserves the right to add to the collection letters that he may write in the future. On the issues of why Pliny released his letters to the public and whether he edited them before publication, see "The Letters of Pliny" in the introduction to this book.

---

C. PLINIUS SEPTICIO SUO S.

1 Frequenter hortatus es, ut epistulas, si quas paulo curatius scripsissem, colligerem publicaremque. Collegi non servato temporis ordine (neque enim historiam componebam), sed ut quaeque in manus venerat.

---

**C. Plinius Septicio Suo S.:** Pliny uses this same form of salutation for all the letters of Books 1 to 9.

**C.:** an abbreviation for Pliny's **praenomen, Gaius.**

**Septicio:** dative of **Septicius**, the man to whom Pliny addresses this letter. The case is dative because **Septicio** is the indirect object of the (understood) verb **dat.**

**Suo** is in the dative case, modifying **Septicio:** *to his (dear friend) Septicius.* Latin sometimes gives the possessive adjective the additional meaning of *dear friend.* Compare **nostri** in Letter 3.11, Section 1.

**S.:** an abbreviation for the noun, **salutem** (in the accusative case), *greeting.* The verb **dat** is understood: *gives* or *sends greeting(s).* (**Dat** is third person singular, present active indicative of **do, dare.**)

1 **hortatus es:** deponent verb: *to urge, encourage.* Supply **me** as a direct object.

**ut:** Translate as *that (I collect and publish)* or, less literally, *to (collect and publish).* The conjunction here introduces a construction that takes the subjunctive mood. The term used to identify the construction differs, depending on the grammar book used. It is variously called *indirect command, final noun* *clause, jussive noun clause, substantive clause of purpose,* or *noun clause of purpose.* In this commentary, the term *indirect command* will be used to identify this construction. Pliny is reporting, that is, stating indirectly, a command that his addressee issued directly: *Collect and publish!*

**epistulas:** the direct object of **colligerem** and **publicarem**.

**si:** *if.* The conjunction introduces a conditional clause.

**quas (indef. adj.):** *some, any.* The more common form of the indefinite adjective is **aliqui, aliqua, aliquod**, but **qui, qua, quod** are used after the conjunctions **si, nisi,** and **ne. Quas** is feminine plural in agreement with **epistulas**. It is the direct object of **scripsissem**.

**curatius:** comparative adverb: *more carefully.*

**scripsissem:** first person singular, pluperfect active subjunctive of **scribere**. The subjunctive here does not denote (as one might expect) a past contrary to fact condition. Instead, the subjunctive denotes a customary or frequent action in a general condition. This usage is not common.

**colligerem, publicarem:** first person singular, imperfect active subjunctive. The subjunctive mood is required because **colligerem** and **publicarem** are the verbs of an indirect command introduced by **ut**. On this construction, see the note above.

**-que:** an enclitic particle attached to the end of a word. It connects this word with a previous word or phrase. It is an alternative for **et**. Translate as *and.* Thus **colligerem publicaremque = colligerem et publicarem**.

**Collegi:** Supply **epistulas** as a direct object.

**servato ... ordine:** ablative absolute.

**tempus, -oris (n.):** *time.* Pliny is here saying that he has not published the letters in the chronological order in which they were written. On the problems of establishing dates for the letters, see "The Letters of Pliny" in the introduction to this book.

**enim:** *for.* The conjunction **enim** is postpositive, that is, it is placed after the first word of its clause, although in English we put *for* as the first word.

**ut:** *as.* Contrast the use of **ut** here with the indicative mood, and above with the subjunctive.

**quisque, quaeque, quidque:** *each one.* **Quaeque**, the subject of **venerat**, is feminine because it agrees with an understood **epistula**.

**manus:** *hands.* Supply **meas**.

**venerat:** We do not know how the letters had come into Pliny's hands. Perhaps he had kept copies of the letters he had sent or perhaps the recipients had returned the letters to him.

## 2 Superest ut nec te consilii nec me paeniteat obsequii. Ita enim fiet, ut eas, quae adhuc neglectae iacent, requiram et, si quas addidero, non supprimam. Vale.

---

2    **supersum, -esse, -fui, -futurus:** *to remain, be left.* **Superest** is being used as an impersonal verb, *it remains*, followed by a subjunctive clause introduced by **ut**. The **ut** construction is a noun (or substantive) clause of result. The entire **ut** clause expresses what will *result* or happen.

**paeniteat:** another impersonal verb, here in the subjunctive mood in the **ut** clause. The meaning of **paeniteat** is *it grieves, makes sorry.* The personal pronouns **te** and **me** are the direct objects.

The cause of the "grieving" is put in the genitive case, hence **consilii** and **obsequii**.

The meaning of the clause is *that it neither grieves you (makes you sorry) of advice, nor grieves me of compliance.* A less literal translation is *that neither you regret your advice, nor I regret my compliance.*

**fio, fieri:** *to happen, come to pass.* **Fiet** is third person singular, future active indicative. Here it is used impersonally and is followed by another noun (or substantive) clause of result introduced by **ut**.

**eas:** direct object of **requiram**; feminine plural accusative because it agrees with an understood **epistulas**.

**qui, quae, quod:** *who, which.* **Quae** (feminine nominative plural) is the subject of the relative clause whose predicate is **iacent**. The antecedent of **quae** is **eas**.

**neglectae:** perfect passive participle, feminine plural nominative, of **neglegere**.

**requiram:** first person singular, present active subjunctive of **requirere**. It is the first verb of the **ut** clause (noun clause of result).

**quas:** indefinite adjective used with **si**. See the note above on **quas**.

**addidero:** first person singular, future perfect active indicative of **addere**.

**supprimam:** first person singular, present active subjunctive of **supprimere**. It is the second verb of the **ut** clause. Supply **eas** as a direct object.

Pliny's statement here is evidence that he published his letters in several volumes, at several different times.

**Vale** is second person singular, present active imperative of **valere**. Here it means *farewell, goodbye.* Pliny closes all his letters thus.

This commemorative Italian stamp, issued on the 1900th anniversary of the birth of Pliny the Younger, celebrates his legacy as a Roman states-man and author. The image on this stamp is a photo of one of two stat-ues that are displayed on the façade of the Cathedral of Santa Maria in Como, the town in northern Italy that Pliny considered his hometown. (The other statue is a representation of Pliny the Elder.) The statues were created during the late fifteenth century CE and are the product of the artist's imagination, rather than historically accurate portraits. We do not know anything about Pliny's appearance. There are no surviving artistic depictions or literary descriptions of him done by any of his contemporaries. (© Shutterstock Images LLC)

# 2. Letter 1.6

Pliny owned many acres of agricultural land throughout Italy. These
farms were a major source of his wealth, and he visited them occasionally to make sure that they were being managed profitably.
Although other landowners enjoyed hunting when they visited their country estates, this activity was of little interest to Pliny, as the following letter
reveals. The letter is addressed to the famous Roman historian Cornelius
Tacitus, whom Pliny considered a friend. (For more information about
Tacitus, see "The Life of Pliny" in the introduction.) Here, Pliny relates an
amusing anecdote about his hunting experience. He apparently wanted
to indicate to Tacitus that he found pleasure in literature and intellectual
stimulation, not in rural diversions.

---

C. PLINIUS CORNELIO TACITO SUO S.
1 Ridebis, et licet rideas. Ego Plinius ille, quem nosti,
apros tres et quidem pulcherrimos cepi. "Ipse?" inquis.
Ipse; non tamen ut omnino ab inertia mea et
5   quiete discederem. Ad retia sedebam; erat in proximo
non venabulum aut lancea, sed stilus et pugillares;
meditabar aliquid enotabamque, ut, si manus vacuas,
plenas tamen ceras reportarem.

---

1    **licet:** *it is allowed (that), permitted (that).* **Licet** is an impersonal verb, followed
by the subjunctive (as here, without an introductory **ut**) or by an infinitive.
Compare the use of **licebit** in Section 3.

**rideas:** second person singular, present active subjunctive, following **licet**.

**quem:** masculine singular accusative because it is the direct object of **nosti**.
Its antecedent is **Plinius ille**.

**nosco, -ere, novi, notum:** present tense: *to learn (about),* perfect tense: *to
have learned (about)* and therefore *to know.* **Nosti** is a contraction (syncopa-
tion) of **novisti**, second person singular, perfect active indicative.

The meaning of the clause is *I, that Pliny whom you know* (and would not
expect to go hunting).

**pulcherrimos:** superlative form of the adjective **pulcher**.

**"Ipse?"**: modifying an understood **tu**: *you yourself.* Pliny imagines that the addressee of the letter, Tacitus, is asking the question.

**inquis**: *you say, you exclaim.* **Inquis** is second person singular, present active indicative. The verb is defective, that is, it is missing many forms of conjugation.

**Ipse**: *(yes) I myself.*

**ut**: *so that*, introducing a result clause with the subjunctive.

**discederem**: first person singular, imperfect active subjunctive of **discedere** in the result clause introduced by **ut**. Pliny is stating that, although he participated in a hunting party, he did not totally depart from (abandon) his usual (and preferred) leisure activities: reading and writing.

**ad (+ acc.)**: usually means *toward*; here it means *at* or *near.*

**rete, -is (n.)**: *hunting net.* When wealthy landowners hunted, they did not pursue the animals. Instead, farmworkers stretched nets in a central location and then drove the animals into the nets. The "hunters" stood or, like Pliny, sat near the nets and killed the animals that were entangled in them. For many Romans, the pleasure of a hunt was the kill, not the pursuit.

**erat**: The verb is singular although there are several subjects.

**in proximo**: *in the nearest* (position), *in the immediate proximity.* The adjective is being used as a substantive. Compare the use in Letter 4.19, Section 3.

**pugillares, -ium (m. pl.)**: *writing tablets.* The Romans wrote on tablets made of wood covered with wax into which they inscribed the letters with a **stilus**, an instrument that had a pointed tip. See the image on page 65.

**meditabar**: first person singular, imperfect indicative of the deponent verb **meditari**.

**ut**: here introducing a purpose (final) clause with the subjunctive. The verb of the purpose clause is **reportarem**.

**si**: introducing the protasis of a future less vivid condition whose verb is not expressed, but is implied by the appearance of **reportarem**. **Manus vacuas** is the direct object of the implied verb: *even if* (I should bring back) *empty hands* (i.e., come home without a dead animal).

**plenas . . . ceras**: *full wax tablets.* He will come home with the notes he has made on his wax tablets. Note the careful juxtaposition of **vacuas - plenas**, *empty - full.* Compare Letter 9.36, Section 6, about returning from a hunt with a literary composition.

**reportarem**: first person singular, imperfect active subjunctive in the purpose (final) clause introduced by **ut**. The tense is imperfect because the sequence is secondary (historic).

2 Non est quod contemnas hoc studendi genus;
10    mirum est, ut animus agitatione motuque corporis
      excitetur; iam undique silvae et solitudo ipsumque illud
      silentium, quod venationi datur, magna cogitationis
      incitamenta sunt. 3 Proinde, cum venabere, licebit
      auctore me ut panarium et lagunculam sic etiam
15    pugillares feras; experieris non Dianam magis
      montibus quam Minervam inerrare. Vale.

---

2    **Non est quod:** *There is no reason why* (or *because of which*). The phrase implies
     a category or group characteristic that the clause that follows does not share.
     Thus the construction that follows is a form of relative clause of characteristic
     and therefore requires a subjunctive, **contemnas**.

     **studendi:** a gerund in the genitive case, formed from **studeo, -ere, -ui:** *to
     pursue, be busy with, apply oneself to.* Here it means *pursuing, keeping busy,* or
     less literally, *pursuit.*

     **ut:** *how.* The construction is a form of indirect exclamation, which uses the
     same construction as an indirect question and therefore requires a subjunc-
     tive, **excitetur.**

     **excitetur:** third person singular, present passive subjunctive of **excitare.** The
     subject is **animus.**

     **silvae et solitudo . . . silentium:** the subjects of **sunt,** which appears at the
     end of the sentence. Note the alliteration.

     **ipsumque:** the enclitic particle **-que. Ipsum** modifies **silentium.**

     **venationi:** in the dative case after **datur,** *is given, granted to.* The implication
     is that hunting requires silence.

     **cogitationis:** objective genitive.

3    **venabere:** the second person singular, future indicative of the deponent verb
     **venari.** (There also exists an alternative form: **venaberis.**)

     **licebit:** future indicative of the impersonal verb **licet,** which is followed by
     **ut** and the subjunctive, **feras.** In Section 1, **licet** was not followed by **ut.**

     **auctore me:** Both words are in the ablative case, in an ablative absolute con-
     struction. However, there is no participle in this instance (because Latin did
     not use a present participle of the verb **esse**). The phrase means *with me (be-
     ing) your advisor* (or *model*). Or translate as *with me as your advisor* (or *model*).

**ut ... sic etiam:** Here **ut** is used in a correlative construction: *not only ... but even.*

**feras:** second person singular, present active subjunctive of **fero, ferre, tuli, latum,** *to carry, take.* The subjunctive is required by **licebit.** The phrase means *it will be permitted that you carry,* or *you may carry.*

**experieris:** second person singular, future indicative of the deponent verb **experiri.** It introduces an accusative infinitive construction in indirect statement. The accusative subjects are **Dianam** and **Minervam.** The infinitive is **inerrare.** Diana was the goddess of hunting; Minerva was the goddess of intellectual endeavors.

**non ... magis ... quam:** *not more than.*

**montibus:** an ablative of place without a preposition.

# 3. Letter 1.11

In this era in which we have many choices of electronic instruments with which we can communicate almost instantaneously with people in almost every region of the world, it is difficult to imagine a period in which there were few ways to communicate with someone absent from us. However, the telegraph came into use comparatively recently, about 1830, the telephone about 1875. Until then, letters or messengers were the only means of keeping in touch with those from whom you were physically separated. And people were frequently separated because a distance of even ten miles was considerable before the age of motorized vehicles. Businesses, governments, and armies utilized letters to convey vital information, and individuals used letters to share personal news. However, letters were also used as a method of fostering and maintaining friendships and alliances at a time when they were the only substitute for meeting in person.

In this letter, Pliny chides the addressee, Fabius Justus, for not having written to him. Fabius Justus was, like Pliny, a senator.

---

C. PLINIUS FABIO IUSTO SUO S.

1 Olim mihi nullas epistulas mittis. "Nihil est," inquis, "quod scribam." At hoc ipsum scribe, nihil esse quod scribas, vel solum illud, unde incipere priores solebant: "Si vales, bene est; ego valeo." Hoc mihi sufficit; est enim maximum. 2 Ludere me putas? serio peto. Fac sciam quid agas, quod sine sollicitudine summa nescire non possum. Vale.

5

---

1 **mittis:** Latin uses the present tense to denote an action that occurred in the past but is continuing into the present. In English, we would write *You have sent.*

**Nihil est . . . quod:** *there is nothing that.* This phrase introduces a relative clause of characteristic (compare the use in Letter 1.6, Section 2), which requires a subjunctive verb, **scribam.** The relative pronoun **quod** is the direct object of **scribam.**

**scribam:** The meaning here is *I can write.*

**hoc ipsum:** *this very thing.* **Hoc ipsum** is the first object of **scribe**.

**nihil esse:** an accusative infinitive construction in indirect statement after the imperative verb **scribe**. It serves as a second object of **scribe**, clarifying the meaning of **hoc ipsum**.

**scribas:** present subjunctive for two reasons: It is the verb in a relative clause of characteristic, and it is the predicate in a subordinate clause in indirect statement.

**solum illud:** *this one (thing).* These words are a third object of the imperative verb **scribe**.

**unde:** *from which, from where.* Translate *this one thing with which* (our forefathers were accustomed to begin their letters).

**bene est:** *it is well* (that is, *I am fine*). This formulaic phrase was occasionally used by Cicero in his letters, about 150 years before Pliny was writing.

**maximum:** *most important, greatest* (thing).

2   **Ludere me:** an accusative infinitive construction in indirect statement after the verb **putas**.

**Fac:** second person singular, present active imperative of **facere**. It is followed by a subjunctive, **sciam**, in a noun (substantive) clause of result (with no introductory **ut**). Translate *See that (make that) I know.*

**quid agas:** an indirect question following **sciam**, and therefore **agas** is present active subjunctive (of **agere**). The phrase can mean *what you are doing*, or, idiomatically, *how you are doing.*

**quod:** *because.* Here **quod** introduces a causal clause with an indicative verb.

**nescire non possum:** *I am not able to be ignorant* (of your health, activities). The meaning of this phrase is that Pliny suffers extreme anxiety if he is kept ignorant of (in the dark about) his friend's health and activities.

# 4. Letter 1.15

Letter 1.15 is addressed to Septicius Clarus. If this man is the same person to whom Pliny addressed Letter 1.1, we now learn that his **cognomen** was Clarus. (On Roman naming practices, see "The Life of Pliny" in the introduction.)

In this letter, Pliny rebukes Septicius for promising to come to dinner but not showing up. Pliny feigns anger at Septicius, but he probably intended the letter to be read with amusement. The two men remained friends, and, in Letter 2.9, Section 4 (not included in this volume), Pliny praises Septicius as a very honest and trustworthy person.

The letter provides interesting information about the foods and entertainments at the dinner parties of wealthy Romans, and also about the concern for cautious conversation.

---

### C. PLINIUS SEPTICIO CLARO SUO S.

1 Heus tu! promittis ad cenam nec venis. Dicitur ius; ad assem impendium reddes, nec id modicum. 2 Paratae erant lactucae singulae, cochleae ternae, ova bina, alica
5   cum mulso et nive (nam hanc quoque computabis, immo hanc in primis, quae periit in ferculo), olivae, betacei, cucurbitae, bulbi, alia mille non minus lauta. Audisses comoedum vel lectorem vel lyristen vel, quae mea liberalitas, omnes.

---

1    **promittis:** Understand with this verb an accusative infinitive in indirect statement: **te venturum esse**. (**Venturum esse** is a future active infinitive.)

**Dicitur ius:** *justice is pronounced.* Pliny is teasing his addressee, Septicius, and humorously declaring that he is being fined for failing to appear at the dinner that Pliny had prepared.

**ad assem:** *to the penny.* The **as** was a copper Roman coin of a very small denomination, i.e., of as little value as a penny today.

**impendium reddes:** Pliny states that Septicius will repay (will reimburse him for) the cost of the dinner. He then proceeds to list in detail all the items that were prepared. Although Pliny declares that the cost of the dinner was not insignificant (**nec ... modicum**), the dinner was, in fact, fairly modest, by the standards of the Roman upper class, to which Pliny belonged.

**id modicum:** Supply the verb **erit**. **Id** refers to **impendium**.

2    **Paratae erant:** The participle of this pluperfect passive form is feminine plural, in agreement with the nearest noun, **lactucae**. However, construe all the following nominative nouns (the names of food items), whether singular or plural, and whatever gender, with this verb.

**ova:** Eggs appeared so frequently in the first course of Roman dinners (and apples at the end) that there arose the expression **ab ovo usque ad mala,** *from the egg to the apples*, an equivalent of our expression *from soup to nuts*.

**alica:** The wheat or spelt may have been boiled to make a porridge or gruel.

**mulso:** The honey-wine (mead) may have been mixed into the wheat dish or drunk separately.

**nive:** The snow was used to cool the wine. Since it rarely snowed in Rome, even in the winter, the snow would have been brought from the mountains in the east. Hence the snow may have been the most expensive item on the dinner menu. Only wealthy people could afford to import snow for their wine.

**computabis:** *You will also add this* (to your debt or fine). **Hanc** = the snow.

**in primis:** *in particular; among the chief* (expenses).

**quae:** feminine nominative singular of the relative pronoun. Its antecedent is **hanc**, and, in turn, **nive**.

**periit:** The snow disappeared, that is, melted.

**alia mille:** Translate together. **Alia** is neuter plural: *other* (things).

**Audisses:** second person singular, pluperfect active subjunctive of **audire**. This form is a contraction of **audivisses**. The subjunctive is a potential subjunctive: *You would have heard* (if you had come). The **audisses** clause is like the apodosis of a past contrary to fact condition.

**comoedum, lectorem, lyristen:** The performers at the dinner may well have been slaves trained in various artistic skills. In Letter 5.19, Section 3 (not in this volume), Pliny reports that he has in his household a former slave who excels in comic acting, reading aloud, and lyre playing. When he read aloud for an audience, he read speeches, histories, and poetry. For more information about entertainment at Pliny's dinner parties, see Letter 9.36, Section 4.

**quae:** Supply the verb **est**. Literally: *which is my generosity*. The relative pronoun **quae** is feminine nominative singular, in agreement with **liberalitas**. In English, we would write *this is* (or *such is*) *my generosity*.

**omnes:** *all* (three entertainers).

10     3 At tu apud nescio quem ostrea, vulvas, echinos,
Gaditanas maluisti. Dabis poenas, non dico quas.
Dure fecisti; invidisti, nescio an tibi, certe mihi, sed
tamen et tibi. Quantum nos lusissemus, risissemus
studuissemus! 4 Potes adparatius cenare apud multos,
15     nusquam hilarius, simplicius, incautius. In summa
experire et, nisi postea te aliis potius excusaveris, mihi
semper excusa. Vale.

---

3    **nescio quem:** *I don't know whom*, or: *someone or other.* The preposition **apud** here means *at the home of.* Translate: *at the home of someone I don't know (someone or other).* The tone is derogatory.

**vulvas:** Sow's udder was a delicacy at Roman banquets. It might be stuffed with meat or eggs.

**Gaditanas:** *women from Gades,* a town in southwestern Spain (modern Cadiz). This word is one of the direct objects of **maluisti**. The women were apparently entertainers whose performances were of a much coarser nature than the comic actor, reader, and lyre player who entertained at Pliny's dinner. Just as Pliny contrasts the simple meal that he served with the luxurious foods served elsewhere, so too he contrasts the refined entertainment he planned with the vulgar entertainment provided elsewhere.

**Dabis poenas:** *You will pay damages (give penalties).*

**quas:** an interrogative adjective. It is feminine accusative plural because it is modifying an understood **poenas**. **Non dico quas (poenas daturus sis).** The tone is a mock threat.

**fecisti:** *you acted.*

**nescio an:** The phrase means *I do not know whether.* It is sometimes followed by an indirect question (with a subjunctive verb). Here, however, its use is adverbial: *perhaps not.*

**tibi:** The dative is required by the verb **invidisti**: *You acted hurtfully, perhaps toward yourself.*

**Quantum:** *how much!* The word is here exclamatory. The accusative singular neuter is used adverbially: *How much we would have laughed!*

**lusissemus, risissemus, studuissemus:** These verbs are first person plural, pluperfect active subjunctive in a potential subjunctive construction. Their clause is like the apodosis of a past contrary to fact condition ("if you had come").

4 **adparatius, hilarius, simplicius, incautius:** These forms are all comparative adverbs.

Pliny's statement offers insight into the social and political climate of his period. He is telling Septicius that, although the food and entertainment at his home were less elaborate than at the homes of other elite men, the evening would have been more enjoyable because Septicius would not have had to worry about what he said or what impression he was making. Pliny's comment implies that social posturing was an element of many fancy dinners and that, in addition, guests had to be very careful about expressing their opinions on current political topics. At his home, Pliny asserts, a person could speak openly, freely, and honestly.

**experire:** present imperative singular of the deponent verb **experior**. Supply **me** as the direct object: *try me* (and my dinner parties).

**excusaveris:** second person singular, future perfect active indicative. The condition is future more vivid and thus uses the indicative in the protasis.

**te aliis potius excusaveris: Te** is the direct object, **aliis** the indirect object of **excusaveris**: *if you will not afterward have excused yourself preferably* (**potius**) (or *instead*) *to other people* (who invite you for dinner).

**mihi . . . excusa:** Supply **te**: *excuse yourself to me.* Although Pliny is quite certain that Septicius would prefer his dinner parties, he tells him that, if he does not decline invitations from others (excuse himself to others), he should at least be polite and inform Pliny that he is declining *his* invitation (make excuses for himself). Pliny is annoyed that Septicius had simply failed to show up for the dinner he had prepared.

# 5. Letter 1.21

The topic of this letter is the purchase of slaves. As was true for other ancient Mediterranean societies, slave ownership was an institution in Roman society. Slaves were bought and sold like horses, oxen, or machines. We do not know whether Pliny planned to use the slaves mentioned in this letter to work on his farms or in his urban residences.

Letter 1.21 is addressed to Plinius Paternus. Although this man has the same **nomen** as Pliny, we have no evidence that they were related. Paternus was also the addressee of Letter 8.16, whose topic is also slavery.

---

C. PLINIUS PLINIO PATERNO SUO S.

1 Ut animi tui iudicio sic oculorum plurimum tribuo, non quia multum (ne tibi placeas) sed quia tantum quantum ego sapis; quamquam hoc quoque multum
5 est. 2 Omissis iocis credo decentes esse servos, qui sunt empti mihi ex consilio tuo. Superest ut frugi sint, quod de venalibus melius auribus quam oculis iudicatur. Vale.

---

1    **Ut ... sic:** a correlative construction: *not only ... but even*, or *even as ... so also.* Construe **iudicio** with both parts of the construction.

**tribuo:** This verb has several meanings, among them *to attribute, yield.* Here **iudicio** is the dative of indirect object with **tribuo.** The genitives **animi** and **oculorum** are dependent on **iudicio. Plurimum** may be considered the accusative direct object of **tribuo:** *I attribute very much (a great deal)*, that is, I grant very much respect. Alternatively **plurimum** may be considered an adverbial accusative (or internal accusative) with **tribuo:** *I very much yield*, that is, I very much grant respect. The adverbial accusative is similar in use to an adverb.

**multum ... sapis:** Construe **multum** as an adverbial accusative with **sapis:** *you know much*, or *you are much wise.*

**ne tibi placeas: Ne** with the second person singular, present active subjunctive, **placeas**, expresses a polite negative command: *Don't flatter yourself.* The dative **tibi** (here a reflexive pronoun) depends on **placeas.**

**tantum quantum:** Literally: *so much, how much*. **Tantum** (like **multum** above) is an adverbial accusative with **sapis**. **Quantum** is an adverbial accusative with an understood verb, **sapio** (of which **ego** is the subject). Literally: *You know so much* (**tantum . . . sapis**), *how much I* (**quantum ego**—understand **sapio**). Less literally: *You know as much as I know.*

**hoc:** *This is much,* that is, a significant accomplishment. By **hoc**, Pliny means *Your knowing as much as I know.* Pliny is attempting to be funny.

2   **Omissis iocis:** ablative absolute construction.

**credo:** The verb introduces an accusative infinitive construction in indirect statement. The accusative subject of the construction is **servos**; the infinitive predicate is **esse**.

**decentes:** an accusative masculine plural agreeing with **servos**. **Decens** can denote good physical appearance and/or good moral behavior. Since Pliny is writing about slaves and his trust in the judgment of his friend's eyes, he is here referring to his friend's ability to assess the physical suitability of the slaves for the jobs to which Pliny will assign them. For example, a slave who appears strong would be suitable for physical labor.

**sunt empti:** We now learn that the slaves have already been purchased by Pliny on the advice of his friend. **Mihi** is a dative of agent, a construction less common than the ablative of agent.

**Superest ut:** For this construction, see the note for Letter 1.1, Section 2.

**frugi:** *useful, honest.* The form is the dative of **frux**, but the word is treated as an indeclinable adjective. Thus here it modifies the understood nominative plural subject of **sint**: **servi**.

**quod:** *because.* Here **quod** introduces a causal clause with an indicative verb.

**venalis, -is (m. and f.):** *slave.* The root meaning of this word is *something that can be bought and sold.* The verb **veneo, venire** means *to be for sale.* Compare Letter 10.96, Section 10.

**auribus, oculis:** ablatives of means. Pliny had praised his friend's ability to assess the physical suitability of a slave by looking at him, but he now remarks that judgments are better made on the basis of what one hears than what one sees. Most of the slaves whom Pliny owned would be under the direct management of a foreman or superintendent (who might also be a slave). Pliny would be dependent on hearing from him whether the slaves had proved to be useful.

**iudicatur:** The subject of this passive verb is impersonal: *it is judged.* Or translate as *one judges (passes judgment).*

# 6. Letter 3.11

D omitian was emperor from 81 to 96 CE, in which year he was assassinated. Many members of the senatorial class disliked his autocratic
style of ruling and resented his measures to deprive them of influence in public affairs. Only a few senators, however, were openly critical of
Domitian, and they and their families suffered for their hostility. Prosecuted
for treason, they were executed or sent into exile. The majority of senators,
wanting to preserve their lives and political careers, concealed their animos-
ity toward Domitian and adopted a policy of acquiescence. It was a time of
anxiety, when the emperor's spies were quick to report any disparaging remarks. However, once Domitian had been assassinated, everyone wanted
to justify his own actions during the reign of terror and to show that he had,
despite the appearance of supporting the emperor, sympathized with and assisted those who were prosecuted. Pliny, for example, had enjoyed a successful political career under Domitian, rising to the rank of **praetor**. (See "The
Life of Pliny" in the introduction to this book.) In Letter 3.11, he describes
to his addressee, Julius Genitor, a teacher, how he took great personal risks to
help Artemidorus, a philosopher who was one of Domitian's critics.

It is not surprising that Pliny chose to publish this letter and thereby
make widely known an incident about which most Romans would not have
known. The letter is a very carefully crafted exercise in self-justification. The
rhetorical complexity of the letter (which may challenge Latin students!)
indicates that Pliny devoted great effort to constructing this account of his
character. (On Pliny's creation of a self-portrait, see "The Letters of Pliny"
in the introduction to this book.) The opening and close of the letter suggest
that its topic is Artemidorus, but Pliny adroitly shifts the focus to himself.
He claims, with feigned modesty, that it is Artemidorus who is spreading
the story that Pliny acted bravely. Pliny implies that, although Artemidorus
may have exaggerated a bit, the account is essentially true, and that we can
trust Artemidorus because he is such an honorable man.

The seven people mentioned in Letter 3.11 as having been executed or
exiled were considered by the emperor Domitian to be a threat to his regime. They and their families had been friends for several decades and had
sustained a resistance to what they believed was Domitian's determination
to destroy the power and dignity of the senatorial class. They maintained
that they were fighting for **libertas**, for the right to speak freely. For his part,
Domitian viewed them as dangerous subversives. The date of their executions and exiles, and of Pliny's praetorship, was probably 93 CE.

## C. PLINIUS IULIO GENITORI SUO S.

1 Est omnino Artemidori nostri tam benigna natura, ut
officia amicorum in maius extollat. Inde etiam meum
meritum ut vera ita supra meritum praedicatione
5    circumfert.

---

1    **Artemidori:** genitive case (possessive genitive) of the proper name
Artemidorus. He was a Stoic philosopher from Syria.

**nostri:** *of our* (supply *friend* or *dear*) Artemidorus. Latin sometimes gives the
possessive adjective the additional meaning of *dear friend*. Compare the note
about **suo** in the salutation to Letter 1.1.

**natura:** nominative case as the subject of **est**.

**ut (conj.):** *so that*, introducing a result clause with the present active subjunctive, **extollat**.

**in maius:** Literally *into the greater*; less literally *into something greater*. Pliny
is suggesting that Artemidorus regularly exaggerates the kindnesses of his
friends.

**meum meritum:** the direct object of **circumfert**.

**meritum:** This word is formed from the perfect passive participle of **merere**
and means *deserved*. In its first appearance in the sentence, it is used as a neuter singular substantive: *something deserved*, or a *kindness*. In its second use,
it is governed by the preposition **supra** and means *beyond what is deserved*.
Pliny is suggesting that Artemidorus is spreading stories about his (Pliny's)
good deed with praise that, while certainly valid, is nonetheless more than is
deserved.

Notice how smoothly Pliny segues from a comment about Artemidorus's
virtues into an account of his own behavior.

**ut . . . ita:** correlative *certainly . . . but*.

**verā:** an ablative singular adjective modifying **praedicatione**.

2 Equidem, cum essent philosophi ab urbe summoti,
fui apud illum in suburbano et, quo notabilius (hoc est,
periculosius) esset, fui praetor. Pecuniam etiam, qua
tunc illi ampliore opus erat, ut aes alienum exsolveret
10    contractum ex pulcherrimis causis, mussantibus
magnis quibusdam et locupletibus amicis mutuatus
ipse gratuitam dedi.

---

2    **cum (conj.):** here introducing a temporal clause whose predicate is the pluperfect passive subjunctive **essent ... summoti**.

**philosophi:** Among the prominent critics, and therefore victims, of
Domitian's regime were Stoic philosophers like Artemidorus. It is not clear
from Pliny's account whether the philosophers were banished only from
Rome (and thus Artemidorus had moved to his suburban home) or whether
they were banished from all of Italy, and thus Artemidorus had gone to his
suburban home to prepare for leaving Italy.

**ab urbe:** *from Rome.* Pliny often uses the word **urbs** to mean specifically
Rome. Compare Letter 4.13, Section 1.

**quo:** *therefore.* **Quo** (literally *by which*) is used instead of **ut eo** (literally *so
that by this*) to introduce a result clause when that clause contains a comparative form, here **notabilius**. The result clause, with the subjunctive **esset**, is
dependent on the main clause, **fui praetor. Quo** is construed closely with the
"more" implied in the comparative form **notabilius**: *by which it was more conspicuous.* A smoother English translation would be *so that it was therefore more
conspicuous.* (Readers who wish to ponder this construction should consider
that **quo** [like the **eo** of **ut eo**] is an ablative of degree of difference.)

**notabilius, periculosius:** neuter singulars in the comparative form: *by which*
(or *so that therefore*) *it was more conspicuous, that is* (**hoc est** = **id est**), *more
dangerous.* **Hoc** is a nominative neuter singular. What was *more conspicuous
and more dangerous* was Pliny's visit. Because he was **praetor** at the time, he
was expected to support the emperor, not his opponents.

**Pecuniam:** the direct object of **dedi**, at the end of the sentence.

**qua, ampliore:** Both words are ablative singular after the impersonal verb
**opus erat** and refer back to **pecuniam**. **Ampliore** is a comparative form: *I
even gave him money, of which more abundant there was need to him* (that is, he
needed; **illi** is dative after **opus erat**). A smoother, though less literal, render-
ing of **ampliore** would be *which he needed in a greater amount*, or *which he
needed more of.*

Artemidorus would have needed money if his property in Rome had been confiscated and he was forced to move out of Italy.

**ut:** introducing a purpose (final) clause with the imperfect subjunctive **exsolveret**.

**contractum:** perfect passive participle of **contrahere**, modifying **aes alienum**.

**ex:** *for.*

**pulcherrimis:** *finest, most honorable.* Pliny wants to assure his reader that the philosopher Artemidorus would have borrowed money only for the most honorable of reasons. He does not, however, tell us what these reasons were.

**mussantibus . . . amicis:** an ablative absolute construction. The intent is concessive: *although certain great and wealthy friends were silent* (that is, did not respond to his need for money). These friends may have ignored Artemidorus's pleas for help because they feared that they would anger the emperor Domitian if they helped someone who had been banished from Rome.

**mutuatus:** The perfect participle of a deponent verb (here **mutuor**) is passive in form but active in meaning. The participle modifies the subject of **dedi: (ego) ipse**. Pliny was a wealthy man, but he claims that he borrowed the money he gave to Artemidorus. He thus makes himself look like a very loyal friend: Not only did he risk his own life by helping Artemidorus, but he even was willing to go into debt to help him, at a time when other friends deserted him. We may be skeptical about his intimation that his generosity to Artemidorus was a financial burden.

**gratuitam:** modifies **pecuniam** at the beginning of the sentence. Pliny gave Artemidorus *(interest) free money*, that is, money without an interest charge.

3 Atque haec feci, cum septem amicis meis aut occisis
aut relegatis, occisis Senecione, Rustico, Helvidio,
15   relegatis Maurico, Gratilla, Arria, Fannia, tot circa
me iactis fulminibus quasi ambustus mihi quoque
impendere idem exitium certis quibusdam notis
augurarer. 4 Non ideo tamen eximiam gloriam
meruisse me, ut ille praedicat, credo, sed tantum
20   effugisse flagitium.

---

3   **haec:** neuter plural accusative.

**cum (conj.):** *although*, here introducing a concessive clause whose predicate
is the imperfect subjunctive deponent verb **augurarer**, several lines below.

**septem amicis meis:** *my seven friends*, or better: *seven of my friends* (because
Pliny had more than seven friends). For the family of three of these people,
see Genealogy Chart 2.

**occisis, relegatis:** These perfect passive participles occur twice in ablative
absolute constructions that are temporal in intent. The first time, they both
modify **septem amicis**: *when seven of my friends had been executed or exiled.*
Then, **occisis** modifies the names (in the ablative case) of the three men who
were executed, while **relegatis** modifies the names (in the ablative case) of
the four people who were sent into exile. The four people who were banished
at this time returned to Italy early in 97 CE, shortly after the assassination of
Domitian in September 96.

**Senecione (abl.):** Herennius Senecio was, like Pliny, a senator and lawyer.
He came to Rome from Spain.

**Rustico (abl.):** Junius Arulenus Rusticus was consul in 92 CE, the year before
his execution.

**Helvidio (abl.):** Helvidius Priscus was, like the other men, a member of the
Senate.

**Maurico (abl.):** Junius Mauricus was the brother of Rusticus.

**Gratilla (abl.):** the wife of Rusticus.

**Arria (abl.):** the mother of Fannia.

**Fannia (abl.):** the stepmother of Helvidius.

**tot:** modifies **fulminibus**.

**fulminibus:** ablative of means with **ambustus**. Of course, Pliny was not really burned by lightning bolts. He uses **fulminibus** figuratively to describe the dangers posed by the angry Domitian. **Quasi** qualifies **ambustus**: *I, having been burned, as it were, by so many lightning bolts hurled* (**iactis**) *around me.*

**ambustus:** perfect passive participle of **amburere**. It is masculine nominative singular, modifying an understood **ego** that is the subject of the **cum . . . augurarer** clause (and also the **feci** at the beginning of the sentence).

**mihi:** the dative case with **impendere**.

**impendere idem exitium:** an accusative infinitive construction in indirect statement after the verb **augurarer**. **Idem exitium** is the accusative subject.

**certis quibusdam notis:** *certain definite signs;* ablative of means. Pliny suggests that he knew that he had fallen out of favor with Domitian, but he does not reveal what definite signs he had that his life was in danger.

**augurarer:** imperfect subjunctive of the deponent verb **augurari**. The verb is subjunctive because it is the predicate of the concessive clause introduced, several lines earlier, by **cum**: **cum . . . ambustus . . . augurarer**: *although . . . having been burned . . . I was predicting . . .*

4  **meruisse me:** an accusative infinitive construction in indirect statement after the verb **credo**. **Me** is the accusative subject; **gloriam** is the accusative object.

**ut:** with the indicative mood.

**effugisse:** another accusative infinitive construction in indirect statement after the verb **credo**. Supply **me** as the accusative subject. **Flagitium** is the accusative object.

5 Nam et C. Musonium, socerum eius, quantum
licitum est per aetatem, cum admiratione dilexi, et
Artemidorum ipsum iam tum, cum in Syria tribunus
militarem, arta familiaritate complexus sum idque
25 primum non nullius indolis dedi specimen, quod virum
aut sapientem aut proximum simillimumque sapienti
intellegere sum visus. 6 Nam ex omnibus, qui nunc se
philosophos vocant, vix unum aut alterum invenies
tanta sinceritate, tanta veritate. Mitto, qua patientia
30 corporis hiemes iuxta et aestates ferat, ut nullis
laboribus cedat, ut nihil in cibo, in potu voluptatibus
tribuat, ut oculos animumque contineat.

---

5    **C(aium) Musonium:** accusative, direct object of **dilexi**. Gaius Musonius
Rufus was an Italian Stoic philosopher; he was the father-in-law of
Artemidorus. **C.** is the abbreviation for the name **Gaius**. This was also Pliny's
**praenomen**, that is, first name; see the salutation at the beginning of the
letter.

**quantum:** subject of **licitum est**: *as much as*.

**per aetatem:** *on account of age*. Pliny was about thirty years younger than
Musonius. Here he means that he developed a friendship with the older man,
despite the difference in their ages.

**cum admiratione dilexi:** *I loved Musonius with admiration*, or less literally *I
loved and admired Musonius*.

**Artemidorum:** accusative case, direct object of the perfect indicative deponent **complexus sum**.

**cum (conj.):** here introducing a temporal clause whose verb is the imperfect
active subjunctive **militarem**.

**tribunus:** in apposition to the understood subject of **militarem** (**ego**).
Translate *as a tribune*.

   Pliny is referring to the position of military tribune (**tribunus militum**).
Young men from wealthy families often served as military tribunes for about
a year, or even less, when they were in their early 20s. They were posted as
officers with a Roman army unit in order to acquire a bit of experience of
military service before they embarked on their first campaign for political
office in Rome. Pliny's duties as a military tribune in Syria, about 81 CE, were

to audit the financial accounts of his army unit. (He discovered a great deal of greed and neglect.) The position of military tribune, **tribunus militum**, was quite different from the office of tribune of the plebs, **tribunus plebis**, an office for which Pliny was selected about 91 or 92 CE.

**idque primum . . . specimen:** Take these words together, as the object of **dedi**; **-que** is an enclitic.

**non nullius:** *not no* = *some*. The expression is an example of the rhetorical figure *litotes*, by which the writer emphasizes something by denying its opposite. **Nullius** is in the genitive case, modifying **indolis**.

**quod:** a conjunction introducing a causal clause with an indicative verb: **sum visus**.

**virum:** direct object of **intellegere**, which is dependent on **sum visus**.

**simillimum:** superlative degree of **similis**; modifying **virum** and followed by the dative case: **sapienti**.

6    **ex:** *from, out of.*

**se:** reflexive direct object of **vocant**. **Philosophos** is in apposition.

**alterum:** Translate as *two*. **Alter** often means *the other of two*.

**sinceritate, veritate:** ablatives of quality/description. This use of the ablative identifies a quality possessed by a person.

**Mitto:** The verb often means *I send* but here means *I dismiss, I say nothing about*. Compare Letter 9.6, Section 3. The verb is followed by a series of present subjunctives: **ferat, cedat, tribuat, contineat**. The construction is a series of indirect exclamations and therefore requires the subjunctives. The direct exclamations would be *With what endurance he bears! How he shrinks from! How he concedes nothing! How he controls!*

**hiemes . . . et aestates:** accusative plural direct objects of **ferat**.

**ut:** *how*, introducing an indirect exclamation, which uses the same construction as an indirect question and therefore requires a subjunctive.

**laboribus:** ablative of separation without the preposition.

**ut . . . tribuat:** *how he concedes nothing to pleasures in food, in drink*. Pliny is stating that Artemidorus never allows pleasure to dictate his choice of when or what to eat and drink. He consumes only the bare necessities for survival. He depicts the virtuous Artemidorus as a model Stoic, abstemious in all aspects of his life.

**contineat:** Artemidorus does not allow his eyes and mind to wander to inappropriate or idle subjects.

7 Sunt haec magna, sed in alio; in hoc vero minima, si
ceteris virtutibus comparentur, quibus meruit, ut a C.
35  Musonio ex omnibus omnium ordinum adsectatoribus
gener adsumeretur. 8 Quae mihi recordanti est quidem
iucundum, quod me cum apud alios tum apud te tantis
laudibus cumulat; vereor tamen, ne modum excedat,
quem benignitas eius (illuc enim, unde coepi, revertor)
40  non solet tenere. 9 Nam in hoc uno interdum vir
alioqui prudentissimus honesto quidem, sed tamen
errore versatur, quod pluris amicos suos, quam sunt,
arbitratur. Vale.

---

7    **haec:** nominative neuter plural: *these* (qualities).

**in alio; in hoc:** *in another man; in this man* (Artemidorus).

**comparentur:** present passive subjunctive of **comparare** in the protasis of
a future less vivid condition. For the apodosis, understand **sunt** with **in hoc
minima**. The subject of both the protasis and apodosis is the **haec** of the
previous clause.

**virtutibus:** dative: *to his virtues.*

**quibus:** *because of which (virtues).*

**ut . . . adsumeretur:** noun (or substantive) clause of result after **meruit**,
requiring a subjunctive verb. The subject of third person singular passive
**adsumeretur** is understood to be Artemidorus.

**a C(aio) Musonio:** ablative of agent. **Caio = Gaio** (the **praenomen** Gaius).
On Roman naming practices, see "The Life of Pliny" in the introduction.

**omnibus:** Construe with **adsectatoribus**, which here means *suitors* (for his
daughter in marriage).

**gener:** predicate nominative. Artemidorus was chosen by Musonius *as his
son-in-law.*

8    **Quae:** *which things.* By **quae**, Pliny means Artemidorus's virtues and selection
as Musonius's son-in-law. This use of the relative pronoun, **qui, quae, quod,** at
the beginning of a sentence is *resumptive*; the pronoun refers to something in
the previous sentence and *resumes* the thought expressed in that sentence. The
relative is used to link its sentence more closely with the preceding sentence.

**Quae** is the accusative neuter plural direct object of **recordanti**, which is modifying the dative **mihi**. English would use a demonstrative pronoun: *these* (deeds and words) or *they*.

**mihi:** The dative is dependent on **iucundum**.

**recordanti:** The present participle of a deponent verb is active in both form and meaning.

**me:** direct object of **cumulat**, whose subject is understood to be Artemidorus.

**cum ... tum:** *both ... and.*

**ne (conj.):** *lest:* introduces a noun (substantive) clause of fearing with the subjunctive verb, **resumam**.

**quem:** The antecedent is **modum**. In its relative clause, **quem** is the accusative direct object of the infinitive **tenere**, which is dependent on **solet**.

**—, —, coepi, coeptum:** *I began.* This defective verb occurs only in the perfect system.

**revertor:** Pliny points out to his reader his use of ring composition. He began his letter with a reference to Artemidorus, leading the reader to believe that the topic of the letter would be Artemidorus. And he concludes the letter with a reference to Artemidorus. The majority of the letter, however, concerns Pliny's alleged generosity and courage during the final years of Domitian's reign.

9   **in hoc uno ... honesto quidem ... tamen errore:** *in this one (fault) ... an honorable (fault) certainly ... nevertheless a fault.*

**quod:** *because.* Here **quod** introduces a causal clause with an indicative verb.

**pluris:** genitive of **plus**: *more.* Here **pluris** is used as a genitive of indefinite value with the verb **arbitratur**: *He considers* (his friends) *of more* (value); that is, *he considers* (his friends) *of greater merit.*

# 7. Letter 3.14

Slaves were ubiquitous in Roman society. They were employed in private residences, public offices, factories, transportation, construction projects, farms, and mines. The wealth of men like Pliny was generated, to a great extent, by the toil of slaves who worked on their properties. Slaves were considered by law the property of their owners, like farm animals, machinery, or tools. (For additional information about slaves, see Letters 1.21 and 8.16.) They could be treated as abusively as their owner might wish to. It was common for slaves to be whipped, both to punish them and to frighten them into being obedient. It was also common for slaves to be sexually abused by their owners.

In any slave-owning society, owners, especially wealthy ones, are vastly outnumbered by their slaves. It is estimated that Pliny owned at least five hundred slaves, employed both in his urban residences and on his rural properties. In slave-owning societies, there develops among owners an anxiety about possible attacks by their slaves. Another Roman writer, Seneca the Younger, claimed that one has as many enemies as slaves (**totidem hostes esse quot servos**, Letter 47.5). Perhaps one reason that owners in ancient Rome (and other societies) frequently physically abused their slaves and threatened to kill them was to reinforce their dominance over people whom they considered inferior, but also essential to their well-being.

In this letter to Acilius (whose identity is otherwise unknown to us), Pliny describes the murder of a cruel slave owner by some of his slaves.

---

## C. PLINIUS ACILIO SUO S.

1 Rem atrocem nec tantum epistula dignam Larcius
Macedo, vir praetorius, a servis suis passus est,
superbus alioqui dominus et saevus, et qui servisse
5     patrem suum parum, immo nimium meminisset.

---

1    **Rem:** direct object of **passus est**; modified by **atrocem** and **dignam**.

   **tantum (adv.):** *only*. Pliny means that the fate of Larcius Macedo was so horrible that it deserves not only a letter but much wider publicity.

   **epistulā:** ablative of specification after **dignam**.

**Larcius Macedo:** subject of **passus est**. His identity is known only from this letter. **Macedo** is declined as a third declension noun.

**vir praetorius:** Larcius Macedo had, at an earlier date, served as a **praetor**. He was henceforth known as a "man of praetorian rank." On the position of **praetor**, see the Vocabulary. There is no other known case from the early imperial period of the son of a slave reaching praetorian rank.

**alioqui:** *moreover.*

**dominus:** in apposition to Larcius Macedo. **Dominus** is modified by **superbus** and **saevus** and is the antecedent of the relative pronoun **qui** (which is the subject of **meminisset**).

**servisse:** contracted (syncopated) perfect active infinitive of **servire**, instead of **servivisse**.

**servisse patrem:** an accusative infinitive construction in indirect statement, dependent on the verb **meminisset**.

Although the father had been a slave, he had at some point been freed and thus had become a *freedman* (**libertus**). His son, in turn, possessed full Roman citizenship and was therefore eligible to run for political office. However, campaigning for office was very expensive, and it was highly unusual, both because of finances and because of prejudice, for the son of a former slave to achieve the rank of senator and the office of **praetor**.

Larcius Macedo was a cruel slave owner. As Pliny suggests, we might expect that the son of a former slave would be sympathetic to his slaves, but Macedo seems to have remembered *too much*, that is, he was acutely aware that he, unlike his elite-born senatorial colleagues, had an ignoble family. He tried to compensate for his feeling of inferiority by acting even more arrogantly than other wealthy men.

**meminisset:** third person singular, pluperfect active subjunctive of the defective verb **memini**. The form is pluperfect, but the meaning is perfect tense: *remembered.* The verb is a subjunctive in a relative clause of characteristic. Larcius Macedo was the *type* of man who remembered *too little, or rather too much*, that his father had been a slave.

2 Lavabatur in villa Formiana. Repente eum servi circumsistunt; alius fauces invadit, alius os verberat, alius pectus et ventrem atque etiam (foedum dictu) verenda contundit; et, cum exanimem putarent,

10 abiciunt in fervens pavimentum, ut experirentur, an viveret. Ille, sive quia non sentiebat, sive quia se non sentire simulabat, immobilis et extentus fidem peractae mortis implevit. 3 Tum demum quasi aestu solutus effertur; excipiunt servi fideliores, concubinae cum

15 ululatu et clamore concurrunt.

---

2     **Lavabatur:** a passive form: *he was being bathed*, that is, he was assisted in his bath by slaves. Letter 3.16, Section 8, provides additional information about personal tasks performed by slaves for their owners. Slaves attended to their owners in situations where the owners were very vulnerable, such as being naked and in a bath. These situations presented opportunities for slaves to do harm. Consequently slave owners were sometimes anxious about being harmed by slaves who might hate them. However, as this letter indicates, the punishment for rebellious slaves was very harsh.

**Formianus, -a, -um:** the adjective Formian, that is, at Formiae, a town on the west coast of Italy, about halfway between Rome and Naples.

**cirumsistunt:** The tense is "historical present." Pliny switches from the imperfect, **lavabatur,** to create a more vivid narrative. This practice is common also in English. *He was taking a bath. His slaves surround him.*

**alius . . . alius:** *one . . . another.*

**foedum:** accusative of exclamation. **Dictu:** supine of **dicere,** ablative of specification (respect): *horrible to say.*

**exanimem:** Supply **eum esse. Putarent** introduces an accusative infinitive in indirect statement: *when they thought* (him to be) *dead.*

**fervens pavimentum:** Wealthy Romans had elaborate bathing rooms with heated floors.

**ut experirentur: Ut** is introducing a purpose (final) clause with the subjunctive. Although the main verb, **abiciunt,** is in the present tense, the subjunctive in the subordinate clause, **experirentur,** is in the imperfect tense, that is, in secondary (historic) sequence because **abiciunt** is a historical present, like **circumsistunt** (above).

**an viveret:** *whether he was alive.* **Viveret** is the subjunctive in an indirect question.

**Ille:** Larcius Macedo.

**se non sentire:** an accusative infinitive in indirect statement, introduced by the verb **simulabat**. The reflexive pronoun **se** is the accusative subject.

**extentus:** perfect passive participle of **extendere**: *stretched out.*

**fidem ... implevit:** *he satisfied their belief,* that is, he convinced them.

**peractae mortis:** *of his death having been achieved.* **Peractae** is the perfect passive participle of **peragere**. The words are objective genitives with **fidem**. A less literal translation: *their belief that his death had been achieved.*

3   **solutus:** perfect passive participle of **solvere**: *loosened.* Here it means *debilitated, devitalized (by the heat).* **Quasi,** *as if,* qualifies the phrase. The slaves who attacked Macedo make it look *as if* he were de**vita**lized (deprived of life, **vita**) by the heat of the bath so that they will not be suspected of causing his death. At this point, they think that he is already dead.

**effertur:** Macedo is carried out, perhaps into an open-air courtyard.

**fideliores:** comparative degree of **fidelis**.

**concubinae:** The Latin word **concubina** is cognate with the verb **concubare**, *to lie together, to have sexual intercourse.* These women were likely to have been slaves or freedwomen (**libertae**), that is, women who had been slaves but had subsequently been freed (as Macedo's own father had been freed). Wealthy men sometimes kept concubines in their homes, but it may have been unusual, and frowned upon, to keep several concubines, as Macedo apparently did. In painting a negative portrait of Domitian, the historian Suetonius reports that the emperor was a man of enormous libido who had many concubines (*Life of Domitian* 22.1).

Ita et vocibus excitatus et recreatus loci frigore sublatis
oculis agitatoque corpore vivere se (et iam tutum erat)
confitetur. 4 Diffugiunt servi; quorum magna pars
comprehensa est, ceteri requiruntur. Ipse
20   paucis diebus aegre focilatus non sine ultionis solacio
decessit ita vivus vindicatus, ut occisi solent. 5 Vides,
quot periculis, quot contumeliis, quot ludibriis simus
obnoxii; nec est quod quisquam possit esse securus,
quia sit remissus et mitis; non enim iudicio domini, sed
25   scelere perimuntur.

---

**loci frigore:** Macedo had been moved out of the hot bathing room to an area where the air was much cooler.

**sublatis oculis:** ablative absolute: *his eyes having been raised*, or *with his eyes opened*. **Sublatis** is the perfect passive participle of **tollere**.

**agitatoque corpore:** another ablative absolute construction.

**vivere se:** accusative infinitive in indirect statement, introduced by the verb **confitetur**.

**tutum:** *safe* (to reveal that he was still alive).

4   **quorum:** The antecedent of this relative pronoun is **servi**. In its own clause, it is a partitive genitive: *a great part of whom*. This use of the relative pronoun, **qui, quae, quod**, at the beginning of a sentence is *resumptive*; the pronoun refers to something in the previous sentence and *resumes* the thought expressed in that sentence. The relative pronoun is used to link its sentence more closely with the preceding sentence. English would use a demonstrative pronoun: *a great part of them*.

**Ipse:** Larcius Macedo.

**paucis diebus:** ablative of time within which. Translate with **decessit**.

**decessit ... solent:** *he died, in this way, while alive, having been avenged as those (slave owners) who have been killed are accustomed* (to be avenged).
        Under Roman law, if a slave owner was killed by one or some of his slaves, all the slaves in his household, even if not involved in the crime, were executed. And the methods of execution were very painful. For example, condemned slaves might be crucified. In 61 CE, four hundred slaves of one murdered slave owner were executed, even though few had participated in the plot. The reasoning behind this extremely harsh practice was to encourage any slave who

became aware that others were conspiring to kill the slave owner to report the plot, in order to avoid being executed himself/herself, although innocent. At the Senate discussion prior to the execution of the four hundred slaves, one senator argued that "we can live safely and securely, though one man among many slaves, if they are afraid" (Tacitus, *Annals* 14.44).

Pliny's words suggest that Macedo's slaves were executed while he was still alive. Officials did not wait until his death to order the executions.

5    **quot periculis:** *how many dangers.* **Periculis** is in the dative case after **obnoxii** (nominative plural masculine adjective).

**simus:** present subjunctive in an indirect question following **vides**. The understood subject of **simus**, *we*, denotes Pliny and his fellow slave owners.

**nec est quod:** *nor is it* (the case) *that.*

**possit:** present subjunctive. The subjunctive implies a future less vivid potentiality: Anyone could be safe if he were kind. **Quia**, *because*, is here similar to the conditional conjunction **si**, *if.* Thus the verb **sit** is also subjunctive.

**iudicio:** here *judgment, rational decision making.* **Domini** is a nominative plural, used as the subject of the verb **perimuntur**: *slave owners are not killed because of (as a result of) rational decision making.* Pliny is asserting that when slaves kill their owner, they do so not because of a rational judgment about the owner's cruelty, but because of their (the slaves') innate wickedness. Thus, in Pliny's view, kind slave owners are as vulnerable to attack as cruel slave owners. Although elsewhere in his letters Pliny appears to have been a less brutal owner than Macedo (see Letter 8.16), he here implies that any murder of an owner, even a despicable owner, is inexcusable and unforgivable.

6 Verum haec hactenus. Quid praeterea novi? quid?
nihil; alioqui subiungerem; nam et charta adhuc
superest, et dies feriatus patitur plura contexi. Addam
quod opportune de eodem Macedone succurrit. Cum
30    in publico Romae lavaretur, notabilis atque etiam, ut
exitus docuit, ominosa res accidit. 7 Eques Romanus a
servo eius, ut transitum daret, manu leviter admonitus
convertit se nec servum, a quo erat tactus, sed ipsum
Macedonem tam graviter palma percussit, ut paene
35    concideret. 8 Ita balineum illi, quasi per gradus
quosdam, primum contumeliae locus, deinde exitii fuit.
Vale.

---

6    **haec hactenus:** *this to this extent;* less literally *so much for this* (story).

**Quid . . . novi:** partitive genitive construction: *what of new?* Less literally: *what's new?*

**subiungerem:** apodosis of a present contrary to fact condition. (The protasis is implied by the word **alioqui**.) Supply a direct object for the verb; I would add *it.* Compare the use of **alioqui** in Letter 6.20, Section 16.

**charta:** The Romans wrote on papyrus (as well as on the wax tablets mentioned in Letter 1.6, Section 1). See the image on page 65.

**dies feriatus:** *holiday day, a day of leisure.* There were many public holidays in the Roman world. We do not know on which holiday Pliny was writing the letter, but he was free of public obligations for the day.

**patitur:** here *allows: a day of leisure allows.* The object of **patitur** is the accusative infinitive construction **plura contexi. Contexi** is the present passive infinitive of **contexere. Plura** is its accusative plural subject.

**eodem:** masculine ablative singular of **idem**, modifying **Macedone** (ablative).

**succurrit:** Supply the dative **mihi:** *what occurs to me.*

**in publico:** Macedo was *in public* at a public bath. (As a substantive, **publico** would mean *a public place.*) There were many public bath complexes in ancient Rome, some of them very large and ornate. In addition to the pool areas, the complexes included facilities such as those found at modern health clubs. People of all social classes regularly visited public baths. However, as is revealed below, people of lower classes were expected to defer to people of higher classes.

**Romae:** locative case.

**lavaretur:** See the note above on **lavabatur** in Section 2.

**Notabilis** and **ominosa** modify **res**.

7     **Eques Romanus** is the subject of two main verbs: **convertit . . . nec . . . percussit**.

      An **eques**, often translated into English as an *equestrian* or *knight*, was a member of a family that was wealthy but not of senatorial rank. Pliny's family was equestrian, but he had successfully pursued a political career and gained a seat in the Roman Senate, thus moving into the senatorial rank.

**a servo eius: A servo** is ablative of agent; **eius** is a possessive genitive referring to Macedo: *of him, his.*

**ut:** here introducing a purpose (final) clause with the subjunctive. **Daret** is the verb of the clause whose understood subject is **eques Romanus**. The clause depends on the phrase that follows it: **manu leviter admonitus**. Macedo's slave lightly touched (alerted) with his hand the Roman knight, in order that he (the knight) would grant passage (step aside) to Macedo.

**admonitus:** perfect passive participle modifying **eques**.

**se:** reflexive direct object of **convertit**.

**servum:** direct object of **percussit**. **Ipsum Macedonem** (accusative case) is the second direct object.

      The Roman knight committed a grave offense by striking a man of senatorial rank with a blow intended for a slave.

**a quo:** ablative of agent.

**palmā:** ablative of means.

**ut:** here introducing a result clause with the subjunctive. **Concĭderet** (not concīderet) is the verb of the clause whose understood subject is **Macedo**.

8     **illi:** dative. The reference is to Macedo. Construe as **balineum fuit illi locus**. The genitives **contumeliae** and **exitii** are dependent on **locus**.

# 8. Letter 3.16

I n Letter 3.16, Pliny describes the fortitude of Arria the Elder and her devotion to her husband, Caecina Paetus. Arria the Elder, who died in 42 CE, was the mother and grandmother of two of the people who had opposed Domitian's reign and were consequently punished in 93 CE. (See Genealogy Chart 2.) They were among the opponents of Domitian whom Pliny claims to have assisted in Letters 3.11 and 7.19. In this letter, Pliny raises a question about defining courage. He presents the argument that Arria's final courageous deed was motivated, at least in part, by her desire to achieve eternal glory. It was therefore, in his opinion, not as remarkable as an earlier instance of her strength of mind, an instance that was unknown to most people and earned her no public praise. This letter and Letter 7.19, which reports the courage of Arria's granddaughter, Fannia, both reveal that Roman women were admired for loyalty to and support of their husbands and families. They would not have been praised for having ambitions that were independent of their husbands' or families' interests.

The letter is addressed to Maecilius (or perhaps Metilius) Nepos, a man of senatorial rank otherwise unknown to us.

---

C. PLINIUS NEPOTI SUO S.

1 Adnotasse videor facta dictaque virorum feminarumque alia clariora esse, alia maiora. 2 Confirmata est opinio mea hesterno Fanniae
5   sermone. Neptis haec Arriae illius, quae marito et solacium mortis et exemplum fuit.

---

1    **Adnotasse:** a contracted (syncopated) perfect active infinitive of **adnotare**. The full form is **adnotavisse**. This infinitive is followed by an accusative infinitive in indirect statement: **facta dictaque ... esse**.

**alia ... alia:** Construe with **facta dictaque**: *some deeds and words, other deeds and words.*

**clariora ... maiora:** Construe these comparative adjectives as predicate adjectives after **esse**. Pliny's observation is that some deeds and words receive renown, while others, although of greater significance, remain uncelebrated.

2   **hesterno Fanniae sermone:** *by yesterday's conversation with Fannia.* The genitive, **Fanniae**, is objective, that is, the noun **Fanniae** is the object of the verbal action of *conversing with*, which is implied in the noun **sermone**.

**Fanniae:** Fannia is mentioned in Letters 3.11 and 7.19 as one of the people condemned to exile in 93 CE. Pliny sets out, in this letter, to record several heroic actions of Fannia's grandmother, Arria the Elder. In doing so, he appears to have been a supporter of this family that, for several generations, criticized imperial rule. In addition, by mentioning that his source of information was a conversation with Fannia, he leads the reader to believe that he was quite friendly with the family. See the introduction to Letter 3.11.

**Neptis haec:** Supply **est**.

**Arriae:** There are two women named Arria mentioned in Pliny's letters. The Arria of Letter 3.11 was the daughter of the Arria of this letter. To differentiate the two, historians have labeled the latter as Arria the Elder and the former as Arria the Younger. Arria the Younger was the mother of Fannia. (See Genealogy Chart 2.) It was customary for women to receive, as their **nomen**, the feminine form of their father's **nomen**. On Roman naming practices, see "The Life of Pliny" in the introduction. It is not known why Arria the Younger was known by the name of her mother's family.

**Arriae illius:** The demonstrative, **illa**, here provides a forceful reference: *that well-known Arria.*

**quae:** The antecedent is **Arriae illius**.

**marito:** dative.

**mortis:** Construe this objective genitive with both **solacium** and **exemplum**. Arria the Elder was, for her husband, both a solace for his death (because he took comfort in knowing that he had such a loyal wife) and an example or model for his death (because she showed him how to die). On the use of real people as models for behavior in Roman moral education, see Letter 7.19, Section 7.

Multa referebat aviae suae non minora hoc, sed
obscuriora; quae tibi existimo tam mirabilia legenti
fore, quam mihi audienti fuerunt. 3 Aegrotabat
Caecina Paetus, maritus eius, aegrotabat et filius,
uterque mortifere, ut videbatur. Filius decessit eximia
pulchritudine, pari verecundia, et parentibus non
minus ob alia carus quam quod filius erat. 4 Huic illa
ita funus paravit, ita duxit exsequias, ut ignoraret
maritus; quin immo, quotiens cubiculum eius intraret,
vivere filium atque etiam commodiorem esse simulabat
ac persaepe interroganti, quid ageret puer, respondebat:
"Bene quievit, libenter cibum sumpsit." 5 Deinde, cum
diu cohibitae lacrimae vincerent prorumperentque,
egrediebatur; tunc se dolori dabat; satiata siccis oculis
composito vultu redibat, tamquam orbitatem foris
reliquisset.

---

**Multa:** Understand **facta dictaque**.

**hoc:** ablative of comparison: *than this* (deed). Pliny alludes to "this deed" in his reference to Arria having been a solace and a model for her husband. Later in the letter, he explains what the deed was.

**quae . . . fore:** indirect statement construction after **existimo**. **Quae** (which is the accusative subject of the indirect statement) is the accusative neuter plural of the relative pronoun: *which* (deeds and words). Its use here is *resumptive*; it refers to something in the previous clause and *resumes* the thought expressed in that clause. English would use a demonstrative pronoun: *these* (deeds and words) or *they*.

**tam . . . quam:** *as . . . as*. There are two correlative constructions: **tibi tam mirabilia legenti (fore)** and **quam mihi audienti (fuerunt)**. **Fuerunt** is perfect indicative.

**mirabilia:** accusative neuter plural; the predicate adjective for **quae**.

**fore:** future infinitive of **esse**. It is an alternative form for **futura esse** (where the participial element, **futura**, would be accusative neuter plural in agreement with **quae**).

**legenti, audienti:** present participles in the dative, modifying the pronouns.

3    **Caecina Paetus:** the husband of Arria the Elder, the father of Arria the Younger. He was a man of senatorial rank and a suffect consul in 37 CE.

**et filius:** *her son was also ill.*

**pulchritudine, verecundia:** ablatives of description or quality with **filius**. This use of the ablative identifies a quality possessed by a person.

**pari:** His modesty was *equal* in the sense that it was as outstanding as his beauty. Pliny means that Arria's son excelled in both virtues and physical appearance.

**parentibus:** dative with **carus**, which modifies **filius**.

**quod:** *because.* Here **quod** introduces a causal clause with an indicative verb.

4    **huic:** dative, *for him* (her son).

**illa:** Arria.

**ut:** introduces a result clause, with the imperfect subjunctive, **ignoraret**.

**intraret:** imperfect subjunctive expressing iterative or frequentative action (an action that happened often or repeatedly). The indicative mood is more common in this construction. The subject is Arria.

**vivere filium atque . . . esse:** two infinitives in an indirect statement construction after **simulabat**. **Filium** is the accusative subject of both.

**interroganti:** dative with **respondebat**. **Interroganti** is modifying an understood *him* (the husband).

**quid ageret puer:** an indirect question, and therefore the verb is subjunctive. This use of **agere** is idiomatic: *how the boy was, how he was doing* (rather than *what he was doing*). Compare Letter 1.11, Section 2.

5    **cohibitae:** perfect passive participle of **cohibere**.

**vincerent prorumperentque:** subjunctives in the **cum** temporal clause. Understand **illam** (**Arriam**) as a direct object of **vincerent**.

**satiata:** feminine nominative singular of the perfect passive participle, modifying the understood subject of **redibat**: Arria.

**siccis oculis, composito vultu:** ablative absolutes expressing manner. **Siccis oculis:** there is no ablative participle in this instance (because Latin did not use a present participle of the verb **esse**). The phrase means *with her eyes (being) dry.*

**reliquisset:** pluperfect subjunctive in a past contrary to fact condition after **tamquam**.

6 Praeclarum quidem illud eiusdem: ferrum stringere,
perfodere pectus, extrahere pugionem, porrigere
25    marito, addere vocem immortalem ac paene divinam:
"Paete, non dolet." Sed tamen ista facienti, ista dicenti,
gloria et aeternitas ante oculos erant; quo maius est
sine praemio aeternitatis, sine praemio gloriae abdere
lacrimas, operire luctum amissoque filio matrem adhuc
30    agere.

7 Scribonianus arma in Illyrico contra Claudium
moverat; fuerat Paetus in partibus et, occiso
Scriboniano, Romam trahebatur.

---

6    **Praeclarum . . . illud:** Supply **est**. With **illud**, understand **factum** (*deed*).
The rest of the sentence, from **ferrum** on, is explanatory of **illud**. The **illud**
anticipates the narration of Arria's deed that follows.

In 42 CE, Arria's husband, Caecina Paetus, was convicted of conspiring against the emperor Claudius and sentenced to death. In similar situations, other members of the senatorial class chose to commit suicide rather
than endure the humiliation of a public execution. There were, in addition,
other incentives for committing suicide. The property of persons who were
executed was confiscated by the state, but the property of those who chose
suicide remained in the possession of their families. When Arria's husband
hesitated to kill himself, she pulled out a knife and stabbed herself, thus becoming for him an **exemplum mortis** (Section 2). The story is told also by
the poet Martial in Epigram 1.13.

**eiusdem:** refers to Arria.

**ferrum stringere:** *to pull out a knife*. This infinitive + object phrase forms the
narration that was anticipated by the **illud** that preceded.

**porrigere:** Understand an object such as **pugionem**.

**vocem:** *voice, utterance*; less literally *words*.

**Paete:** vocative case of **Paetus**.

**dolet:** The understood subject, *it*, refers to the self-inflicted stabbing.

**ista:** accusative neuter plural, direct object of **facienti** and **dicenti**, which
are present participles in the dative case (dative of reference). The participles
modify an understood **Arriae**, *for Arria*.

**quo maius:** *greater than which*; less literally *greater than this*. As often in Latin, the relative pronoun is used instead of the demonstrative pronoun in a resumptive function (see the note in Section 2). **Quo** is an ablative of comparison and refers to Arria's suicide.

Pliny cites two occasions on which Arria displayed great fortitude: when she concealed her son's death and when she committed suicide. In both cases, she acted to protect her husband. On the former occasion, he was not physically strong enough to bear the news about his son. On the latter occasion, he seemed to lack the courage to save himself from the humiliation of a public execution. Pliny considered the former occasion of greater significance because only the family knew of Arria's fortitude. She gained no reward of fame. Of course, Pliny was able to grant her this reward by publishing this letter. Two thousand years later, we can still admire Arria's bravery.

**abdere, operire, agere:** the infinitive subjects of **est**. **Maius** is a predicate adjective: *to conceal is greater.*

**amissoque filio:** ablative absolute. Note that **-que** is an enclitic.

**agere:** another idiomatic use of **agere**: *to play the role of.*

7   **Scribonianus:** Camillus Scribonianus was the commander of two legions in the Roman province of Illyricum. He was the instigator of a failed plot to overthrow the emperor Claudius in 42 CE.

**arma . . . moverat:** *he had taken up arms.*

**Illyrico:** Roman territory on the eastern Adriatic coast. The southern part of Illyricum was the province of Dalmatia.

**Claudium:** Claudius was emperor 41–54 CE.

**in partibus: Pars** (singular) and **partes** (plural) can both mean *division, political faction* (singular). Here: *in the faction (plot).* We do not know why Caecina Paetus and Arria were in Illyricum. Perhaps he had an official government posting.

**occiso Scroboniano:** ablative absolute. The plot was discovered, Scribonianus was killed, and Paetus was taken to Rome for trial.

**Romam:** accusative of motion without the preposition.

8 Erat ascensurus navem. Arria milites orabat ut
35   simul imponeretur. "Nempe enim" inquit "daturi estis
consulari viro servulos aliquos, quorum e manu cibum
capiat, a quibus vestiatur, a quibus calcietur; omnia sola
praestabo." 9 Non impetravit; conduxit piscatoriam
naviculam ingensque navigium minimo secuta est.
40   Eadem apud Claudium uxori Scriboniani, cum illa
profiteretur indicium, "Ego" inquit "te audiam, cuius
in gremio Scribonianus occisus est, et vivis?" Ex quo
manifestum est ei consilium pulcherrimae mortis non
subitum fuisse.

---

8   **Erat ascensurus navem:** active (first) periphrastic construction (the future active participle with a form of the verb **esse** to express an action about to happen): *he was about to board.* **Navem:** accusative of direct object, *to board the ship.* **Ascendere** can be used with or without the preposition **in** or **ad**. Compare Letter 6.16, Section 5.

**ut simul imponeretur:** indirect command. The subject is *she*, Arria.

**daturi estis:** active (first) periphrastic construction: *you are about to give, you are going to give.*

**consulari:** dative case, modifying the indirect object **viro**. Paetus had, at an earlier date, served as a consul. He was henceforth known as a "man of consular rank."

**servulos aliquos:** *some little slaves*, that is, *some paltry slaves.* The meaning is not that the slaves were small or young, but rather that they were of mediocre quality. Arria's tone is deprecatory. The phrase may also imply *a few paltry slaves.*

**quorum, a quibus:** The antecedent is **servulos**.

**capiat, vestiatur, calcietur:** subjunctives in relative clauses of purpose (a purpose clause introduced by a relative pronoun or a relative adverb).
     This sentence indicates how dependent wealthy people were on their slaves. Compare the information in Letter 3.14 that Macedo was being bathed by his slaves.

**calcietur:** This present subjunctive form has an *i* in order to avoid a double *e*: **calceetur**.

**omnia:** accusative neuter plural, referring to the dressing and feeding of Paetus.

**sola:** nominative feminine singular, referring to Arria.

9    **minimo:** ablative of means: *with a very small* (one). It is modifying an understood **navigium**. Although Arria had rented a little boat, **navicula**, which is feminine in gender, and the adjective **minimo** is referring to this little boat, **minimo** is attracted into the neuter gender by the word next to it, **navigium**, *ship*, the vessel in which Paetus was being transported.

**Eadem:** nominative feminine singular, the subject of **inquit**.

**apud Claudium:** The trial of Caecina Paetus was held in Rome, in the Senate, in the presence of Claudius, the emperor against whom Paetus had plotted.

**cum:** introducing a temporal clause.

**illa:** the wife of Scribonianus, whose name was Vibia.

**profiteretur indicium:** Vibia turned state's evidence, thereby ensuring the conviction of Paetus and the other conspirators, and gaining a lighter sentence for herself.

**audiam:** deliberative subjunctive, present active. Arria expresses indignation: *Am I to listen to you?* Here **et** has an adversative use, not *and*, but *and yet*.

**cuius in gremio:** *in the lap of whom, in whose arms.*

**et vivis:** an exasperated Arria berates Vibia in court for not sharing the fate of her husband: *and yet you are still alive!*

**Ex quo:** *from which* (i.e., outburst or incident); a resumptive use of the relative pronoun; less literally: *from this.*

**manifestum est:** introduces an indirect statement, **consilium . . . fuisse**.

**ei:** dative of possession, referring to Arria. Construe with **fuisse**.

**non subitum:** modifies **consilium**. The point that Pliny wants to make is that Arria had been thinking for some time that she would gain everlasting glory if she died with her husband.

45    10 Quin etiam, cum Thrasea, gener eius, deprecaretur,
      ne mori pergeret, interque alia dixisset: "Vis ergo
      filiam tuam, si mihi pereundum fuerit, mori mecum?",
      respondit: "Si tam diu tantaque concordia vixerit tecum
      quam ego cum Paeto, volo." 11 Auxerat hoc responso
50    curam suorum, attentius custodiebatur. Sensit et "Nihil
      agitis" inquit; "potestis enim efficere, ut male moriar, ut
      non moriar, non potestis." 12 Dum haec dicit, exsiluit
      cathedra adversoque parieti caput ingenti impetu
      impegit et corruit. Focilata "Dixeram" inquit "vobis
55    inventuram me quamlibet duram ad mortem viam, si
      vos facilem negassetis."

---

10    **Thrasea:** Publius Clodius Thrasea Paetus, the husband of Arria the Elder's
      daughter, Arria the Younger, who is mentioned in Letter 3.11. He was a critic
      of the regime of the emperor Nero (54–68 CE). He was sentenced to execution
      in 66 CE but chose to preempt execution by committing suicide.

      **ne:** introducing an indirect command.

      **Vis:** second person singular, present active indicative of **volo, velle**. The verb
      is followed by an accusative infinitive: **filiam ... mori**.

      **pereundum fuerit:** passive (second) periphrastic construction: the verb **esse**
      + the gerundive, which expresses obligation and is here used impersonally.
      **Mihi** is the dative (rather than ablative) of agent with the periphrastic con-
      struction. **Fuerit** is future perfect indicative: *if it will have had to be died by
      me*; less literally: *if I will have had to die*.

      **mecum:** = **cum me**. The preposition **cum**, which usually precedes the word it
      governs (for example, **cum Paeto**), is joined enclitically to personal pronouns.

      **respondit:** The subject is Arria.

      **tam ... quam:** *as ... as.*

      **concordia:** In Letter 4.19, Section 5, Pliny expresses the hope that he and his
      wife will enjoy perpetual **concordia**.

      **vixerit:** future perfect indicative of **vivere**. Understand the subject as *she* (my
      daughter).

**ego cum Paeto:** Supply **vivebam**.

In 66 CE, when Thrasea was facing execution, his wife, Arria the Younger, wanted to follow her mother's example, but Thrasea persuaded her to stay alive for the sake of their daughter, Fannia (for whom see Letters 3.11 and 7.19).

11  **Auxerat:** The subject is Arria.

**suorum:** *of her* (family members, loved ones).

**attentius:** comparative degree of the adverb.

**Sensit:** Arria was aware that her family (and slaves) were watching her vigilantly to prevent her from harming herself.

**Nihil agitis:** Arria means that they are acting futilely, wasting their time.

**efficere:** Construe with both appearances of **potestis** and both appearances of **moriar**. **Efficere ut** (**ut non** for the negative) is followed by noun clauses of result that require a subjunctive. Arria tells her family that they can bring it about that she dies badly (**male**), but they cannot bring it about that she does not die. By **male**, she may mean *painfully*, or she may mean *unheroically*.

12  **Dum:** *while*. This conjunction uses a present indicative tense to denote a past action.

**adversoque parieti:** dative with the verb **impegit**. Note the repetition of the explosive *p* sounds to emphasize the violence of Arria's action: **parieti caput . . . impetu impegit**.

**inventuram:** Supply **esse** to form the future active infinitive of the indirect statement construction. The accusative subject is **me** (I, Arria) and therefore the participle element of the infinitive has a feminine ending.

**quamlibet duram:** *however harsh*. Construe with **viam**, which is the direct object of **inventuram** (**esse**). The adverb **quamlibet** is formed from the two words **quam** and **libet**, literally *how it pleases*.

**negassetis:** a contracted (syncopated) form, for **negavissetis**. Arria's direct statement was a future condition: I will find a route to death, however harsh, if you will have denied me an easy one. In the indirect statement, the apodosis becomes an accusative infinitive construction, and the verb of the protasis is put into a pluperfect subjunctive, but without implying that the condition is contrary to fact. (A subordinate clause in indirect statement requires the subjunctive mood; there is no future subjunctive form.)

13 Videnturne haec tibi maiora illo "Paete, non dolet,"
ad quod per haec perventum est—cum interim illud
quidem ingens fama, haec nulla circumfert? Unde
60   colligitur, quod initio dixi, alia esse clariora, alia
maiora. Vale.

---

13   **Videnturne: -Ne** is an enclitic particle attached to the end of a word to indicate a question. **Videri** = *to seem.*

**haec, maiora:** modifying an understood **facta dictaque**.

**illo:** *that well-known* (word/deed), ablative of comparison. On the use of **illo**
to mean *well-known*, see Section 2 (above).

**ad quod:** *to which (deed).* The *deed* is the moment at which Arria stabbed
herself in order to inspire her husband to do the same. Her previous intrepid
deeds led her to the point where she was able to kill herself to save her husband's reputation. In doing so, she earned for herself an everlasting reputation
for courage and loyalty.

**per haec:** Understand **facta dictaque**.

**perventum est:** an impersonal use of the perfect passive: *it was arrived.*

**cum:** introducing a concessive clause.

**haec nulla: Haec** is accusative neuter plural, direct object of **circumfert**. **Nulla** (understand **fama**) is nominative feminine singular, subject of
**circumfert**.

**circumfert:** This verb has two subjects: **ingens fama** and **nulla (fama)**.

The Anglo-American painter Benjamin West (1738–1820) based his *Paetus and Arria* on Pliny's account of the deaths of Caecina Paetus and Arria the Elder. The painting, now located at the Yale Center for British Art, is sometimes titled *Non Dolet* after Arria's words recorded in Section 13 of this letter. (Public Domain)

# 9. Letter 4.6

Pliny's wealth was derived mainly from land ownership. Profit resulted from sales of the crops and animals raised on his properties and
also from rental of land to tenant farmers. In this letter, he reports
two situations that have reduced his profits. The addressee of this letter is
Julius Naso, a young man aspiring to a senatorial career.

---

C. PLINIUS IULIO NASONI SUO S.

1 Tusci grandine excussi, in regione Transpadana
summa abundantia, sed par vilitas nuntiatur. Solum
mihi Laurentinum meum in reditu. 2 Nihil quidem ibi
possideo praeter tectum et hortum statimque harenas,
solum tamen mihi in reditu. Ibi enim plurimum scribo
nec agrum, quem non habeo, sed ipsum me studiis
excolo; ac iam possum tibi ut aliis in locis horreum
plenum, sic ibi scrinium ostendere. 3 Igitur tu quoque,
si certa et fructuosa praedia concupiscis, aliquid in hoc
litore para. Vale.

---

1   **Tusci grandine excussi:** more fully: **Tusci (agri) grandine excussi (sunt).**
Pliny was raised in northern Italy, in the area of Lake Como, where his family
owned income-producing property. He also owned estates in Tuscany that
he had inherited from family members.

**in regione Transpadana:** *in the Transpadane region,* that is, north of the Po
River. The Lake Como area, where much of Pliny's family property was located, was north of the Po River. (See Map 1.)

**abundantia:** *abundance* in terms of crop harvests or yields. **Abundantia** is
the first subject of **nuntiatur. Vilitas** is the second subject.

**par vilitas:** The low selling price of the crops was **par,** *equal,* to the abundance
of the crops in the sense that it was low to the highest degree, that is, that it
was extremely low. Translate **par** as *corresponding.* It is still true today that
when a very good harvest produces an abundance of a food supply, the prices
for that food drop.

**Sōlum:** neuter nominative singular, modifying **Laurentinum meum.**

**Laurentinum meum:** Supply **praedium**. Pliny's estate at Laurentum, a town on the coastline, was about sixteen miles southwest of Rome. This word is the subject of an understood **est**. This sentence makes clear the range of Pliny's land ownership—from northern Italy to south of Rome.

**in reditu:** *in revenue*; less literally *in the black, profitable*.

2    **statimque harenas:** Pliny means the sands of the nearby seashore. **Statim**, *immediately, right there*, describes the sandy shoreline as being *immediately* beyond his estate.

**excolo:** Pliny is attempting to be witty. He has already let the reader know that his seaside estate at Laurentum has no land devoted to raising market crops. After saying that he writes a great deal at his Laurentine estate, he remarks: I do not *cultivate* agricultural land, which I do not have (at Laurentum), but I *cultivate* me myself by means of my literary pursuits. The focus of this letter is thus not really to report a loss of income but to convince the reader that Pliny is interested in literary activities rather than financial matters. In other letters, Pliny similarly presents an image of himself as a man devoted to literature. In Letter 9.36, for example, he portrays himself as spending most of his time at his Tuscan estate with his books, and only begrudgingly attending to the management of the income-producing agricultural activities. However, because Pliny's financial skills were recognized by several emperors, who appointed him to treasury positions and a governorship, perhaps the reader may conclude that Pliny was a more astute and involved property manager than he presents himself to be.

**ut ... sic:** *even as ... so also*.

**horreum plenum ... scrinium: Plenum** modifies both **horreum** and **scrinium**. Both are objects of the infinitive **ostendere**.

**scrinium:** On ancient writing materials, see Letters 1.6, Section 1, and 3.14, Section 6. In Letter 1.6, Pliny reports to Tacitus that he was able to continue his writing projects, even during a hunt in the countryside. In Letter 9.6, he announces that he prefers literary activities to watching chariot races. In this letter, he asserts that he has been very productive as a writer (if not as a landowner) at his seaside estate. He ends the letter by drolly suggesting to Julius Naso that a seaside **praedium** is profitable, but he means, of course, in terms of inspiring literary composition.

3    **para:** present imperative. **Parare** here means *to buy*.

# 10. Letter 4.11

## (Sections 6 to 9)

The Vestal Virgins were priestesses who tended to the cult of Vesta at her temple in the Roman Forum. There were six Vestal Virgins, ranging in age from about eight years to about sixty years. (For additional information about the Vestal Virgins, see Letter 7.19, Sections 1 and 2.) Upon entering the priesthood, a young Vestal took a vow of celibacy. Unchastity, **incestum**, was punished severely. A Vestal who was convicted of **incestum** could be buried alive. There were eleven reported executions of Vestal Virgins from Rome's earliest history until 113 BCE, but there are no further reports until the reign of Domitian, who revived the gruesome practice on at least one occasion. In Sections 6 to 9 of Letter 4.11, Pliny discusses this event, which occurred at some point in the late 80s CE. The Vestal Virgin, named Cornelia, who was buried alive was not just a Vestal but the chief or senior Vestal, the **Virgo Vestalis Maxima**.

Pliny's letter was written several years after Domitian's assassination in 96 CE. Although Pliny's career had flourished under Domitian, he was not hesitant, once Domitian was dead, to vilify him. The letter reveals well Pliny's rhetorical skills. His aim is to deflect attention from Cornelia's sexual impropriety and instead to malign Domitian as savagely cruel in demanding her execution. A contemporary historian, Suetonius, provides a different interpretation of events. He reports that Domitian was trying to curb immorality in the state and thus he put on trial the **Virgo Vestalis Maxima** who was accused of breaking her vow of celibacy.

The letter is addressed to C. (Gaius) Cornelius Minicianus, who was a wealthy **eques** and, like Pliny, a native of the Transpadane region of Italy. (For the definition of **eques**, see the note on Letter 3.14, Section 7.)

The passage below is an excerpt from Letter 4.11. In earlier sections of the letter, Pliny informs his addressee that one of the men accused of having been a lover of Cornelia is now living in Sicily. He had apparently been punished by a sentence of exile. He was fortunate. We know from sources other than Pliny that the other men involved in the sexual scandal were flogged to death in public.

## C. PLINIUS CORNELIO MINICIANO SUO S.

6 Cum Corneliam, Vestalium maximam, defodere vivam
concupisset, ut qui inlustrari saeculum suum eiusmodi
exemplis arbitraretur, pontificis maximi iure seu potius
immanitate tyranni, licentia domini, reliquos pontifices
non in Regiam, sed in Albanam villam convocavit.

5

---

6 **Cum:** introducing a temporal clause.

**Corneliam:** object of **concupisset**.

**Vestalium maximam:** *the senior of the Vestal* (Virgins), that is, the senior
Vestal Virgin. **Vestalium** is a (partitive) genitive plural.

**vivam:** modifies **Corneliam** predicatively: *to bury Cornelia alive*.

**concupisset:** The understood subject is the emperor Domitian. The pluperfect subjunctive form is syncopated from **concupivisset**.

**ut qui:** *inasmuch as he; as being one who*. In this type of relative causal clause,
**ut qui** requires the subjunctive mood, here **arbitraretur**.

**exemplis:** ablative of means.

**arbitraretur:** governs an accusative (**saeculum**) and infinitive (**inlustrari**)
in indirect statement.

**pontificis maximi:** The **pontifex maximus** was the highest priest and head
of the Roman clergy. The emperor was also the **pontifex maximus**, and it was
his duty and right to investigate and punish other priests' misconduct.

**seu potius:** Pliny does not deny that the emperor, as Pontifex Maximus, had a
right (**pontificis maximi iure**) to investigate charges of unchastity by a Vestal
Virgin. However, with **seu potius**, *or rather*, he skillfully introduces the question of whether Domitian's actions were motivated by his possession of the
savage character of a tyrant and the unrestrained power of an absolute ruler.

**reliquos pontifices:** Although Pliny leads his readers to believe that
Domitian had made the decision to execute Cornelia unilaterally, the emper-
or had, in fact, convoked a council of the other priests to hear the case against
Cornelia. Pliny insinuates, moreover, that it was irregular for Domitian to
convoke a council of priests at his Alban villa, but some historians argue that
it was not.

**Regiam:** The Regia was the office of the **pontifex maximus** in the Forum.

**Albanan villam:** Domitian had a villa in the area of the Alban Hills and Lake
Alba, about twelve miles southeast of Rome.

Nec minore scelere quam quod ulcisci videbatur,
absentem inauditamque damnavit incesti, cum ipse
fratris filiam incesto non polluisset solum, verum etiam
occidisset; nam vidua abortu periit. 7 Missi statim
pontifices, qui defodiendam necandamque curarent.
Illa nunc ad Vestam, nunc ad ceteros deos manus
tendens multa, sed hoc frequentissime clamitabat: "Me
Caesar incestam putat, qua sacra faciente vicit,
triumphavit?"

10

15

---

**quam:** *than.* Construe with the comparative **minore**.

**quod:** The antecedent is an understood **scelus**: *with a wickedness not lesser than (the wickedness) that he was seen to punish.*

**videbatur:** *he was seen.*

**absentem inauditamque:** These words modify an understood **Corneliam**.

**incesti:** genitive of charge. Here **incestum** means *unchastity.* Domitian charged Cornelia with *unchastity,* breaking her vow of chastity. However, the word **incestum** can sometimes mean, more narrowly, *incest,* sexual relations with a close relative. This is its meaning in the next clause, where Pliny alleges that Domitian was guilty of incest with his niece.

**cum:** introducing a concessive clause with the subjunctives **polluisset** and **occidisset**.

**incesto:** ablative. The story that Domitian was responsible for his niece's death is probably fictitious and invented by his enemies. However, Pliny was happy to repeat it because it portrayed the emperor as a depraved hypocrite. Domitian's enemies alleged that he had slept with his brother's daughter, Julia, a widow, and, when she became pregnant, he forced her to have an abortion that resulted in her death. The Latin word **abortus** can mean either *abortion* or *miscarriage.* There is thus some ambiguity in Pliny's words **abortu periit**. Julia may have died as a result of either an *abortion* or a natural *miscarriage.*

**non . . . solum:** Translate together: *not only.* Construe with **polluisset**.

**vidua:** *widow,* a reference to Julia. The historian Suetonius (*Life of Domitian* 10.4) reports that Domitian killed Julia's husband because he suspected him of plotting against him.

7   **Missi:** Supply **sunt** (to form a third plural, perfect passive indicative). Priests were sent back to Rome from the Alban villa.

**qui:** introducing a relative clause of purpose with the subjunctive, **curarent**.

**defodiendam necandamque:** gerundives modifying an understood **illam**: *her* (Cornelia) *to be buried alive and killed.*

**curarent:** When used with an accusative and gerundive, **curare** means *to cause* (something to be done), *to order.*

**Illa:** Just before she is carried on a litter through the streets of Rome to the site of her burial, Cornelia appeals to Vesta and other gods. Once she was placed on the litter, she was gagged so that she could not make a sound. The burial site was just inside the city walls. There, steps led down to a subterranean chamber. In it were a couch, lamp, and small portions of bread, water, and oil. Once the condemned Vestal had stepped down into the chamber, it was sealed.

**multa, hoc:** two objects of **clamitabat**.

**Caesar:** Domitian. All emperors after Augustus assumed his family name, Caesar, as a title.

**qua:** The antecedent is **me**. **Qua** is part of the ablative absolute construction with the participle **faciente**: *who doing (performing) the sacred rites*; less literally *although when I (= who) was performing the sacred rites.*

**vicit, triumphavit:** The subject is Domitian. Cornelia is trying to make the point that she must be innocent and the gods must be pleased with her work as the senior Vestal Virgin because they granted many military victories to Domitian.

8 Blandiens haec an inridens, ex fiducia sui an ex
contemptu principis dixerit, dubium est. Dixit, donec
ad supplicium, nescio an innocens, certe tamquam
innocens ducta est. 9 Quin etiam, cum in illud
20    subterraneum cubiculum demitteretur, haesissetque
descendenti stola, vertit se ac recollegit, cumque
ei manum carnifex daret, aversata est et resiluit
foedumque contactum quasi plane a casto puroque
corpore novissima sanctitate reiecit.

---

8      **sui:** objective genitive of the reflexive pronoun **se**; construe with the **fiducia**:
       *confidence in herself.*

       **dubium est:** the main verb of this complex sentence. The phrase introduces
       an indirect question, which requires a subjunctive verb: **dixerit**. In fact, there
       are four indirect questions in all, because Pliny offers two pairs of alternative
       interpretations (two sets of disjunctive questions) for Cornelia's behavior. All
       four indirect questions use the verb **dixerit** (whose object is the neuter plural
       accusative **haec**). Pliny might have used the words **utrum ... an,** *whether ...
       or,* to introduce the indirect questions, but he uses only **an**. **Blandiens** and
       **inridens** are present participles modifying the understood subject, Cornelia,
       and presenting the first two options: *it is uncertain whether she said these things
       flattering* (to flatter Domitian) *or whether she said these things mocking* (to
       mock him). Pliny then provides two further options: **ex fiducia sui an ex
       contemptu principis**.

       **nescio an:** literally: *I do not know whether;* less literally: *perhaps.* Our other
       ancient sources are certain that Cornelia was guilty. Pliny attempts to cast
       doubt on her guilt because he wants to make Domitian look like a monster.

9      **demitteretur, haesissetque:** Both verbs are subjunctive in the temporal
       clause introduced by **cum**. However, **demitteretur** is imperfect subjunc-
       tive while **haesisset** is pluperfect. The subject of **demitteretur** is Cornelia;
       the subject of **haesisset** is **stola**. *Her dress had caught* (on something) *as she
       descended.* **Descendenti** is dative of reference.

       **cumque** = **et cum**. The conjunction **cum** is joined to the sentence by the
       enclitic **-que**.

       **ei:** dative of indirect object; the reference is to Cornelia.

**carnifex:** Strictly speaking, there was no executioner present because the guilty Vestal Virgin was simply left in the chamber with a small amount of food and water. The Romans thus absolved themselves of any responsibility for killing a priestess. However, someone was at the scene to make sure that the Vestal descended into the underground chamber. It is possible that the "someone" may have been the Pontifex Maximus, that is, Domitian himself. Pliny uses the word **carnifex** to color the scene with more horror and pathos.

**novissima sanctitate:** ablative: *in her final* (act of) *purity*. **Novissimus**, the superlative of **novus**, can mean *most recent* in the sense of *last, final*. Compare Letter 5.16, Section 3, and Letter 6.16, Section 20.

# 11. Letter 4.13

Letter 4.13 is, like Letter 1.6, addressed to Cornelius Tacitus. There are several possible reasons for Pliny's decision to publish this letter. First, it provides a permanent record of Pliny's generosity. In addition, it creates a paper trail to demonstrate that Pliny considered himself a friend of the famous historian. In the letter, moreover, Pliny ingratiates himself with Tacitus by flattering him and requesting his assistance.

We know from inscriptional evidence that Pliny was a generous patron to his hometown of Comum. (On this inscription, see "The Life of Pliny" in the introduction to this book and the Appendix of Inscriptions.) The inscription records that he paid for the construction and maintenance of a public bath building, for the upkeep of a public library, and for financial support for boys and girls and for freedmen (former slaves) in the town. In this letter, he outlines his plan to fund a school in Comum.

---

### C. PLINIUS CORNELIO TACITO SUO S.

1 Salvum te in urbem venisse gaudeo; venisti autem, si quando alias, nunc maxime mihi desideratus. Ipse pauculis adhuc diebus in Tusculano commorabor, ut
5  opusculum, quod est in manibus, absolvam. 2 Vereor enim ne, si hanc intentionem iam in fine laxavero, aegre resumam.

Interim, ne quid festinationi meae pereat, quod sum praesens petiturus, hac quasi praecursoria epistula
10  rogo. 3 Sed prius accipe causas rogandi, deinde ipsum, quod peto.

---

1   **Salvum te: Salvum** is the adjective, *safe*, but in English we would use the adverb: *safely*.

**te . . . venisse:** the accusative infinitive construction in indirect statement.

**urbem:** Rome. On the use of **urbs** to designate specifically Rome, compare Letter 3.11, Section 2; also Letters 9.6, Section 1, and 10.96, Section 4.

**si quando alias:** *if ever at another time.*

**mihi:** dative of agent, instead of ablative of agent with **ab**.

**pauculis . . . diebus:** ablative of duration of time, instead of the accusative. Compare Letter 8.5, Section 1.

**in Tusculano:** Supply **praedio**. The estate was near the town of Tusculum, which was about sixteen miles southeast of Rome in the Alban Hills. (See Map 2; Letter 4.11, Section 6, mentions the Alban villa of the emperor Domitian.)

**ut:** introducing a purpose clause with the subjunctive verb **absolvam**.

**opusculum:** Pliny means a literary work that he (perhaps modestly) considers minor.

**in manibus:** English uses the singular, *in hand*, to mean *in progress*.

2    **ne:** *lest*; introducing a subjunctive verb, **resumam**, after a verb of fearing.

**in fine:** *at the end*. Pliny is close to finishing his small work.

**laxavero:** future perfect indicative in a future more vivid protasis. (The apodosis is the **ne . . . resumam** clause.)

**ne:** introducing a negative purpose clause with the verb **pereat**.

**quid (indef. pron.):** *something, anything*. The more common form of the indefinite adjective is **aliqui, aliqua, aliquod**, but **qui, qua, quod** are used after the conjunctions **si, nisi, ne**, and **num**.

**festinationi meae:** dative of separation (a subcategory of the dative of reference).

**pereat:** *be lost*: *in order that not anything be lost from my urgency*. The *urgency* of which Pliny speaks is his eagerness to accomplish a project that he describes below (the establishment of a school). Less literally: *in order that my urgency not suffer any loss (become weaker)*.

**quod . . . rogo:** The relative pronoun **quod** is the direct object of **sum . . . petiturus**. Its antecedent is an understood **id**, which would be the direct object of **rogo**: *I am asking (that) which*.

**sum . . . petiturus:** active (first) periphrastic construction: *I am about to request, going to request*. Pliny will make this request also in person when he returns to Rome from the Tusculan estate.

**hāc . . . epistulā:** ablative of means.

3    **rogandi:** gerund in the genitive case (objective gen.).

**ipsum:** *the very thing, the thing itself*.

Proxime cum in patria mea fui, venit ad me salutandum
municipis mei filius praetextatus. Huic ego "Studes?"
inquam. Respondit: "Etiam." "Ubi?" "Mediolani." "Cur
15   non hic?" Et pater eius (erat enim una atque etiam ipse
adduxerat puerum): "Quia nullos hic praeceptores
habemus." 4 "Quare nullos? nam vehementer intererat
vestra, qui patres estis" (et opportune complures patres
audiebant) "liberos vestros hic potissimum discere.
20   Ubi enim aut iucundius morarentur quam in patria aut
pudicius continerentur quam sub oculis parentum aut
minore sumptu quam domi?

---

**patria mea:** Pliny's homeland was in the area of Comum (now Como), in
northern Italy, about twenty-five miles north of Mediolanum (now Milan).

**salutandum:** a gerundive modifying the accusative **me.** The accusative of the
gerundive used after the preposition **ad** denotes purpose: *to me to be greeted.*
Less literally: *to greet me.* A wealthy landowner, such as Pliny, was expected
to help the residents of his homeland, particularly with financial support for
municipal projects. He was the town's patron and he was treated with great
deference. It was customary for people of a lower social status to indicate their
respect for the patron by visiting his home. The visit was called a **salutatio**,
a *greeting.* Most people simply stood outside; a few might be invited in for an
audience, during which they could request the patron's assistance.

**praetextatus:** wearing a **toga praetexta,** a toga with a border of purple worn
by boys until they came of age at about fifteen or sixteen years. The adjective
indicates that the boy was less than midteen.

**Studes:** *Do you study? Are you a student?*

**"Etiam":** the Latin equivalent of English *yes.*

**Mediolani:** locative case. Mediolanum (now Milan) was about twenty-five
miles south of Comum. (See Map 1.)

**hīc:** *here,* that is, in Comum.

**praeceptores:** The father means that the residents of the town do not have a
higher-level teacher (**rhetor**). There were undoubtedly teachers in Comum
who taught younger children the three Rs, but none who taught advanced
classes. Pliny had likely received his higher education in Rome. (See "The Life
of Pliny" in the introduction to this book.) Education in the ancient Roman

world was not publicly funded. Parents had to pay teachers for their children's lessons. Thus boys from wealthy families received more education than boys from poor families. And most families were not willing or could not afford to spend much money for the education of girls.

4     **intererat:** The impersonal verb **interest** often governs a genitive, for example, **interest vestrum** (genitive plural of **vos**): *it is of importance to you.* Sometimes, however, it governs the ablative feminine singular of the possessive adjective, **vester**, as here for example, **interest vestrā**: *it is of importance to you.* The adjective **vestrā** modifies an understood **rē**: *your (situation).* (The use of the feminine ablative is idiomatic and cannot be translated literally into English.) The verb **intererat** is here in the imperfect tense, denoting a situation existing in the past and continuing into the present: *it was (and still is).*

**qui patres estis:** The antecedent of the relative pronoun **qui** is **vos**, *you*, understood from the **vestrā**.

**liberos . . . discere:** Although we may translate the subject of the impersonal verb **intererat** as *it*, the grammatical subject is the accusative infinitive construction: *that your children learn.*

**iucundius, pudicius:** comparative degree of the adverb.

**morarentur, continerentur:** imperfect subjunctives. **Morarentur** is a deponent form. The use of the imperfect subjunctive indicates that the question contains a "disguised" or implied present contrary to fact condition. Pliny is suggesting that the boys *would* be happier and more closely supervised, *if* they remained at home. Compare Letter 6.4, Section 3.

5 Quantulum est ergo collata pecunia conducere
praeceptores, quodque nunc in habitationes, in
25   viatica, in ea, quae peregre emuntur (omnia autem
peregre emuntur), impenditis, adicere mercedibus?
Atque adeo ego, qui nondum liberos habeo, paratus
sum pro re publica nostra, quasi pro filia vel parente,
tertiam partem eius, quod conferre vobis placebit,
30   dare. 6 Totum etiam pollicerer, nisi timerem ne hoc
munus meum quandoque ambitu corrumperetur, ut
accidere multis in locis video, in quibus praeceptores
publice conducuntur. 7 Huic vitio occurri uno remedio
potest, si parentibus solis ius conducendi relinquatur,
35   isdemque religio recte iudicandi necessitate collationis
addatur. 8 Nam, qui fortasse de alieno neglegentes,
certe de suo diligentes erunt dabuntque operam, ne a
me pecuniam [non] nisi dignus accipiat, si accepturus
et ab ipsis erit.

---

5   **Quantulum est:** *How little (a thing) it is.* The subjects of **est** are the infinitives
**conducere** and **adicere** (which appears several lines below).

**collatā:** ablative singular, perfect passive participle of **conferre**.

**quod:** direct object of **impenditis**. The antecedent of **quod** is an understood
**id**, which would be the direct object of **adicere**: *to apply* (that) *what you spend.*

**paratus sum:** Here **paratus** is used as an adjective, thus *I am prepared*, rather
than *I have been prepared*.

**pro re publica nostra:** Pliny here means the Comum community.

**eius quod:** *of that* (amount) *which.* **Quod** is the subject of **placebit**.

**dare:** complementary infinitive with **paratus sum**.

6   **pollicerer, nisi timerem:** present contrary to fact condition, followed by
a noun (substantive) clause of fearing. **Timerem ne** introduces a clause of
fearing whose subjunctive verb is **corrumperetur**.

**corrumperetur:** Pliny is concerned that, if the students' families do not make a financial investment in the school, they will not be vigilant about its management and about the hiring and oversight of the teachers.

**ut:** *as.*

**publice conducuntur:** *hired with community funds.* This phrase does not have the same connotation as it does for modern school funding, which is raised through taxes. *Community funds* might mean a donation given to the community by a private patron like Pliny. Beginning in the reign of Vespasian, emperor 69–79 CE, **rhetores** (advanced-level teachers) were sometimes hired in Rome and paid from state funds. Later emperors extended the practice to other towns. However, there was never a comprehensive public education system.

7    **occurri ... potest: Potest** is impersonal. **Occurri** is the present passive infinitive and governs the dative case (**vitio**). *It can be resisted to this flaw.* Less literally: *One can resist (prevent) this flaw,* or *this flaw can be prevented.*

**conducendi, iudicandi:** gerunds in the genitive case.

**relinquatur, addatur:** present subjunctives in the protasis of future less vivid conditions. (However, the verb of the apodosis is present indicative, **potest**, creating a "mixed condition.")

**isdem:** dative case, corresponding with **parentibus solis**.

8    **qui:** Understand the verb **sunt:** (those) *who are.*

**alieno:** *someone else's* (money).

**dabuntque operam:** followed by a negative purpose (final) clause introduced by **ne**.

**[non] nisi:** The square brackets are used to indicate that the modern editor of the Latin text believes that the word (or letter) enclosed in the brackets, although appearing in the manuscript, was not written by Pliny, that is, that it was inserted in error by the people who later copied the epistles. The **ne** that introduces the purpose clause supplies the necessary negative meaning. Contrast the use of chevron brackets in Letter 10.96, Section 2.

**accipiat:** The understood subject is the hypothetical teacher whom the shareholders in the school hire. He will not receive payment unless he is worthy (**nisi dignus**). The direct object is **pecuniam**.

**accepturus ... erit:** active (first) periphrastic construction. The subject is the understood hired teacher. The direct object is **pecuniam**.

**a me ... ab ipsis:** These words are correlative: *money from me* and *money from themselves* (the parents).

40    9 Proinde consentite, conspirate maioremque animum
      ex meo sumite, qui cupio esse quam plurimum, quod
      debeam conferre. Nihil honestius praestare liberis
      vestris, nihil gratius patriae potestis. Educentur hic, qui
      hic nascuntur, statimque ab infantia natale solum
45    amare, frequentare consuescant. Atque utinam tam
      claros praeceptores inducatis, ut finitimis oppidis
      studia hinc petantur, utque nunc liberi vestri aliena in
      loca, ita mox alieni in hunc locum confluant!"

      10 Haec putavi altius et quasi a fonte repetenda,
50    quo magis scires, quam gratum mihi foret, si
      susciperes, quod iniungo. Iniungo autem et pro rei
      magnitudine rogo, ut ex copia studiosorum, quae ad
      te ex admiratione ingenii tui convenit, circumspicias
      praeceptores, quos sollicitare possimus, sub ea tamen
55    condicione, ne cui fidem meam obstringam.

---

9    **animum:** here means *resolve, initiative.*

**meo:** Understand **animo.**

**qui:** The antecedent of the relative pronoun is **ego,** *I*, understood from **meo.**

**cupio:** This verb is followed by an accusative-infinitive construction in indirect statement. The accusative subject of the construction is an understood **id,** which is the antecedent of the **quod** of the **quod debeam conferre** clause: *(that) which I must contribute.* The infinitive predicate after **cupio** is **esse.** Modifying the **quod debeam conferre** clause as a predicate adjective is **quam plurimum. Quam** with a superlative means *as . . . as possible.* Thus: *I wish (that) which I must contribute to be as much as possible.*

**debeam:** This verb is in the subjunctive mood because it is in a subordinate clause in indirect statement.

**honestius, gratius:** comparative degree of the adjectives.

**educentur, consuescant:** jussive subjunctives. The subjects are the sons of the men to whom Pliny is speaking.

**solum:** Note the short *o.* **Solum** = *land, soil;* **sōlum** = *alone, single.*

**utinam:** introduces an optative subjunctive.

**ut:** introduces two result clauses, one with the verb **petantur** whose subject is **studia**, the other with the verb **confluant**, whose subject is **alieni**.

**oppidis:** dative of agent. Pliny means *by (families in) neighboring towns.*

**studia:** *studies, educations.*

**utque:** This second **ut** (**ut + que**) means *(and) just as* and is not introducing a subjunctive clause. It introduces a clause where an indicative verb is understood: **utque nunc liberi vestri (confluunt)**: *(and) just as now your children (flock).* The -**que** is joining **petantur** and **confluant**.

10    **putavi:** followed by an accusative infinitive construction in indirect statement. The accusative subject is **haec**, *these* (things, details). The infinitive predicate is **repetenda** (**esse** is understood). **Repetenda esse** is a passive (second) periphrastic construction, which expresses obligation. *I thought that these things were to be (should be) recounted.*

**altius:** the comparative adverb: *more deeply*, that is, *in greater depth.*

**quo:** *in order that.* **Quo** is used instead of **ut** to introduce a purpose (final) clause that contains a comparative degree form, here **magis**. **Quo** (an ablative of degree of difference) is construed closely with the "more" implied in the comparative form **magis**. **Quo . . . magis** means literally *by which . . . more.* A smoother English translation would be *in order that* (you may know) *more* (or *better*). Compare Letter 6.16, Section 1.

**quam . . . foret: Foret** is an alternative form for **esset**. The construction is a form of indirect exclamation, which uses the same construction as an indirect question and therefore requires a subjunctive, **foret**.

**susciperes:** The condition is future less vivid, but the tense is imperfect rather than present within the indirect statement construction in secondary sequence.

**rogo:** followed by an indirect command, whose subjunctive verb is **circumspicias**.

**quae:** The antecedent is **copia**.

**possimus:** subjunctive mood in a relative clause of characteristic.

**cui:** instead of **alicui**, after **ne**.

**ne . . . obstringam:** present subjunctive in a clause of proviso.

Omnia enim libera parentibus servo; illi iudicent, illi
eligant; ego mihi curam tantum et impendium vindico.
11 Proinde, si quis fuerit repertus, qui ingenio suo fidat,
eat illuc ea lege, ut hinc nihil aliud certum quam
60  fiduciam suam ferat. Vale.

---

**Omnia . . . libera . . . servo:** *I am keeping all things unrestricted (open).* Pliny indicates that he will be a silent financial partner, leaving all the management decisions to the parents.

**iudicent, eligant:** jussive subjunctives.

11  **quis:** instead of **aliquis,** after **si.**

**fuerit repertus = erit repertus:** future perfect passive indicative in a future more vivid condition.

**ingenio suo:** *his own talent.* The dative is dependent on the verb **fidat.**

**fidat:** subjunctive mood in a relative clause of characteristic.

**eat:** jussive subjunctive from **ire.**

**illuc:** *to that place.* Pliny means *to Comum.* He is in the Tusculan area, writing to Tacitus in Rome.

**ea lege:** *with this agreement, under this condition.*

**hinc:** *from this place.* Pliny means *from Rome,* or *from me and you.* Pliny wants Tacitus to warn the prospective teacher that he has been given no guarantee of employment in Comum. The decision about hiring rests with the parents whom he will meet in Comum.

**ferat:** present subjunctive in a clause of proviso introduced by **ut.**

This wall painting, discovered at the estate of Julia Felix in Pompeii, displays items intended to suggest to viewers that the owner of the property was a wealthy and successful
businessperson. In the upper section are depictions of a pile of silver coins, a money bag,
and a pile of gold coins. In the lower section are depictions of articles of writing equipment
that would be used to record business transactions: a bronze container of ink, a pen, a papyrus roll, two wax tablets (*pugillares*) and a *stilus* for writing in the wax. The same equipment
would also, of course, be used by literary authors and by schoolboys. (Public Domain)

# 12. Letter 4.19

About 100 CE, Pliny married for the third time. His wife's death ended his second marriage. We do not know whether death or divorce ended the first. And we know almost nothing about the first two wives, although we learn, from his published letters, that he remained on very good terms with his second mother-in-law. Pliny was about forty years old at the time of his third marriage. His bride was in her midteens. This age discrepancy was not unusual. It was not uncommon for girls to be married when they were thirteen or fourteen years old. In fact, Letter 5.16 records that a girl of twelve years of age was about to be married. When an older man was looking for a wife, he often sought a young bride who had many years of childbearing ahead of her. It is important to realize that life expectancy in the ancient world was very low. Many children died before they were even five years old, and therefore a wife was expected to have many pregnancies to ensure that at least one or two of the children survived to adulthood. The mortality rate among young adults was also high, and thus many people lost spouses to death. It was therefore not unusual for a middle-aged man to have had two or three wives.

Pliny's third wife, whose name was Calpurnia (the feminine form of the family **nomen**, Calpurnius), was raised in his hometown, Comum. Their families had been friends for several generations. (See Genealogy Chart 1.) At the time of the marriage, she was living with her paternal grandfather, Calpurnius Fabatus, and her paternal aunt, Calpurnia Hispulla. Her father was dead. Her mother may also have been dead or perhaps had lost custody of her because, under Roman law, children belonged to the family of their father. This letter is addressed to Calpurnia's aunt, Calpurnia Hispulla, who was about the same age as Pliny, who had known him since childhood, and who seems to have played a major role in arranging the marriage.

To avoid confusion, Pliny's wife will henceforth be identified as Calpurnia and her aunt as Hispulla, although the aunt's full name was Calpurnia Hispulla. It was customary for women to receive, as their **nomen**, the feminine form of their father's **nomen**. (On Roman naming practices, see "The Life of Pliny" in the introduction.) Calpurnia Hispulla had, in addition, a **cognomen**. Hispulla is presumably the feminine form of the **nomen gentilicium** Hispullus, but we do not know what Calpurnia's relationship to that family may have been.

## C. PLINIUS CALPURNIAE HISPULLAE SUAE S.

1 Cum sis pietatis exemplum, fratremque optimum et amantissimum tui pari caritate dilexeris, filiamque eius ut tuam diligas, nec tantum amitae ei, verum

5   etiam patris amissi adfectum repraesentes, non dubito maximo tibi gaudio fore, cum cognoveris dignam patre, dignam te, dignam avo evadere.

---

1   **Cum:** introducing causal clauses with the subjunctive verbs **sis**, **dilexeris**, **diligas**, and **repraesentes**.

**pietatis: Pietas** means *devotion*, here particularly to one's family.

**amantissimum tui:** *very loving of you*; less literally *very loving toward you*. **Amantissimum** modifies **fratrem**. **Tui** is objective genitive of the personal pronoun **tu**.

**pari caritate:** *with equal affection*; ablative of manner. The brother (Calpurnia's deceased father) and sister (Calpurnia's aunt) loved one another equally.

**ut tuam:** *as if your own* (daughter).

**amitae:** genitive singular. Construe with **adfectum**.

**ei:** feminine singular, dative of indirect object with **repraesentes**; referring to the niece, Calpurnia.

**amissi:** perfect passive participle, genitive singular of **amittere**.

**dubito:** The main verb of the sentence. The use of **dubitare** with an infinitive (here **fore**) was used by Pliny instead of **dubito quin** + subjunctive.

**maximo tibi gaudio:** a double dative construction (dative of purpose and dative of reference): *it will be a very great joy to you*.

**fore:** alternative form of the future infinitive of **esse**, which is **futurum esse**.

**cum:** introducing a temporal clause.

**dignam:** modifying an understood **Calpurniam**, which is the accusative subject of **evadere** in an indirect statement after **cognoveris**. **Dignam** is an adjective modifying the understood **Calpurniam** predicatively: *that Calpurnia* (or *she*) *is turning out worthy*. **Dignus** takes the ablative case.

**evadere:** Pliny reports that his new wife is proving worthy of her family. Pliny wrote this letter to reassure Hispulla, who had arranged the marriage, that the marriage was going well and that she, who had raised Calpurnia in the absence of her parents, had done a good job of preparing her for marriage.

2 Summum est acumen, summa frugalitas; amat me,
quod castitatis indicium est. Accedit his studium
10   litterarum, quod ex mei caritate concepit. 3 Meos
libellos habet, lectitat, ediscit etiam. Qua illa
sollicitudine, cum videor acturus, quanto, cum egi,
gaudio adficitur! Disponit qui nuntient sibi, quem
adsensum, quos clamores excitarim, quem eventum
15   iudicii tulerim. Eadem, si quando recito, in proximo
discreta velo sedet laudesque nostras avidissimis
auribus excipit. 4 Versus quidem meos cantat etiam
formatque cithara, non artifice aliquo docente, sed
amore, qui magister est optimus.

---

2    **Summum est acumen:** Supply a dative of possession: **ei (Calpurniae).**
**Acumen** here means Calpurnia's astuteness in managing the household.
Pliny also praises her **frugalitas,** *thriftiness.* Pliny was a very wealthy man,
and his wife did not need to be frugal, but **frugalitas** was a virtue convention-
ally associated with good wives.

It is important to keep in mind that Calpurnia was only about fifteen
years old and had been transported from a sheltered life in Comum to the
crowded city of Rome, where she assumed the role of wife to a man more than
twice her age and the duties of managing a large household with many slaves.

**his:** dative: *to these (qualities).*

**mei:** objective genitive. Construe as **ex caritate mei.**

3    **libellos:** *small literary works.* Pliny may truly mean that his literary works
are not long and substantial, or he may be adopting a posture of modesty.
Compare the note on **opusculum** in Letter 4.13, Section 1.

**lectitat, ediscit: Lectitare** is a frequentative form of its cognate **legere:** *she
reads again and again.* **Ediscere** is an emphatic form of its cognate **discere:**
*she learns thoroughly.*

Although quite young, Calpurnia had astutely figured out that she could
win her husband's affection by showing interest in his work as a writer and
speaker.

**Qua:** ablative of the interrogative adjective. Construe with **sollicitudine.**

**illa:** nominative singular feminine.

**acturus:** future active participle of **agere**, which can mean *to speak in court, plead a case*. In this context, the perfect indicative **egi** has the same meaning.

**qui:** introducing a relative clause of purpose, with the subjunctive verb **nuntient**.

Understand **eos** as the direct object of **disponit** and as the antecedent of **qui:** *she posts (those, i.e., men) who announce*.

**sibi:** *to her*; indirect reflexive pronoun. The accusative form is **se**. There is no nominative form.

**clamores:** *shouts* (of approval).

**excitarim:** a syncopated (contracted) form of **excitaverim**, the first person singular perfect subjunctive. The subjunctives **excitarim** and **tulerim** are required for the indirect questions.

**Eadem:** Calpurnia.

**si quando:** *if ever*. Better: *whenever*.

**recito:** It was common for men of Pliny's social class to host gatherings at which they read aloud their own literary compositions.

**in proximo:** *in the immediate proximity, close by*. The adjective is being used as a substantive. Compare the use of **proximo** in Letter 1.6, Section 1.

**discreta velo:** Pliny's wife Calpurnia listened to his recitations, but her presence was concealed behind a curtain from the male audience. Tacitus, *Annals* 13.5.2, uses the same phrase to describe a scene where Nero's mother, Agrippina, surreptitiously listened in on a Senate meeting, concealed by a curtain.

**nostras:** *my* (not *our*). It was not uncommon in Latin for the adjective **noster** to refer to one person, *my*, rather than several, *our*. Similarly the pronoun **nos** on occasion can mean *I* rather than *we*.

4     **cithara:** ablative case. *She arranges my verses (poetry) with the lyre*; less literally *for the lyre*. Calpurnia sets his poetry to music.

**non artifice aliquo docente:** ablative absolute: *not with some musician teaching* (her).

**amore:** Understand **docente**, to form another ablative absolute.

20    5 His ex causis in spem certissimam adducor
perpetuam nobis maioremque in dies futuram esse
concordiam. Non enim aetatem meam aut corpus,
quae paulatim occidunt ac senescunt, sed gloriam
diligit. 6 Nec aliud decet tuis manibus educatam, tuis
25    praeceptis institutam, quae nihil in contubernio tuo
viderit nisi sanctum honestumque, quae denique amare
me ex tua praedicatione consueverit. 7 Nam, cum
matrem meam parentis loco verereris, me a pueritia
statim formare, laudare, talemque, qualis nunc uxori
30    meae videor, ominari solebas. 8 Certatim ergo tibi
gratias agimus, ego, quod illam mihi, illa, quod me sibi
dederis, quasi invicem elegeris. Vale.

---

5    **in dies:** *day by day.*

**futuram esse concordiam:** accusative infinitive construction in indirect
statement, dependent on the verbal action of hoping implied in the noun
**spem**.

Note that the **concordia** that Pliny believes he finds in his marriage is
achieved when his young wife devotes herself to *his* interests. Although the
etymology of the word suggests mutual efforts to live together harmoniously,
in practice it was generally the wife who was expected to adapt herself to her
husband's interests. In Letter 3.16, Section 10, Arria the Elder told her family
that she had lived in harmony, **concordia**, with her husband for a long time.

**quae:** nominative neuter plural, referring to **aetatem meam aut corpus** (objects of **diligit**).

6    **aliud:** here used as a substantive, *anything else,* and as the subject of **decet**.

**manibus, praeceptis:** ablatives of means: *at your hands, by your instructions.*

**educatam, institutam:** perfect passive participles, accusative direct objects
of **decet**. The participles modify an understood **illam**: *her* or *one educated.*

**quae:** feminine nominative singular. The antecedent is the **illam**, *her,* implied
in the participles **educatam** and **institutam**.

**viderit, consueverit:** subjunctive verbs in a relative clause of characteristic.

Pliny's comments, that Calpurnia had been raised by Hispulla, inform us that Calpurnia's father had died when she was quite young and that she had lived with her father's family after his death. As noted above, her mother may also have died or perhaps had lost custody of her daughter when her husband died because, under Roman law, children belonged to the family of their father. Calpurnia, Hispulla, and Calpurnius Fabatus had formed a three-generation household. At a time when many people died when quite young, a multigenerational household of "survivors" was not unusual. It seems that Hispulla was a widow or divorcee who had returned home to live with her father.

7    **cum:** introducing a causal clause with **verereris**, second person singular, imperfect subjunctive. The main verb of the sentence, **solebas**, does not appear until the very end.

**parentis loco:** *in the place of a parent.* It seems that Hispulla's mother had died when Hispulla was a child and that Pliny's mother had served as a surrogate mother to her. Hispulla, in turn, took on the role of an older sister for Pliny, shaping his character, praising him, and predicting that he would be an outstanding person.

**formare, laudare:** dependent on **solebas**. Me is the direct object of these infinitives. Also dependent on **solebas** is **ominari**. **Ominari** introduces an indirect statement, of which the same **me** now serves as the accusative subject of an implied infinitive predicate: **futurum esse:** *to predict me* (to be), or better: *to predict that I* (would be).

**talemque:** In the indirect statement after the verb **ominari**, **talem** modifies **me** predicatively: *to predict that I* (would be) *such* (a person).

**talem ... qualis:** correlative.

8    **agimus:** The subjects are **ego** and **illa**. **Gratias agere** = *to thank.* Compare Letter 6.16, Section 1.

**quod ... dederis:** The subjunctive mood, used here, is less common than the indicative after **quod** causal.

**illam, illa:** Calpurnia.

**sibi:** *to her*; indirect reflexive pronoun.

**invicem:** *each in turn for the other.*

**elegeris:** perfect subjunctive following a primary tense main verb in a conditional clause of comparison.

# 13. Letter 5.16

Pliny reports the death of the daughter of one of his friends, Mini-cius Fundanus, at the young age of twelve or thirteen. The letter is a reminder of how fragile life was in the ancient world. It is also testimony to the universality of grief and of parents' love for their children.

By chance, in the late nineteenth century, the girl's epitaph was discovered in her family tomb just north of Rome. From the epitaph on her tombstone, we have learned that her name was Minicia Marcella. There was also in the tomb an epitaph for a woman who we believe was her mother, Statoria Marcella. (Note the use of **cognomina** for these women. See the comment about the name Calpurnia Hispulla in the introduction to Letter 4.19.)

Letter 5.16 is addressed to Aefulanus Marcellinus, about whom we know nothing.

---

C. PLINIUS AEFULANO MARCELLINO SUO S.
1 Tristissimus haec tibi scribo, Fundani nostri filia minore defuncta. Qua puella nihil umquam festivius, amabilius, nec modo longiore vita, sed prope
5 immortalitate dignius vidi. 2 Nondum annos XIIII impleverat, et iam illi anilis prudentia, matronalis gravitas erat et tamen suavitas puellaris cum virginali verecundia.

---

1    **Tristissimus:** a superlative adjective, modifying the subject of **scribo**. In English we would use an adverb: *very sadly.*

**filia minore defuncta:** an ablative absolute construction. From the word **minore**, we know that Minicia had an older sister who may already have been married.

**Qua:** ablative of comparison of the relative adjective: *than which* (**puella**, *girl*). This use of the relative pronoun, **qui, quae, quod**, at the beginning of a sentence is *resumptive*; the pronoun refers to something in the previous sentence and *resumes* the thought expressed in that sentence. The relative is used to link its sentence more closely with the preceding sentence. In English: *than this girl.*

**festivius, amabilius, dignius:** comparative degree. The adjectives are neuter because they modify **nihil**, which is the direct object of **vidi**. It seems perhaps odd that Pliny would compare the girl to "nothing," but the idiom is not uncommon in Latin. Compare the use of **aliud** in Letter 7.19, Section 4.

**vita, immortalitate:** ablatives of respect or specification with **dignius**.

2     **annos XIIII:** The manuscripts record that Minicia had not yet completed fourteen years, that is, that she was still thirteen years old. Her tomb inscription, however, provides the information that she lived XII (12) years, XI (11) months, and VII (7) days, that is, that she was still twelve years old when she died. The manuscripts we have date back to the ninth and tenth centuries CE, about eight hundred years after Pliny wrote his letters, and they are copies of copies. Perhaps Pliny originally wrote XIII, not XIIII, but a later copier added the extra stroke. XIII would correspond to the information on the tombstone, which is likely to be correct because it was commissioned by the family and inscribed at the time of the death.

**illi ... erat:** dative of possession. According to Pliny, Minicia was remarkable because she had, although still a girl, cultivated the virtues of an adult woman. On age-appropriate virtues, see also Letter 8.5.

**verecundia:** In Letter 3.16, Section 3, Arria the Elder's son (who died) is described as possessing **verecundia**.

3 Ut illa patris cervicibus inhaerebat! ut nos amicos

10   paternos et amanter et modeste complectebatur!
ut nutrices, ut paedagogos, ut praeceptores pro suo
quemque officio diligebat! quam studiose, quam
intellegenter lectitabat! ut parce custoditeque ludebat!
Qua illa temperantia, qua patientia, qua etiam

15   constantia novissimam valetudinem tulit! 4 Medicis
obsequebatur, sororem, patrem adhortabatur ipsamque
se destitutam corporis viribus vigore animi sustinebat.

---

3    **Ut:** an exclamatory adverb: *How she used to cling!*

**cervicibus:** plural, where English uses the singular: *neck*. The dative case is governed by the verb **inhaerebat**.

**nutrices, paedagogos:** *nannies, attendants*. These people would be slaves. A **nutrix** was often a woman who had been a wet nurse for an infant (because some upper-class women preferred not to nurse their own children) and then served as a nanny after the child was weaned. Of course, Minicia may have needed a wet nurse if her mother had died while she, Minicia, was an infant. **Nutrix** has the same root as the Latin verb **nutrire**, *to nourish*.

**praeceptores:** Minicia's family was wealthy and hired tutors who came to the house to teach her. Or perhaps they purchased educated slaves to do the job. We need not assume that the level of her education was equivalent to that of the boys mentioned in Letter 4.13. In any case, Minicia's time as a student may have been coming to an end. At the time of her death, at not quite thirteen years of age, she was on the verge of being married and taking on the duties of a wife and mother.

**pro suo quemque officio: Quemque**, *each one*, is the accusative corresponding to the previous accusative direct objects of **diligebat**. Construe as **quemque pro suo officio**. Minicia *loved each one* (of her nannies, attendants, and teachers) *in accordance with each one's* (**suo**) *service* (to her).

**quam studiose:** *how studiously*.

**lectitabat:** On the frequentative verb, see Letter 4.19, Section 3.

**Quā illa temperantiā: Quā temperantiā** is ablative; **illa** is nominative. Construe as **illa quā temperantiā**.

**novissimam valetudinem:** either *most recent illness* or *final illness*. Compare Letter 4.11, Section 9.

4   **sororem, patrem adhortabatur:** Since there is no mention of Minicia's mother, it is likely that she was already dead, although divorce may have separated her from her daughter. Under Roman law, custody of children belonged to the family of their father; see the introduction to Letter 4.19. On the mother's tombstone, see the introduction to this letter.

**viribus:** ablative with the participle **destitutam** (which modifies **ipsamque se**).

**vigore:** ablative of means with **sustinebat**. Note the chiastic arrangement (ABBA) of **corporis viribus vigore animi** (genitive ablative, ablative genitive) and the juxtaposition of *body . . . mind*. (Note, however, that the uses of the ablative differ.)

The tombstone of Minicia Marcella is now housed in the National Roman Museum at the Palazzo Massimo. The inscription reads *D(is) M(anibus), Miniciae Marcellae, Fundani F(iliae), V(ixit) A(nnos) XII, M(enses) XI, D(ies) VII.* (Courtesy of Rebecca Bush/ By kind permission of the Ministero dei beni e delle attività culturali e del turismo—Soprintendenza Speciale per il Colosseo, il Museo Nazionale Romano e l'Area archeologica di Roma)

5 Duravit hic illi usque ad extremum, nec aut spatio
valetudinis aut metu mortis infractus est, quo plures
20    gravioresque nobis causas relinqueret et desiderii et
doloris. 6 O triste plane acerbumque funus! o morte
ipsa mortis tempus indignius! iam destinata erat
egregio iuveni, iam electus nuptiarum dies, iam nos
vocati. Quod gaudium quo maerore mutatum est!
25    7 Non possum exprimere verbis quantum animo
vulnus acceperim, cum audivi Fundanum ipsum, ut
multa luctuosa dolor invenit, praecipientem, quod in
vestes, margaritas, gemmas fuerat erogaturus, hoc in
tura et unguenta et odores impenderetur.

---

5      **hic:** nominative masculine singular. The reference is to **vigor animi**.

**illi:** dative of reference.

**quo:** *so that therefore.* **Quo** (literally *by which*) is used instead of **ut eo** (literally *so that by this*) to introduce a result clause when that clause contains a
comparative form, here the adjectives **plures gravioresque**. The result clause,
with the subjunctive **relinqueret**, is dependent on the main clause: **duravit
... infractus est**. **Quo** is construed closely with the "more" implied in the
comparative forms **plures** (*more* numerous) **gravioresque** (which modify
**causas**). Translate as *so that therefore she left more* (numerous) *and more grievous reasons.* (**Quo** is an ablative of degree of difference. Compare Letter 3.11,
Section 2.)

**relinqueret:** The subject may be either Minicia or **hic vigor animi**.

**desiderii et doloris:** objective genitives after **causas**.

6      **acerbumque:** The primary meaning is *bitter*, as for an unripe fruit, and hence,
by extension, *untimely.*

**funus, tempus:** accusatives of exclamation.

**mortis tempus:** a rhetorical flourish by Pliny: the time of Minicia's death,
just before her wedding, was more cruel than death itself.

**iuveni:** We do not know who the man was who had been selected as Minicia's
husband. Nor do we know his age. Young men married for the first time when
they were about twenty. However, the word **iuvenis** was used of men between

twenty and forty years of age. He was certainly older than the twelve-year-old Minicia. Compare the discrepancy in age between Pliny and Calpurnia.

**electus, vocati:** Supply **erat**, **eramus**.

7     **quo maerore:** ablative of price with a verb of exchanging. **Quod** and **quo** are interrogative adjectives.

**acceperim:** perfect subjunctive in an indirect exclamation (which uses the same construction as an indirect question).

**ut:** here + the indicative *as grief finds many sorrowful things* (to deal with). The meaning is that the person who suffers a loss and is grieving discovers that s/he must attend to situations that cause sorrow, such as planning the funeral. Arria the Elder had to plan her son's funeral even as she was concealing his death from her ill husband (Letter 3.16).

**praecipientem:** modifies **Fundanum**. The participle introduces an indirect command: **hoc . . . impenderetur:** (that) *this* (money) *be spent.* There is no introductory conjunction such as **ut**, *that*.

**quod:** *what* (money). **Quod** is correlative with the **hoc** in the following clause.

**vestes, margaritas, gemmas:** These were items that Minicia's father had planned to give her.

**fuerat erogaturus:** *he had been about to expend, pay out;* active (first) periphrastic with a pluperfect tense.

**tura, unguenta, odores:** These items were used at funerals.

30   8 Est quidem ille eruditus et sapiens, ut qui se ab
ineunte aetate altioribus studiis artibusque dediderit;
sed nunc omnia, quae audiit saepe, quae dixit,
aspernatur expulsisque virtutibus aliis pietatis est
totus. 9 Ignosces, laudabis etiam, si cogitaveris, quid
35   amiserit. Amisit enim filiam, quae non minus mores
eius quam os vultumque referebat, totumque patrem
mira similitudine exscripserat. 10 Proinde, si quas
ad eum de dolore tam iusto litteras mittes, memento
adhibere solacium non quasi castigatorium et nimis
40   forte, sed molle et humanum. Quod ut facilius admittat,
multum faciet medii temporis spatium. 11 Ut enim
crudum adhuc vulnus medentium manus reformidat,
deinde patitur atque ultro requirit, sic recens animi
dolor consolationes reicit ac refugit, mox desiderat et
45   clementer admotis adquiescit. Vale.

---

8   **ut qui:** *as one who, because.* The construction is a relative causal clause, using a subjunctive verb, **dediderit.** Compare Letter 4.11, Section 6.

**audiit:** syncopated (contracted) form of **audivit.**

**expulsisque virtutibus aliis:** ablative absolute.

**pietatis est totus:** **Totus** + the genitive creates an idiom: *totally absorbed with family devotion.* On the meaning of **pietas,** compare Letter 4.19, Section 1.

9   **Ignosces:** The understood object is Fundanus. The Latin form would be **Fundano** because the verb **ignosces** requires a dative.

**quid amiserit:** indirect question.

**quae . . . referebat:** Minicia mirrored her father's character no less than his physical appearance.

**eius:** referring to Fundanus.

**quam:** *than,* with **non minus.**

**totumque patrem:** *the total father.* English would prefer an adverb, *totally.*

10   **quas:** instead of **aliquas,** after **si. Quas** modifies **litteras.** The plural may mean one *epistle, letter.*

**memento:** imperative singular of the defective verb **memini:** *remember.*

**solacium:** Pliny recommends that his addressee, Aefulanus, offer words of consolation that are gentle. It was not uncommon for men, especially Stoic philosophers, to chastise people for grieving excessively.

**Quod:** another resumptive use of the relative pronoun. Translate as *this.* The antecedent is **solacium** in the previous sentence. Within its own clause, **quod** is the direct object of **admittat.**

**ut ... admittat:** a result clause that is dependent on the verb **faciet.** The subject of **faciet** is **spatium.** The subject of **admittat** is an understood Fundanus.

**facilius:** comparative degree of the adverb.

**multum faciet:** *will do much* (with the result that . . .).

**medii temporis:** *of middle time, of intervening time.*

11   **Ut:** *as* + indicative.

**vulnus:** the subject of **reformidat.**

**medentium:** genitive plural, present participle of the deponent verb **mederi.** (The present participle of deponent verbs is active in form and meaning.) Translate as *those healing,* i.e., *doctors.*

**clementer admotis:** (consolations) *gently offered.* The dative case is required by the verb **adquiescit.**

# 14. Letter 6.4

Pliny addressed this letter to his wife, Calpurnia, whose virtues he extolled in Letter 4.19. Here we learn that Calpurnia had traveled south from Rome to Campania (a region that includes Naples; see Map 2) to recuperate from an illness. Pliny may have owned a villa in the Bay of Naples area, which was a favorite vacation spot for wealthy Romans. As Letter 4.19 reveals, Pliny was enamored of his young wife who had learned how to gain his affection. In this letter, he declares how much he misses her.

## C. PLINIUS CALPURNIAE SUAE S.

1 Numquam sum magis de occupationibus meis questus, quae me non sunt passae aut proficiscentem te valetudinis causa in Campaniam prosequi aut
5 profectam e vestigio subsequi. 2 Nunc enim praecipue simul esse cupiebam, ut oculis meis crederem, quid viribus, quid corpusculo adparares, ecquid denique secessus voluptates regionisque abundantiam inoffensa transmitteres.

1   **sum ... questus:** perfect indicative; construe together.

**sunt passae:** perfect indicative of the deponent **patior**. This verb is followed by an accusative-infinitive construction with two infinitives: **me ... prosequi aut ... subsequi**.

**proficiscentem, profectam:** These two participles, the present and the perfect tenses of **proficiscor**, modify **te**. **Te** is the direct object of **prosequi** and **subsequi**. Construe as **prosequi te proficiscentem aut subsequi te profectam**.

**causā:** In the ablative case, **causā** serves as a preposition governing the genitive case, and often (as here) it is postpositive, that is, it follows the word it governs.

**Campaniam:** Campania is an area south of Rome, including the Bay of Naples region.

**e vestigio:** literally *from your footstep*; as an idiom *immediately*.

2    **cupiebam:** The tense is an epistolary imperfect: *I was wishing*. The writer is projecting into the future, knowing that, when the recipient reads the letter, she will think *he was wishing* (while he was writing), rather than *he is wishing*. Because the tense of the verb is imperfect, that is, a secondary sequence tense, the verbs in dependent clauses are also in secondary sequence. For another example, see Letter 7.19, Section 11.

**ut . . . crederem:** a purpose clause, in the imperfect subjunctive because it follows a verb of secondary sequence.

**quid . . . quid . . . ecquid:** interrogative pronouns introducing indirect questions. The subjunctive verbs of the indirect questions, **adparares** and **transmitteres**, are imperfect tense, secondary sequence.

**viribus, corpusculo:** datives: *to* (your) *bodily strength* and *to* (your) *little body*. Pliny is wondering whether Calpurnia has gained back the weight she lost during her illness. The diminutive, **corpusculum** (instead of **corpus**), reminds modern readers that Calpurnia is still quite young.

**secessus:** genitive singular: (pleasures) *of seclusion*. Calpurnia had apparently traveled to Campania to escape the noise and hectic activity of life in Rome.

**abundantiam:** Pliny is referring to the abundance of good food in the Campania region and wondering if Calpurnia has enjoyed the food without ill effects to her health.

**inoffensa:** nominative singular.

10    3 Equidem etiam fortem te non sine cura desiderarem; est enim suspensum et anxium de eo, quem ardentissime diligas, interdum nihil scire. 4 Nunc vero me cum absentiae tum infirmitatis tuae ratio incerta et varia sollicitudine exterret. Vereor omnia, imaginor omnia, quaeque natura metuentium est, ea maxime mihi, quae maxime abominor, fingo. 5 Quo impensius rogo, ut timori meo cotidie singulis vel etiam binis epistulis consulas. Ero enim securior, dum lego, statimque timebo, cum legero. Vale.

---

3    **desiderarem:** imperfect subjunctive. The subjunctive is used because the clause is the apodosis of a present contrary to fact condition. The protasis is implied ("disguised") in the words **etiam fortem:** *even* (if you were) *strong.* Compare Letter 4.13, Section 4.

     **non sine cura:** Pliny is referring to his own anxiety.

     **est:** The subject of this verb is the infinitive phrase **nihil scire.** The adjectives **suspensum et anxium** modify **nihil scire** as neuter singular predicate adjectives: *To know nothing is suspenseful and troubling.*

     **de eo, quem:** Although Pliny is addressing Calpurnia, he uses a generic masculine, instead of a specific feminine: *about one whom.* Therefore the verb **diligas** is a subjunctive in a relative clause of characteristic.

4    **cum … tum:** *both … and.*

     **incertā:** ablative.

     **quaeque:** = **et quae** (-que is the enclitic). **Quae** is nominative feminine singular, agreeing grammatically with **natura:** *what is the nature,* or, less literally, *as is the nature.* The phrase is explained by the words that follow.

     **metuentium:** genitive plural, present participle of **metuere.**

     **ea:** accusative neuter plural, direct object of **fingo. Ea** serves as the antecedent of **quae.**

     **mihi:** dative of reference. Construe closely with **fingo.**

5    **Quo:** *by which, whereby, therefore;* an ablative of degree of difference with the comparative adverb, **impensius. Quo** is resumptive. It refers to the entire thought of the previous sentences: I fear everything, *whereby (therefore)* I more vehemently ask.

**epistulis:** ablative of means.

**consulas:** subjunctive in an indirect command after **rogo**. Pliny is asking Calpurnia to send him one or even two letters a day. There was no official public mail service in the ancient Roman world. The letters between Pliny and his correspondents would have been delivered by messengers.

**legero:** future perfect of **legere**, *when I will have read*, i.e., *after I have read*.

# 15. Letter 6.16

Pliny's maternal uncle is also known to us by the name Pliny. To avoid confusion, he is generally identified as Pliny the Elder, while the author of the letters in this book is known as Pliny the Younger. The father of Pliny the Younger was Lucius Caecilius. We know nothing about him except his name, which is included in inscriptions relating to the life of Pliny the Younger. (On these inscriptions, see "The Life of Pliny" in the introduction to this book and the introduction to Letter 4.13 and the Appendix of Inscriptions.) He died when Pliny the Younger was quite young, perhaps before he had reached his teen years. After his father's death, it seems that Pliny continued to live with his mother, whose name we assume to have been Plinia. Since his father's family could legally have claimed custody of him, it is possible that there were no close paternal relatives alive to provide a home. Plinia's brother, Pliny the Elder (Gaius Plinius Secundus), adopted his nephew, but not until his own death, when the adoption was made official in his will. Until that time, the nephew, who had been born about 61 or 62 CE, had the name of his birth father, Lucius Caecilius. Upon adoption by his uncle, his name was changed to Gaius Plinius Caecilius Secundus. This nomenclature gave recognition to the fact that he was now legally the son of Plinius but had been born a Caecilius.

Pliny the Elder is best known to us as a prolific author who wrote extensively about natural phenomena as well as military history. He also had a distinguished career in public service, including several administrative posts overseas. About 76 CE, Pliny the Elder was appointed prefect of the Roman naval fleet at Misenum, a town on the northwest end of the Bay of Naples. (See Map 2.) Plinia and Pliny the Younger (then about seventeen years old) were staying at his villa at Misenum in the summer of 79 CE. We don't know if they had been living with him for several years or were simply visiting at that time. In any case, they were present at the time of the calamitous eruption of Mount Vesuvius. And Pliny's letter is our only extensive eyewitness account of the eruption. Even today, it remains an important source of information for scientists who study the phenomena of volcanoes. And volcanic eruptions similar in nature to that of Mount Vesuvius in 79 CE are labeled as "Plinian." For more information about volcanic and seismic activity in the Mount Vesuvius area, see Letter 6.20, Section 3 and note.

This volume contains four letters addressed to the Roman historian Cornelius Tacitus. In Letters 1.6 and 4.13, the manuscripts record both his **nomen** and **cognomen**, that is, Cornelius Tacitus. In Letters 6.16 and 6.20, the manuscripts record only his **cognomen**: Tacitus. His **praenomen** may have been Publius or Gaius. There is no certainty.

---

## C. PLINIUS TACITO SUO S.

1 Petis ut tibi avunculi mei exitum scribam, quo verius tradere posteris possis. Gratias ago; nam video morti eius, si celebretur a te, immortalem gloriam esse
5   propositam.

---

1    **tibi:** Pliny implies that Tacitus had requested from him a report on the death of his uncle, Pliny the Elder, in 79 CE, a report that Tacitus could use in his historical writing. We do not know, however, whether Tacitus ever used Pliny's report. Tacitus was planning to write an account of the period from 69 to 96 CE (from the Year of the Four Emperors to the death of Domitian), and he would presumably have reported the eruption of Vesuvius and the death of Pliny the Elder. One of his major works, the *Histories*, begins with the year 69 CE, but the surviving portions of the book extend only to the year 70.

**scribam:** subjunctive in an indirect command.

**quo ... possis:** a purpose (final) clause introduced by **quo** (instead of **ut**) because the clause contains a comparative degree form, here the adverb **verius**. **Quo** (an ablative of degree of difference) is construed closely with the "more" implied in the comparative form **verius**. **Quo verius** means literally *by which more accurately*. A smoother English translation would be *in order that* (you can transmit) *more accurately*. Compare Letter 4.13, Section 10.

**tradere:** Understand **exitum** as the direct object. **Exitum** here means (*a report on*) *the death*.

**Gratias ago:** *I thank you*. Compare Letter 4.19, Section 8.

**morti ... immortalem:** Notice the juxtaposition of *death* and *deathless*. **Morti** is a dative of indirect object.

**morti ... propositam:** This part of the sentence is an indirect statement after the verb **video**. The accusative subject is **gloriam**. **Propositam** is better translated as an adjective with the present infinitive **esse**, rather than as the participial element of a perfect infinitive: *is promised*, rather than *has been promised*.

**Celebretur** (whose subject is an understood **mors eius**) is subjunctive because it is a subordinate clause in an indirect statement.

2 Quamvis enim pulcherrimarum clade terrarum
(ut populi, ut urbes), memorabili casu, quasi semper
victurus occiderit, quamvis ipse plurima opera et
mansura condiderit, multum tamen perpetuitati eius
10      scriptorum tuorum aeternitas addet. 3 Equidem beatos
puto, quibus deorum munere datum est aut facere
scribenda aut scribere legenda, beatissimos vero, quibus
utrumque. Horum in numero avunculus meus et suis
libris et tuis erit. Quo libentius suscipio, deposco etiam,
15      quod iniungis.

---

2      **Quamvis . . . addet: Addet** is the main verb of this long sentence, which contains two subordinate clauses introduced by **quamvis** (which appears twice).
The meaning of the sentence is that the eternal nature of Tacitus's historical
writing will add much to the immortality of Pliny the Elder, although Pliny
the Elder already seems about to live forever, both because he died during a
catastrophe that will be remembered forever and because his literary works
are deathless.

**clade, casu:** ablatives of attendant circumstances: *at* (the same time as) *the
destruction, catastrophe.*

**ut:** *as.* Supply **occĭderunt** (not **occīderunt**): *as peoples, as cities* (have died).
Pliny is referring to the peoples and cities killed in the 79 CE eruption of Mount
Vesuvius, for example, the cities and residents of Pompeii and Herculaneum.

**quasi semper:** *as if;* modifying **victurus.**

**victurus:** future active participle of **vivere.** Pliny is suggesting that his uncle
will live forever (that is, be remembered) because he perished during a catastrophe that will be remembered forever. Notice the juxtaposition of **victurus**
and **occĭderit.**

**occĭderit, condiderit:** The subject is Pliny the Elder. The verbs are subjunctive in the concessive clauses introduced by **quamvis.** Their tenses are perfect
because the introductory verb, **addet,** is future indicative, that is, a primary
sequence tense.

**mansura:** future active participle, modifying **opera.**

**scriptorum tuorum:** Construe with **aeternitas.**

**addet:** Finally—the main verb of the sentence! **Addet** is future indicative.
The subject is **aeternitas.**

3    **beatos puto:** *I consider* (those people) *blessed.* **Beatos** is the antecedent of the dative of indirect object, **quibus.**

**datum est:** The subjects are the infinitives **facere** and **scribere.**

**scribenda, legenda:** gerundives in the neuter plural accusative case: (things) *to be written about,* (things) *to be read;* less literally *worthy of being written about, worthy of being read.*

**quibus utrumque:** Supply **datum est. Quibus** is dative of indirect object. **Utrumque,** the subject of **datum est,** means *both* (to do things worthy of being written about and to write things worthy of being read).

**libris:** ablative of cause; modified by both **suis** and **tuis.**

**Quo:** *by which, whereby, therefore;* ablative of degree of difference with the comparative adverb, **libentius. Quo** is resumptive. It refers to the entire thought of the previous sentences: My uncle will be in the number of the most blessed men if you write about him, *whereby (therefore)* I more readily urge you.

This photo offers a view of Mount Vesuvius as seen from the remains of the ancient Forum of Pompeii. The buildings in the Forum and throughout the city were damaged by an earthquake in 62 CE and then shattered and buried by the volcanic eruption of Mount Vesuvius in 79 CE. The volcano has erupted several times since 79 CE, most recently in 1944. The active cone is the higher peak on the left side of the photo. The mountain was higher before the eruption of 79, which caused it to collapse. (Creative Commons 3.0)

4 Erat Miseni classemque imperio praesens regebat. Nonum Kal. Septembres hora fere septima mater mea indicat ei adparere nubem invisitata et magnitudine et specie. 5 Usus ille sole, mox frigida, gustaverat iacens

20   studebatque; poscit soleas, ascendit locum, ex quo maxime miraculum illud conspici poterat. Nubes— incertum procul intuentibus ex quo monte (Vesuvium fuisse postea cognitum est)—oriebatur, cuius similitudinem et formam non alia magis arbor quam

25   pinus expresserit.

---

4   **Miseni:** locative case. Misenum was a port town at the northwest end of the Bay of Naples, about eighteen miles from Mount Vesuvius and about twelve miles from the city of Naples. (See Map 2.) It had a good natural harbor and was used as the main naval base for the Roman fleet on the west coast of Italy. It was also a popular vacation area for wealthy Romans.

**imperio praesens regebat:** *He (Pliny the Elder), being present, commanded* (the fleet) *with authority.* Less literally: *he was present and held command* (of the fleet). It may seem odd that Pliny would specify that his uncle was present in Misenum. However, his position as prefect did not require that he be in that area at all times.

**Nonum Kal. Septembres:** Translate as *on the ninth day before the September Kalends.* **Kal. = Kalendas.** Pliny could have included the word **ante: ante nonum (diem) Kal. Septembres**. The entire phrase is regularly placed in the accusative case after **ante. Septembres** is an adjective modifying **Kalendas.** The September Kalends (nominative **Kalendae**) were the first day of that month. **Nonum (diem)** is the ninth day before the Kalends of September, which, according to the Roman method of calculating, was, in our terms, *August 24.* (On the Roman custom of counting days inclusively, see the note on Section 20 of this letter.)

**horā ... septimā:** ablative of time when. For the Romans, the seventh hour was the one after midday. The first hour began at sunrise. On the length of Roman hours, see Section 6 of Letter 6.20.

**ei:** dative case; Pliny the Elder.

**adparere nubem:** accusative infinitive in indirect statement.

**invisitata:** modifies **et magnitudine et specie**, which are ablatives of description. Some editors prefer the reading **inusitata**, *unusual, strange,* instead of **invisitata**, *unseen before, strange.*

5    **usus:** It was shortly after noon. Pliny the Elder had enjoyed a sun bath and a dip in cold water before having a light lunch and returning to his studies.

**frigidā:** in the ablative case after **usus**, modifying an understood **aquā**, *water.*

**iacens:** The Romans reclined both for eating and for reading.

**locum:** *to a spot*; accusative. **Ascendere** can be used with or without the preposition **in** or **ad**. Compare Letter 3.16, Section 8.

**Nubes:** subject of **oriebatur**. It is also the unexpressed subject of several verbs in the next sentence.

**incertum:** Supply **erat**. The construction is impersonal.

**intuentibus:** dative with **incertum**.

**Vesuvium:** Mount Vesuvius was (and still is) a volcanic mountain about six miles east of Naples, about eighteen miles east of Misenum. The people living in the area in 79 CE did not realize that it was volcanic. Today its activities are closely monitored.

**cognitum est:** impersonal use: *it was learned*; governing an accusative infinitive construction: **Vesuvium fuisse**.

**cuius:** The antecedent is **nubes**.

**alia:** modifies **arbor**.

**magis . . . quam:** Construe together.

**pinus:** subject of **expresserit**, which is a potential subjunctive. The type of pine tree to which Pliny compared the cloud rising from Vesuvius is common in the Mediterranean area. It does not have the conical shape of "Christmas tree" pines. It is, rather, an umbrella pine whose shape resembles an umbrella. Its trunk rises up several feet without branches (like the stick of an umbrella), and then the branches spread out horizontally to form a canopy that resembles the ribs and canopy of an umbrella.

6 Nam longissimo velut trunco elata in altum
quibusdam ramis diffundebatur, credo, quia recenti
spiritu evecta, dein senescente eo destituta, aut etiam
pondere suo victa, in latitudinem vanescebat, candida
interdum, interdum sordida et maculosa, prout
terram cineremve sustulerat. 7 Magnum propiusque
noscendum ut eruditissimo viro visum. Iubet
Liburnicam aptari; mihi, si venire una vellem, facit
copiam. Respondi studere me malle, et forte ipse, quod
scriberem, dederat.

30

35

---

6   **elata, evecta, destituta, victa:** nominative participles, modifying an understood **nubes**, which was the subject of the previous sentence. **Nubes** is also
the understood subject of the verbs **vanescebat** and **sustulerat**. **Elata** is the
perfect participle of **effere**.

**longissimo velut trunco:** Pliny expands on his comparison of the cloud of
volcanic material to the shape of an umbrella pine tree. The "trunk" is the
initial vertical cloud rising up from the volcano.

**elata . . . diffundebatur:** The understood subject is **nubes**.

**in altum:** *up high, on high.*

**quibusdam:** ablative plural of **quidam**. Translate as *so to speak.* Pliny continues his comparison of the form of the **nubes** to an umbrella pine.

**credo:** *I believe;* an interjection, intended to alert the reader that the explanation that follows is Pliny's own. The **credo** is not followed by an indirect
statement.

**evecta:** nominative perfect participle, modifying an understood **nubes**.

**senescente eo:** ablatives; *by this* (blast of air) *as it decreased in strength.*
**Senescente** is a present participle. **Eo** refers to **spiritus**.

**destituta:** nominative perfect participle, modifying the understood **nubes**.

**victa:** nominative perfect participle, modifying the understood **nubes**.

**in latitudinem:** *laterally, horizontally.* The cloud rose up vertically in a thick
column, but when it reached a great height, it began to spread horizontally
(at which point it resembled the canopy of an umbrella pine tree).

**vanescebat:** The subject is the understood **nubes**.

**candida, sordida, maculosa:** nominative adjectives, modifying the understood **nubes**.

**sustulerat:** pluperfect indicative of **tollere**.

7 **Magnum:** Supply an indefinite substantive: *something great.*

**noscendum:** gerundive of **noscere**, with the implication of necessity or urgency. Supply an indefinite substantive: *something to be learned about (investigated).* The gerundive is modified by the adverb **propius**.

**ut . . . visum:** Supply **est**: *as it seemed.*

**eruditissimo viro:** The *very learned man* is, of course, Pliny's uncle. He wrote an encyclopedia, titled *Naturalis Historia*, in which he collected material from a very wide range of fields, including biology, astronomy, geology, and geography. The strange cloud issuing from Mount Vesuvius seemed to him worthy of closer observation.

**Iubet, facit:** Pliny uses the present tense (termed the historical present) for a more vivid narration.

**vellem:** The imperfect subjunctive may express potentiality: *if I should wish.*

**facit copiam:** *He makes the opportunity*; less literally *he gives the opportunity.*

**respondi:** Pliny switches back to a secondary tense. The verb is followed by an accusative-infinitive construction in indirect statement.

It is perhaps surprising that Pliny would leave for posterity a portrait of himself, at the age of about seventeen, preferring to stay home and read, rather than joining his uncle's bold voyage toward the volcano. His statement explains why he lived to write his account but does not depict him as an adventurous spirit.

**ipse:** refers to Pliny the Elder.

**quod scriberem:** relative clause of purpose. Supply *something* as an antecedent for **quod**.

8 Egrediebatur domo; accipit codicillos Rectinae
Tasci imminenti periculo exterritae (nam villa eius
subiacebat, nec ulla nisi navibus fuga); ut se tanto
discrimini eriperet orabat. 9 Vertit ille consilium
40 et, quod studioso animo incohaverat, obit maximo.
Deducit quadriremes, ascendit ipse non Rectinae
modo, sed multis (erat enim frequens amoenitas orae)
laturus auxilium. 10 Properat illuc, unde alii fugiunt,
rectumque cursum, recta gubernacula in
45 periculum tenet adeo solutus metu, ut omnes illius mali
motus, omnes figuras, ut deprenderat oculis, dictaret
enotaretque.

---

8  **Rectinae Tasci:** both words are in the genitive case. **Rectinae** is a possessive
genitive with **codicillos**. **Tasci** is a masculine name, also a possessive genitive, but dependent on **Rectinae** and meaning *belonging to Tascius*, that is,
(wife) *of Tascius*. We know nothing about these people.

**exterritae:** in the genitive case, modifying **Rectinae**.

**subiacebat:** Supply **monti**. (The verb requires the dative case.) Her villa
was situated at the foot of Mount Vesuvius, perhaps near the seaside town of
Herculaneum.

**nec . . . nisi:** *nor . . . except.*

**ulla . . . fuga:** Supply **erat**.

**ut:** introduces an indirect command after **orabat**.

**se:** *her*, referring to Rectina, who is making the request.

**tanto discrimini:** dative of separation (a subcategory of the dative of
reference).

**eriperet:** the subjunctive verb of the indirect command. The subject is Pliny
the Elder.

9  **quod:** (that) *which* (or *what*), object of **incohaverat**.

**studioso animo . . . maximo:** *with scholarly intent . . . with very great courage.*
Pliny the Elder had first planned to approach the Vesuvius area on a scientific
mission, but, having learned that lives were in danger, he changed his plans
to a rescue mission. **Animo** is construed with both **studioso** and **maximo**.

With the former it means *scholarly spirit*; with the latter it means *very great spirit*, that is, *courage*. To facilitate rescue measures, Pliny dismissed the one Liburnica and ordered several larger ships, known as quadriremes.

**Deducit:** a return to the historical present for a more vivid narration.

**ipse:** This word emphasizes that Pliny the Elder was personally directing the rescue mission.

**Rectinae, multis:** datives of indirect object, following **laturus auxilium**.

**erat ... orae:** Literally *the beauty of the shore was heavily populated.* Less literally *that beautiful stretch of coastline was heavily populated.*

**laturus:** future active participle of **ferre**; the subject is **ipse**. The future active participle often expresses purpose.

10 **metu:** ablative of separation. **Solutus** modifies the understood subject (Pliny the Elder) of all the verbs in the sentence (except **fugiunt**). Free of fear (fearlessly), he headed to the very place from which others were fleeing.

**ut:** introduces a result clause with two subjunctive verbs. These verbs, **dictaret enotaretque**, are imperfect subjunctive (i.e., secondary sequence) because the historical present is often construed as a secondary sequence tense.

**omnes ... motus, omnes figuras:** accusative plurals, direct objects of the two verbs in the result clause.

**ut deprenderat:** This second **ut** means *as* and uses an indicative verb, here in the pluperfect tense. Pliny the Elder's scientific curiosity made him eager, despite the dangers of the situation, to be an eyewitness to events and to record them for posterity.

**oculis:** ablative of means.

**dictaret:** He dictated his observations to an assistant, probably a slave.

11 Iam navibus cinis incidebat, quo propius accederent,
calidior et densior; iam pumices etiam nigrique et
50 ambusti et fracti igne lapides; iam vadum subitum
ruinaque montis litora obstantia. Cunctatus paulum an
retro flecteret, mox gubernatori, ut ita faceret, monenti
"Fortes" inquit "fortuna iuvat. Pomponianum pete."
12 Stabiis erat diremptus sinu medio (nam sensim
55 circumactis curvatisque litoribus mare infunditur);
ibi, quamquam nondum periculo adpropinquante,
conspicuo tamen et, cum cresceret, proximo, sarcinas
contulerat in naves certus fugae, si contrarius ventus
resedisset.

---

11 **quo propius accederent:** *by which, by what amount*; an ablative of degree
of difference with the comparative adverb **propius**; literally *by what amount
they* (the ships) *approached more closely, hotter and thicker ash fell.* Less literally *the more closely they approached, the hotter and thicker fell the ash.* The **quo**
clause has a causal aspect in this type of construction and may, as here, use a
subjunctive verb, although the indicative may also be used.

**pumices . . . lapides:** These two nouns are both subjects of an understood
verb: **incidebant.** The enclitic **-que** at the end of **nigri** joins the two subjects.
However, the three adjectives modify only **lapides.**

**vadum . . . litora:** Supply **erant.**

**ruināque montis: Ruinā** is ablative of means. The whole mountain had not
collapsed, but the debris from the eruption was raining down.

**litora obstantia: Obstantia** is a nominative plural, present active participle:
*the shores blocking.* Understand *blocking the way for anyone trying to sail in.* Less
literally *the shores blocked.*

Pliny the Elder was not able to reach the shore and rescue Rectina because the water was filled with debris from the volcano and because the water
had become too shallow for his ships, due to movement along the floor of the
Bay of Naples caused by the volcanic activity.

**Cunctatus . . . inquit:** The subject is Pliny the Elder, speaking to the helmsman. The word **cunctatus** includes the idea of wondering: *while hesitating and
wondering whether.* It is therefore followed by **an** and an indirect question with
the imperfect subjunctive verb **flecteret.**

**gubernatori . . . monenti:** dative, with **inquit**. The helmsman was advising Pliny to do so (turn back). **Ut ita faceret:** an indirect command following **monenti**. Pliny did not follow his helmsman's advice.

**Fortes . . . fortuna iuvat:** This maxim was common in Latin literature.

**Pomponianum:** Pomponianus was a resident of the area close to Mount Vesuvius. His identity is unknown to us.

12   **Stabiis:** locative case (plural). Stabiae (the name of the town is a feminine plural) was a town on the east coast of the Bay of Naples, about ten miles south of Mount Vesuvius.

**erat diremptus:** The subject of **erat** is Pomponianus: *he was at Stabiae*. **Diremptus** is an adjective with **erat**, rather than the participial element of a pluperfect form: *he was at Stabiae, separated, cut off* (from Pliny and the ships).

**sinu medio:** *by the middle bay;* less literally *by the bay in between*.

**circumactis curvatisque litoribus:** ablative absolute construction. Pliny is describing the natural curve of the shoreline of the Bay of Naples, not changes caused by the eruption.

**infunditur:** a passive form with a middle (reflexive) meaning: *the sea pours (itself) in*.

**quamquam:** used here concessively with the ablative absolute **periculo adpropinquante** (rather than as a concessive conjunction with a subordinate clause). It correlates with **tamen**.

**conspicuo, proximo:** Both words modify **periculo**.

**cum:** introduces a temporal clause. When the danger (from the volcanic activity) increased, it would be very near, **proximo**.

**contulerat:** The subject is Pomponianus.

**certus fugae:** *certain of flight;* an objective genitive with the adjective. Less literally *determined on flight*.

**contrarius ventus:** The wind, blowing from the northwest, had enabled Pliny to reach the eastern shore of the Bay of Naples but prevented anyone from sailing away from the area of the volcano on the east side of the bay.

**resedisset:** *if the wind had abated*—but it did not: contrary to fact condition.

60    Quo tunc avunculus meus secundissimo invectus
      complectitur trepidantem, consolatur, hortatur, utque
      timorem eius sua securitate leniret, deferri in balineum
      iubet; lotus accubat, cenat, aut hilaris aut (quod est
      aeque magnum) similis hilari. 13 Interim e Vesuvio
65    monte pluribus locis latissimae flammae altaque
      incendia relucebant, quorum fulgor et claritas tenebris
      noctis excitabatur. Ille agrestium trepidatione ignes
      relictos desertasque villas per solitudinem ardere in
      remedium formidinis dictitabat. Tum se quieti dedit
70    et quievit verissimo quidem somno. Nam meatus
      animae, qui illi propter amplitudinem corporis gravior
      et sonantior erat, ab iis, qui limini obversabantur,
      audiebatur. 14 Sed area, ex qua diaeta adibatur, ita iam
      cinere mixtisque pumicibus oppleta surrexerat,
75    ut, si longior in cubiculo mora, exitus negaretur.
      Excitatus procedit, seque Pomponiano ceterisque, qui
      pervigilaverant, reddit.

---

**Quo:** *to which place;* less literally *to that place.*

**secundissimo:** Supply **vento**, ablative of means. This same wind, however, was **contrarius** for anyone trying to sail west, away from the volcanic activity.

**complectitur:** historical present.

**trepidantem:** Pomponianus.

**ut . . . leniret:** a purpose clause, dependent upon **deferri . . . iubet. Leniret** is in the imperfect tense because **iubet** is considered a historical present and thus secondary sequence.

**eius, sua:** referring respectively to Pomponianus and Pliny the Elder. Note the juxtaposition: **timorem eius sua securitate,** *the fear of him—his confidence.*

**deferri:** Supply the reflexive pronoun **se** (Pliny) as the accusative subject.

**lotus:** irregular perfect passive participle of **lavare**. In Letter 3.14, Larcius Macedo is described as having been bathed, presumably by his slaves.

**similis hilari:** *like a cheerful* (person). **Similis** governs the dative case. Pliny the Elder may have been truly cheerful or pretending to be cheerful.

13  **Ille ... dictitabat:** requires an indirect statement construction. The accusative subjects are **ignes** and **villas**; the infinitive predicate is **ardere**. To calm the fears of Pomponianus and the others, Pliny the Elder suggests that the flames they can see on Mount Vesuvius are not coming from the volcano but rather are (1) flames that spread when panicked peasants living on the slopes abandoned their cooking fires and (2) deserted villas in the uninhabited areas of the slopes. The villas caught fire, and there were no residents to put out the flames.

Construe the two accusative infinitive constructions as **ignes relictos trepidatione agrestium ardere, et desertas villas ardere per solitudinem**.

**dictitabat:** frequentative form of **dicere**. Compare Letter 4.19, Section 3.

**in remedium formidinis:** *in remedy of*; less literally *as a remedy for*. **In** + the accusative may denote purpose. **Formidinis** (objective genitive) means the fear that other people were experiencing.

**meatus animae:** *the movement of his breath*. The overweight Pliny the Elder was snoring. **Meatus** is the subject of **audiebatur** and the antecedent for the clause **qui ... erat**.

**illi:** dative of reference, referring to Pliny the Elder.

14  **oppleta:** perfect passive participle, nominative feminine singular, modifying **area**.

**surrexerat:** The floor level of the courtyard had increased because of the downfall of ash and pumice.

**ut ... exitus negaretur:** a result clause, thus requiring a subjunctive (imperfect, in secondary sequence). However, it does not mean, as one might at first expect, (the courtyard was filled) *with the result that exit was denied*. The result clause is also the apodosis of a future less vivid condition: *with the result that (if the delay were longer) exit would be denied*.

**si longior ... mora:** *if the delay (were) longer*; the protasis of the future less vivid condition. Supply **esset** as the verb. Although future less vivid conditions usually require a present subjunctive, the imperfect subjunctive here reflects the past time of the narration.

**se ... reddit:** a reflexive construction. The subject is Pliny.

15 In commune consultant, intra tecta subsistant an in
aperto vagentur. Nam crebris vastisque tremoribus
80    tecta nutabant et, quasi emota sedibus suis, nunc huc,
nunc illuc abire aut referri videbantur. 16 Sub dio
rursus quamquam levium exesorumque pumicum
casus metuebatur; quod tamen periculorum collatio
elegit. Et apud illum quidem ratio rationem, apud alios
85    timorem timor vicit. Cervicalia capitibus imposita
linteis constringunt; id munimentum adversus
incidentia fuit. 17 Iam dies alibi, illic nox omnibus
noctibus nigrior densiorque; quam tamen faces multae
variaque lumina solabantur. Placuit egredi in litus et ex
90    proximo adspicere, ecquid iam mare admitteret; quod
adhuc vastum et adversum permanebat.

---

15    **In commune:** *in common*. Either *among themselves* or *for a mutual objective*.
For **in** + accusative to denote purpose, see **in remedium** above.

**consultant:** There is a double (alternative) question after **consultant**, which,
in English, would be introduced by a *whether … or*. Pliny does not here use the
Latin equivalent for *whether*, but he does use **an**, *or*. Because the construction
is an indirect question, subjunctive verbs are required.

One option is to remain **intra tecta**. The other is to be **in aperto** (**sub
dio**). There were considerable dangers attached to either option.

**tecta:** neuter plural, but translate as a singular: *the house*. **Tecta** (modified by
**emota**) is the subject of **nutabant** and **videbantur**.

**sedibus suis:** ablative of place from which.

16    **sub dio:** *under the sky, under heaven*. **Dius** is an alternative form for **divus**,
which means *god* or, as here, *heaven, the sky*.

**quamquam:** Translate with the adjectives **levium exesorumque**, not the
verb: *although* (or *however*) *light*.

**quod:** *which* (alternative); a resumptive relative pronoun referring to the
option of being **sub dio**. Less literally *this alternative*. **Quod** is the accusative
direct object of **elegit**.

**apud illum:** *for him.* For Pliny the Elder, one rational alternative prevailed over (**vicit**) the other (to go outside rather than to stay inside). For the others, one fear prevailed over (**vicit**) the other (the collapse of the house rather than the downfall of pumice).

**linteis:** ablative of means. Perhaps they tore sheets into strips.

**id:** *this* = the placing of pillows on their heads.

**incidentia:** accusative neuter plural of the present participle of **incidere**, used as a substantive; *falling* (objects).

17   **dies alibi:** Supply **erat**. *It was day, there was daylight elsewhere.* **Dies** can mean either *day* or *daylight.* Farther away from Vesuvius, perhaps at Misenum where Pliny the Younger and his mother were, the sunrise could be seen. It was now August 25.

    Note the chiastic arrangement (ABBA), emphasizing the opposition of *day* and *night*: **dies alibi, illic nox**.

**illic:** at Pomponianus's villa.

**noctibus:** ablative of comparison, with the adjectives **nigrior densiorque** (which modify **nox**).

**quam:** The antecedent is **nox**.

**Placuit:** an impersonal verb.

**ex proximo:** *from the nearest* (position), *from close by.* The adjective is being used as a substantive. Compare the use in Letter 4.19, Section 3.

**admitteret:** imperfect subjunctive in an indirect question introduced by **ecquid**. **Ecquid**, which means *whether anything at all*, is an accusative neuter singular, direct object of **admitteret**. The question in Pliny the Elder's mind was *whether* the sea would now allow *anything*, in particular, would allow them to sail away from shore.

**quod:** The antecedent is **mare**.

**vastum:** This word can mean *rough, wild* or *empty, devastated.* Either meaning would work here. The sea was still wild and empty of other ships.

**adversum:** The sea (more precisely, the bay) remained *opposite* in the sense that winds from the northwest were blowing huge waves toward the eastern shore where Stabiae was located. Compare **contrarius ventus** in Section 12 above. Translate **adversum** as *hostile*.

18 Ibi super abiectum linteum recubans semel atque
iterum frigidam aquam poposcit hausitque. Deinde
flammae flammarumque praenuntius, odor sulpuris,
95    alios in fugam vertunt, excitant illum. 19 Innitens
servulis duobus adsurrexit et statim concidit, ut ego
colligo, crassiore caligine spiritu obstructo clausoque
stomacho qui illi natura invalidus et angustus et
frequenter aestuans erat. 20 Ubi dies redditus (is ab
100   eo, quem novissime viderat, tertius), corpus inventum
integrum, inlaesum opertumque, ut fuerat indutus;
habitus corporis quiescenti quam defuncto similior.

---

18   **alios . . . vertunt, excitant illum:** another chiastic arrangement. The verbs
     are historical present.

19   **ut:** *as*, with the indicative mood.

     **crassiore caligine:** ablative of means. **Crassiore** is the comparative form of
     the adjective **crassus**.

     **spiritu obstructo clausoque stomacho:** ablatives absolute or of attendant
     circumstances.

     **stomacho: Stomachus** usually means *esophagus*, but Pliny here uses it to
     mean *trachea* (*windpipe*). (See Letter 9.36, Section 3.) The thick smog of poi-
     sonous vapors from the volcano congested Pliny the Elder's trachea and lungs.
     He may have had a fatal asthmatic episode, or been suffocated by the vapors,
     or had a heart attack. He died on the beach at Stabiae. The survivors reported
     his final moments and death to his nephew, Pliny the Younger. We don't know
     if the nephew embellished the accounts of his uncle's courage.

     **qui:** The antecedent is **stomacho**.

     **illi:** dative of reference.

     **naturā:** ablative of respect or specification. **Natura** refers to Pliny the Elder's
     nature, that is, physical makeup or constitution.

20   **redditus:** Supply **est**. In contrast to the active (though reflexive) use of **red-
     dere** in Section 14, the construction here is middle voice (though passive
     form): *when day(light) returned itself*. However, the active voice is preferable
     in English: *when day(light) returned*. Compare **infunditur** in Section 12 of
     this letter. On the meaning of **dies**, see Section 17.

**is, eo:** These words modify an understood **dies** and **die** respectively. Supply **erat**. **Eo** is the antecedent of **quem**.

**novissime:** *most recently, last* (as an adverb). The superlative of **novus** can mean *most recent* in the sense of *last, final*. (Compare Letter 4.11, Section 9, and Letter 5.16, Section 3.) Because Pliny the Elder died on August 25, a day on which the sun was blocked from view, he *last* saw the day(light) on August 24. On August 25, **dies alibi, illic nox (erat)** (Section 17).

**tertius:** *third*; modifies **is**. The third day was August 26. Pliny the Elder had sailed from Misenum on August 24. The Romans counted inclusively. *Inclusively* means that the Romans counted the time period from August 24 to August 26 as three days, whereas we count it as two days. The Romans counted the days at both ends of the time period.

**inventum:** Supply **est**. The subject is **corpus**.

**opertum:** perfect passive participle of **operire**.

**indutus:** masculine singular, thus modifying an understood **Plinius** (not the neuter noun **corpus**).

**quiescenti quam defuncto:** the datives, modifying an understood *someone*, are dependent on the comparative adjective **similior**. Construe **quam**, *than*, with the comparative: *more ... than*.

**similior:** Supply **erat**. It is not known if the people who were with Pliny the Elder were able to return his body to his sister and nephew at Misenum. Those who made the report, especially the slaves, were careful to state that his body showed no signs of foul play. Roman slave owners feared being attacked by their slaves, as Letter 3.14 reveals. In turn, slaves feared that, if their owner died, they would be accused of murder. Perhaps the slaves who had accompanied Pliny the Elder on this rescue mission were anxious to prove that they had not killed him in order to escape.

21 Interim Miseni ego et mater—sed nihil ad
historiam, nec tu aliud quam de exitu eius scire voluisti.
Finem ergo faciam. 22 Unum adiciam, omnia me
quibus interfueram quaeque statim, cum maxime vera
memorantur, audieram, persecutum. Tu potissima
excerpes. Aliud est enim epistulam, aliud historiam,
aliud amico, aliud omnibus scribere. Vale.

105

---

21   **ego et mater:** Supply **eramus**.

    **sed . . . historiam:** Supply **id pertinet**: *This pertains not at all to history.* **Nihil**
is here used adverbially.

    **aliud quam:** *anything other than.*

    **eius:** Pliny the Elder.

22   **Unum adiciam: Unum** is the direct object of **adiciam**, but this verb also
introduces an indirect statement construction that explains the **unum**. In
the indirect statement construction, the accusative subject is **me**, and the
infinitive predicate is **persecutum**. Supply **esse** to form the perfect infinitive
**persecutum esse**.

    **omnia:** This word is the object of **persecutum (esse)**. **Omnia** is also the
antecedent for the two relative pronouns in the relative clauses, **quibus interfueram** and **quae . . . audieram**.

    **quibus:** dative case with **interfueram**.

    **statim:** *immediately,* in the sense of *immediately after the event.*

    **cum maxime:** *when especially.*

    **vera:** neuter plural nominative as the subject of **memorantur**: *true things,* but
the use is close to adverbial: *things are remembered truly, accurately.*

    **Aliud est . . . aliud:** *it is one thing . . . another thing.*

    **amico, omnibus:** *for a friend, for everyone.*

This engraving by Sir William Hamilton (1730–1803) depicts Mount Vesuvius erupting on October 20, 1767. The boats in the foreground are reminiscent of Pliny the Elder leading his fleet from Misenum in response to the letter he received from Rectina. (Getty Museum, California) (Public Domain)

# 16. Letter 6.20

At the beginning of Letter 6.16, Pliny wrote that Tacitus had requested from him a report on the death of his uncle, Pliny the Elder, during the eruption of Mount Vesuvius in 79 CE, a report that Tacitus could use in his historical writing. At the end of the letter (Section 21), Pliny began to describe how he and his mother had fared during the eruption but then abruptly broke off, commenting that their experiences were not pertinent to the writing of history. Letter 6.20 is also addressed to Tacitus, and, in the opening, Pliny states that, subsequent to receiving the account of Pliny the Elder's fate, Tacitus had expressed an interest in learning about the experiences of Pliny and his mother. Letter 6.20 is Pliny's account of these experiences. In Letter 6.16, Pliny informed readers that he had preferred to stay at Misenum and read, rather than joining his uncle's bold reconnaissance and rescue mission. In Letter 6.20, Pliny depicts himself as having acted calmly and bravely during the panic and chaos that ensued when the volcanic activity struck Misenum, which was about eighteen miles northwest of Mount Vesuvius. (See Map 2.)

---

C. PLINIUS TACITO SUO S.

1 Ais te adductum litteris, quas exigenti tibi de morte
avunculi mei scripsi, cupere cognoscere quos ego
Miseni relictus (id enim ingressus abruperam)
5    non solum metus, verum etiam casus pertulerim.
"Quamquam animus meminisse horret, incipiam."

2 Profecto avunculo, ipse reliquum tempus studiis
(ideo enim remanseram) impendi; mox balineum,
cena, somnus inquietus et brevis.

---

1    **te:** the accusative subject of the infinitive **cupere** in an indirect statement. **Te** is modified by the perfect passive participle **adductum**.

**exigenti tibi:** indirect object with **scripsi**.

**quos:** interrogative adjective modifying **metus** and **casus**.

**Miseni:** locative case.

**id:** accusative direct object of **ingressus**. By **id**, Pliny means an account of his experiences at Misenum. When composing Letter 6.16, Pliny had begun to describe his own experiences (Sections 4 to 7) but then focused on the activities of his uncle.

**pertulerim:** perfect subjunctive of **perferre**. The subjunctive is used because the clause is an indirect question. The tense is determined by the primary sequence of tenses.

**Quamquam . . . incipiam:** The quotation is taken from Vergil, *Aeneid* 2.12 and 13. With these words, Aeneas reluctantly agrees to describe to Dido the fall of Troy.

2 **Profecto avunculo:** ablative absolute.

**studiis:** dative of indirect object.

**remanseram:** Pliny here explains his decision not to accompany his uncle on the fateful voyage. Compare Letter 6.16, Section 7.

**mox:** *then.* Supply **fuit** in this clause.

10 **3** Praecesserat per multos dies tremor terrae, minus
formidolosus quia Campaniae solitus; illa vero nocte
ita invaluit, ut non moveri omnia, sed verti crederentur.
**4** Inrumpit cubiculum meum mater; surgebam invicem,
si quiesceret, excitaturus. Resedimus in area domus,
15 quae mare a tectis modico spatio dividebat. **5** Dubito,
constantiam vocare an imprudentiam debeam (agebam
enim duodevicensimum annum). Posco librum Titi
Livi et, quasi per otium, lego atque etiam, ut coeperam,
excerpo.

---

3    **tremor terrae: Tremor** is the subject of **praecesserat**. Although it is a singular noun, the phrase **per multos dies** tells us that Pliny means not *one tremor*, but rather (repeated) *trembling of the earth*.

**Campaniae:** dative of reference. Campania was (and still is) a region of Italy that included Mount Vesuvius and the cities of Naples, Misenum, Stabiae, Pompeii, and Herculaneum. (See Map 2.) It is situated at the meeting point of the Eurasian Plate and the African Plate and is part of an area of intense volcanic and seismic activity that includes Mount Etna, an active volcano in Sicily. A large earthquake in 62 CE destroyed a substantial portion of the city of Pompeii, which was in the process of rebuilding when buried by the volcanic eruption of 79 CE that Pliny describes in Letters 6.16 and 20.

**solitus:** modifies **tremor**. The trembling was less frightening (**formidolosus**) than it would have been at, for example, Rome, because such trembling was common (**solitus**) in the Campania region.

**illa . . . nocte:** the night of August 24.

**ut . . . crederentur:** result clause, requiring a subjunctive verb. The subject is **omnia**.

**verti:** present passive infinitive; *to be turned over, upside down.*

4    **cubiculum:** accusative of motion without the preposition (which is contained in the compound verb: **in-rumpit**).

**surgebam:** imperfect tense: Pliny was in the act of getting up when his mother burst into his bedroom.

**si quiesceret:** Supply **ea** (*she, Pliny's mother*) as the subject. This clause is the protasis of a future less vivid condition: *if she were asleep*. The apodosis is contained in the participle **excitaturus**. Although future less vivid conditions usually require a present subjunctive, the subjunctive verb, **quiesceret**, is imperfect tense here because it is in secondary sequence.

**excitaturus:** future active participle, with an implication of intention or purpose. Supply **eam** as the direct object of the participle. Pliny was getting up, and about to wake his mother, if she were asleep.

**area:** often means *courtyard* (see Letter 6.16, Section 14), but here means *yard* or *backyard*.

**tectis:** plural, but referring to one house. Compare Letter 6.16, Section 15. The yard *divided the sea from the house by a small space*. Pliny is explaining that there was a small yard between the house and the sea.

5     **Dubito:** There is a double (alternative) question after **dubito**, which, in English, would be introduced by a *whether . . . or*. Pliny does not here use the Latin equivalent for *whether*, but he does use **an**, *or*. Because the construction is an indirect question, a subjunctive verb, **debeam**, is required.

**vocare:** Supply **id**: *to call it* (his behavior, as described in a subsequent clause), or translate **vocare** as *use the word*.

**agebam . . . duodevicensimum annum:** *I was living my eighteenth year*, or: *I was seventeen years old*.

**Titi Livi:** genitive case. Titus Livius (English: Livy) was a Roman author who wrote a history of Rome. He lived from about 60 BCE to 17 CE.

**ut coeperam:** After his uncle had departed on the afternoon of August 25, Pliny had apparently begun reading and excerpting the Livy text.

20    Ecce amicus avunculi, qui nuper ad eum ex Hispania
venerat, ut me et matrem sedentes, me vero etiam
legentem videt, illius patientiam, securitatem meam
corripit. Nihilo segnius ego intentus in librum.

6 Iam hora diei prima, et adhuc dubius et quasi
25    languidus dies. Iam quassatis circumiacentibus tectis,
quamquam in aperto loco, angusto tamen, magnus et
certus ruinae metus. 7 Tum demum excedere oppido
visum. Sequitur vulgus attonitum, quodque in pavore
simile prudentiae, alienum consilium suo praefert,
30    ingentique agmine abeuntes premit et impellit.

---

5    **Hispania:** The word is translated as *Spain,* but the area it denotes was the
Iberian peninsula and thus included what is now modern Portugal. Pliny the
Elder had once held an administrative post there.

**ut (with indic.):** *when.*

**videt, corripit:** Here, and elsewhere in the letter, Pliny uses the historical
present to create a more vivid narrative.

**illius:** Pliny's mother.

**securitatem:** Pliny used the same word in Letter 6.16, Section 12, to describe
his uncle's fearless composure. Here he implies that his own composure may
have been owed, at least in part, to a youthful audacity.

**segnius:** comparative adverb.

**intentus:** Supply **sum.**

6    **hora:** Supply **est.**

**hora diei prima:** the first hour of the day. There were twelve hours in a Roman
day, and the first hour began at sunrise. The day was counted from sunrise
to sunset. Because there are more minutes of daylight in the summer than in
the winter, the length of a Roman hour varied from summer to winter. On
August 25, one might have expected about seventy minutes of daylight in the
first hour. On the seventh hour, see Letter 6.16, Section 4.

**tectis:** modified by both the present participle, **circumiacentibus**, and the perfect participle, **quassatis**. However, the participles have different uses. **Quassatis . . . tectis** is an ablative absolute expressing cause. Here the plural **tectis** means the houses of the town, rather than just Pliny's house. **Circumiacentibus** does not mean that the buildings were lying on the ground (it is not an ablative absolute), but that the buildings situated (lying) near Pliny's villa had been shaken (**quassatis**).

**quamquam:** Supply **sumus**.

**metus:** Supply **est nobis**.

7    **oppido:** ablative of place from which without a preposition.

**visum:** Supply **est**: *seemed best*. The subject is **excedere**.

**quodque: Quod** is a pronoun; **-que** is an enclitic. Supply **est**: **quod (est) simile prudentiae**. The clause refers to the subsequent statement about the crowd preferring someone else's plan.

**suo:** dative case with **praefert**, whose subject is **vulgus**. Supply **consilio** with **suo**. Pliny is suggesting that the crowd looked to him for a plan.

**abeuntes:** the direct object of **premit et impellit**; accusative plural of the present participle of **abire**. Supply **nos**. Pliny is referring to himself and his mother.

**premit, impellit:** The subject is **vulgus**.

8 Egressi tecta consistimus. Multa ibi miranda, multas
formidines patimur. Nam vehicula, quae produci
iusseramus, quamquam in planissimo campo, in
contrarias partes agebantur ac ne lapidibus quidem
35  fulta in eodem vestigio quiescebant. 9 Praeterea
mare in se resorberi et tremore terrae quasi repelli
videbamus. Certe processerat litus, multaque animalia
maris siccis harenis detinebat. Ab altero latere, nubes
atra et horrenda, ignei spiritus tortis vibratisque
40  discursibus rupta, in longas flammarum figuras
dehiscebat; fulguribus illae et similes et maiores erant.
10 Tum vero idem ille ex Hispania amicus acrius et
instantius "Si frater" inquit "tuus, tuus avunculus vivit,
vult esse vos salvos; si periit, superstites voluit. Proinde
45  quid cessatis evadere?" Respondimus non commissuros
nos, ut de salute illius incerti nostrae consuleremus.

---

8    **tecta:** Again the plural means the houses of the town, rather than just Pliny's
house. Once Pliny and his mother had left behind the buildings of the town,
which were in danger of collapsing, they stopped to rest.

**miranda:** accusative plural gerundive.

**in contrarias . . . quiescebant:** The vehicles, although wedged with rocks to
prevent them from moving, were being moved in opposing directions by the
earth tremors. In his description, Pliny effectively uses the imperfect tense
to develop an image of the horrifying events happening continuously.

**ne . . . quidem:** Construe together: *not even* (although wedged with rocks).

9    **mare . . . resorberi et . . . repelli:** accusative infinitives in indirect statement.

**processerat litus:** The shore seemed to have expanded and extended into
where the receding water had once been.

**maris:** genitive case. Construe with **animalia**.

**harenis:** ablative of place where without a preposition. According to Letter 6.16, Section 11, a similar situation had existed on the east side of the bay. As Pliny the Elder tried to approach the coastline near the home of Rectina, he discovered that his ships could not proceed closer because the volcanic activity had caused the water to recede and created a shoal: **vadum subitum.**

**detinebat:** The subject is **litus.**

**ignei spiritus:** genitive. Pliny is describing *lightning.*

**rupta:** feminine nominative of the perfect participle, modifying **nubes,** which is the subject of **dehiscebat.**

**fulguribus:** both dative, with **similes,** and ablative (of comparison) with **maiores.**

**illae:** nominative plural; the **figurae flammarum.**

**et . . . et:** *both . . . and.*

10    **acrius et instantius:** comparative adverbs.

**quid:** interrogative pronoun: *With respect to what? Why?*

**commissuros nos:** Supply **esse** to form the future active infinitive, which is the verb in the indirect statement after **respondimus. Nos** is the accusative subject of the construction.

**illius:** *of him (our brother/uncle).*

**incerti:** nominative plural, modifying the understood subject (*we,* that is, Pliny and his mother) of **consuleremus.**

**nostrae:** dative with **consuleremus.** Supply **saluti.**

**consuleremus:** subjunctive in a noun (substantive) clause of result. Pliny and his mother reply that they will not allow (it to happen) that they would consider their own safety while uncertain about the safety of him.

11 Non moratus ultra proripit se effusoque cursu
periculo aufertur. Nec multo post illa nubes
50 descendere in terras, operire maria; cinxerat Capreas et
absconderat, Miseni quod procurrit abstulerat. 12 Tum
mater orare, hortari, iubere, quoquo modo fugerem;
posse enim iuvenem, se et annis et corpore gravem
bene morituram, si mihi causa mortis non fuisset.
55 Ego contra salvum me nisi una non futurum; deinde
manum eius amplexus addere gradum cogo. Paret aegre
incusatque se, quod me moretur.

---

11 **moratus:** perfect participle of a deponent verb.

**periculo:** ablative of place from which without a preposition.

**multo:** ablative of degree of difference.

**post:** used here as an adverb: *afterward*. Construe with **nec multo**.

**descendere, operire:** historical infinitives. This construction—of a subject in the nominative case with an infinitive verb—is sometimes used in historical narration instead of an indicative form. Translate as if the infinitives were third person singular indicative forms, with **illa nubes** as the subject. Note that Pliny switches back to indicative forms (pluperfect) with **cinxerat, absconderat, abstulerat**.

**maria:** Pliny may have used the plural to designate the Bay of Naples and, beyond it, the Tyrrhenian Sea. From his location on the promontory at Misenum, Pliny could have seen both bodies of water.

**Capreae, -arum (f. pl.):** an island in the southern part of the Bay of Naples, known today as Capri. It is about 20 miles southeast, across the Bay, from Misenum, where the Pliny family lived.

**Miseni quod procurrit:** literally *what of Misenum juts out*; less literally *that (part) of Misenum (that) juts out*. **Miseni** is a partitive genitive. Pliny is describing the promontory of Misenum. Supply an **et** before **Miseni**.

**abstulerat:** third person singular pluperfect active indicative of **auferre**. The cloud had removed the promontory, that is, made it disappear from view.

12 **orare, hortari, iubere:** historical infinitives.

**iubere:** This verb is usually followed by an infinitive. Occasionally it is followed by an **ut** + the subjunctive in an indirect command. Here, however, the **ut** has been omitted before the subjunctive verb, **fugerem**.

**quoquo:** ablative of **quisquis**. Construe **quoquo modo** with **fugerem**.

**posse:** Understand a verb of saying that would introduce an accusative infinitive in indirect statement: (she said) *that* (I) *a young man was able* (to flee).

**se ... morituram:** another accusative infinitive construction after the understood verb of saying. (Supply **esse** to form the future active infinitive **morituram esse**.) This accusative infinitive is the apodosis of a condition for which **si ... fuisset** is the protasis.

**gravem:** modifies **se**. Plinia describes herself as weighed down by her years and body. There are only about ten references in Pliny's letters to physical appearance, and most do not allow us to form much of a mental image of the person. In Letter 6.16, Section 13, we learn that Plinia's brother, Pliny the Elder, snored **propter amplitudinem corporis**.

**bene:** Construe with **morituram (esse)**.

**fuisset:** pluperfect subjunctive. The subject is Plinia. **Causa** is a predicate noun. The verb occurs in the protasis of a conditional sentence, but the condition is not contrary to fact. It is, rather, a future more vivid condition, and, if it were not in indirect statement, the verb of the protasis would have been in the future perfect indicative. Since, however, the subordinate clause is in indirect statement, its verb must be subjunctive. The pluperfect subjunctive is used because there is no future subjunctive in Latin.

**Ego:** Understand a verb of saying that would introduce the accusative infinitive in indirect statement: **me ... futurum (esse)**.

**contrā:** adverbial.

**manum eius:** *her* (Plinia's) *hand*.

**addere gradum:** *to step up her pace, hurry*. Supply **eam** (*her*, Plinia) after **cogo**.

**moretur:** Pliny uses the subjunctive in this **quod** causal clause because he is reporting the reason given by his mother.

Plinia survived the eruption. However, we do not know when or how she died. We suspect that she had died well before the composition of this letter, which was written at least twenty years after the eruption of 79 CE and the death of her brother. In Letter 4.19, Section 7, Pliny reminds Calpurnia Hispulla, the paternal aunt of his wife, that his mother, Plinia, had served as a mother figure for her, presumably after her own mother had died.

13 Iam cinis, adhuc tamen rarus. Respicio; densa caligo
tergis imminebat, quae nos torrentis modo

60   infusa terrae sequebatur. "Deflectamus," inquam, "dum
videmus, ne in via strati comitantium turba in tenebris
obteramur." 14 Vix consideramus, et nox, non qualis
inlunis aut nubila, sed qualis in locis clausis lumine
extincto. Audires ululatus feminarum,

65   infantium quiritatus, clamores virorum; alii parentes,
alii liberos, alii coniuges vocibus requirebant, vocibus
noscitabant; hi suum casum, illi suorum miserabantur;
erant qui metu mortis mortem precarentur; 15 multi ad
deos manus tollere, plures nusquam iam deos ullos

70   aeternamque illam et novissimam noctem mundo
interpretabantur. Nec defuerunt qui fictis mentitisque
terroribus vera pericula augerent.

---

13   **cinis:** Supply **est** or **erat**.

**modo:** *in the manner of* (+ gen.). **Modo** is here postpositive, that is, it follows the word it governs, **torrentis**. See the note for Letter 6.4, Section 1, on **causā**, another noun in the ablative case used postpositively as a preposition governing the genitive.

**Deflectamus:** hortatory subjunctive.

**dum videmus:** *while we (can) see.*

**ne:** introducing a negative purpose clause.

**strati:** nominative plural of the perfect passive participle of **sternere**: (we) *having been knocked down.* The participle modifies the understood subject of **obteramur**.

**comitantium:** genitive plural, present participle. Construe with **turbā** (ablative).

14   **et:** almost temporal: *and then.*

**nox:** Understand **erat**.

**clausis:** perfect passive participle of **claudere**, modifying **locis**.

**lumine extincto:** ablative absolute.

**Audires:** potential subjunctive.

**ululatus:** This word (accusative plural) is onomatopoeic, that is, the sound of the word imitates the sound of wailing.

**parentes, liberos, coniuges:** accusative plurals, direct objects of **requirebant**.

**suorum:** *of their own* (loved ones). Supply **casum**.

**erant qui . . . precarentur:** *there were some who prayed.* **Precarentur** is a subjunctive verb in a relative clause of characteristic. Pliny, like several other Latin writers, comments on the paradox of people longing for death because they fear it.

**metu:** ablative of cause. Construe with **mortis**, an objective genitive.

15  **tollere:** historical infinitive. Note that Pliny switches back to an indicative form with **interpretabantur**.

**deos, illam . . . noctem:** These words are the accusative subjects of an understood infinitive, **esse**, in an indirect statement construction with **interpretabantur**. They are linked by the enclitic -**que** at the end of **aeternam**.

**aeternam, novissimam:** predicate adjectives with **illam . . . noctem**. They are linked by the **et**.

**mundo:** dative of reference.

The terrified refugees declare that there are no gods anywhere and that that night is the eternal and final one for the world. In ancient culture, there was a widely held belief that someday the arrival of an intense darkness would signal the end of the world, hence the panic during solar eclipses. For **novissimam** meaning *final*, see Letter 6.16, Section 20.

**augerent:** subjunctive in a relative clause of characteristic.

Aderant qui Miseni illud ruisse, illud ardere falso, sed
credentibus, nuntiabant. 16 Paulum reluxit, quod non
75   dies nobis, sed adventantis ignis indicium videbatur. Et
ignis quidem longius substitit; tenebrae rursus, cinis
rursus multus et gravis. Hunc identidem adsurgentes
excutiebamus; operti alioqui atque etiam oblisi pondere
essemus. 17 Possem gloriari non gemitum mihi, non
80   vocem parum fortem in tantis periculis excidisse, nisi
me cum omnibus, omnia mecum perire misero, magno
tamen mortalitatis solacio credidissem. 18 Tandem illa
caligo tenuata quasi in fumum nebulamve discessit;
mox dies verus; sol etiam effulsit, luridus tamen, qualis
85   esse, cum deficit, solet. Occursabant trepidantibus
adhuc oculis mutata omnia altoque cinere tamquam
nive obducta.

---

**Aderant qui . . . nuntiabant:** Pliny here uses the indicative in the relative
clause, although in the previous sentence he used a subjunctive (relative
clause of characteristic).

**Miseni illud . . . illud:** Translate as *one part of Misenum, one part.* These words
are the accusative subjects of, respectively, the infinitives **ruisse** and **ardere**,
in the indirect statement after **nuntiabant.** Note that the two infinitives are
in different tenses. **Miseni** is partitive genitive.

**falso** (adv.): Construe with **nuntiabant,** which introduces the two accusative-
infinitive constructions.

**credentibus:** dative of indirect object. People readily believed these false
reports.

16   **Paulum:** an adverbial accusative. *It became a little bit bright.*

**quod:** a reference to the preceding clause: *which = this little bit of brightening.*

**adventantis:** present active participle of **adventare,** in the genitive singular,
modifying **ignis.**

**longius:** The comparative adverb here indicates a measure of distance, not
time.

**tenebrae . . . gravis:** Understand **erant**.

**cinis:** Pliny uses the singular (modified by **multus et gravis**), but translate as plural: *ashes*.

**Hunc:** Supply **cinem**.

**operti . . . oblisi . . . essemus:** These pluperfect subjunctives form the apodosis of a past contrary to fact condition whose protasis is not expressed, or is expressed only by the word **alioqui**: *otherwise*. **Alioqui** conveys the idea: *if we had not stood up and shaken off the ashes.* Compare the use of **alioqui** in Letter 3.14, Section 6.

17   **Possem . . . credidissem:** These two verbs form a mixed contrary to fact condition. The apodosis (**possem**) is present contrary to fact, while the protasis (**nisi credidissem**) is past contrary to fact. *I could* (now) *boast, if I had not* (then) *believed.*

**gloriari:** introduces an indirect statement in which **gemitum** and **vocem** are the accusative subjects and **excidisse** is the infinitive verb.

**mihi:** dative of reference (separation).

**parum fortem:** Pliny uses the rhetorical figure *litotes*. By *too little strong,* he means *weak*.

**misero, magno tamen mortalitatis solacio:** ablative of attendant circumstance. Pliny is expressing a view not uncommon in the ancient world, that to die, when everyone and everything around you is dying, is a lamentable, yet great consolation of one's human mortality.

**credidissem:** introduces an indirect statement. The infinitive verb of the construction is **perire**, which has two accusative subjects, **me** and **omnia**.

18   **nebulamve: -ve** = *or*; an enclitic particle attached to the end of a word.

**dies:** *daylight*. Supply **erat**.

**Occursabant:** The subject is **omnia**, which is modified by the two participles, **mutata** and **obducta**. The Latin imperfect tense often represents an action that continues to occur over a period of time. Pliny's use of the imperfect tense here provides a vivid impression of the process of gradually adjusting to the sights of a changed landscape.

**trepidantibus adhuc oculis:** *eyes still trembling (still confused).* The dative is required by the verb **occursabant**.

19 Regressi Misenum, curatis utcumque corporibus, suspensam dubiamque noctem spe ac metu exegimus.
90 Metus praevalebat; nam et tremor terrae perseverabat, et plerique lymphati terrificis vaticinationibus et sua et aliena mala ludificabantur. 20 Nobis tamen ne tunc quidem, quamquam et expertis periculum et exspectantibus, abeundi consilium, donec de avunculo
95 nuntius.

Haec nequaquam historia digna non scripturus leges et tibi, scilicet qui requisisti, imputabis, si digna ne epistula quidem videbuntur. Vale.

---

**19** **curatis ... corporibus:** ablative absolute.

**spe ac metu:** ablatives of cause.

**praevalebat, perseverabat, ludificabantur:** The imperfects indicate that the tremors, and the fear and the hysteria that they generated, continued for a long period.

**terrificis vaticinationibus:** ablative of means.

**mala:** accusative of direct object with the deponent verb **ludificabantur**.

**20** **Nobis:** dative of possession, modified by the participles **expertis** and **exspectantibus**. **Quamquam** is used here with the participles rather than with a finite verb: *although having* (already) *experienced and* (still) *anticipating danger.*

**abeundi:** gerund of **abire**.

**consilium:** Supply **erat**. Construe with **nobis**.

**nuntius:** Supply **esset**. **Donec** uses a subjunctive when expectancy is implied. Contrast the use of **donec** in Letter 4.11, Section 19.

**Haec:** neuter accusative plural, object of both **leges** and **scripturus**: *these things.* Pliny means the things that he has described in the letter, that is, how he witnessed and responded to the eruption of Vesuvius. **Haec** is modified by **digna**.

**historiā:** ablative because it is dependent on **digna**.

**non:** Construe with **scripturus**.

**scripturus:** future active participle. Pliny suggests that Tacitus will read his description of his (Pliny's) experiences (**haec**), but will not write about them when composing his historical account of the eruption. Pliny depicts himself as quite unperturbed about the possibility that his story will not be included. However, his statement may be disingenuous. He may well have hoped that Tacitus would indeed include his description and thus grant him the immortality of being recorded in a history book. Because only a small portion of Tacitus's *Histories* is extant, we do not know whether he mentioned Pliny's experiences.

**qui:** The antecedent is **tibi**, which is here a reflexive pronoun: *yourself.*

**requisisti:** Understand the **haec** (which begins the sentence) as the object. In the opening of the letter, Pliny stated that Tacitus had written that he wanted to know what experiences he (Pliny) had had at Misenum while Vesuvius was erupting.

**epistulā:** ablative because it is dependent on **digna**.

**videbuntur:** The subject of this verb is an understood **haec**, *they, these things,* modified by **digna**. Here the understood **haec**, which denotes, as above, *these experiences of mine,* would be a nominative neuter plural because it would be the subject. **Digna**, also a nominative neuter plural because it modifies the understood **haec**, serves as a predicate adjective after **videbuntur**. Pliny is suggesting (with perhaps feigned modesty) that his descriptions of his experiences (**haec**) may not seem to Tacitus worthy of a history book or even a letter.

# 17. Letter 6.34

L etter 6.34 is addressed to a man named Maximus who had family ties to northern Italy. He is otherwise unknown to us. The topic of this brief letter is Maximus's sponsorship of gladiatorial performances in the city of Verona. Maximus had funded this public entertainment as a memorial to his deceased wife, who was a native of the city. He might have chosen to fund a more permanent memorial, such as a public building, or a more beneficial one, such as food provisions for poor children. It was not, however, unusual for wealthy men to sponsor gladiatorial performances as memorials. Indeed, some scholars believe that gladiatorial matches originated as displays at funerals.

Wealthy people were expected to be benefactors of the cities and towns in which they resided or had been raised, and to provide the financing for municipal projects. In return, their fellow townspeople treated them with great deference. In Letter 4.13, in which he outlines his plan to fund a school in Comum, Pliny describes a scene in which local men had gathered at his home to pay their respects. Pliny was, in fact, a generous patron to his hometown. A fragmentary inscription records several of his contributions to the community. (On the inscriptional evidence, see "The Life of Pliny" in the introduction to this book and the Appendix of Inscriptions.)

This letter is of interest not only because of the information it supplies about municipal patronage. It also encourages the reader to consider marital relationships in the ancient Roman world. We know from Letters 4.19, 6.4, and 7.5 that Pliny wanted his readers to conclude that his marriage to Calpurnia was blissfully happy. In Letter 6.34, he depicts the marriage of Maximus and his wife as also having been felicitous. We cannot know if these marriages were truly blissful, but Pliny believed that it was important to a man's public image that he be portrayed as being happily married.

---

## C. PLINIUS MAXIMO SUO S.

1 Recte fecisti quod gladiatorium munus Veronensibus nostris promisisti, a quibus olim amaris, suspiceris, ornaris. Inde etiam uxorem carissimam tibi et
5  probatissimam habuisti, cuius memoriae aut opus aliquod aut spectaculum, atque hoc potissimum, quod maxime funeri, debebatur.

1     **quod:** *with respect to the fact that, because.*

**munus:** The word here means *public exhibition*, but elsewhere it can mean *gift* or *duty*. There was a correlation between the *gift* of an *exhibition* to the townspeople and the *duty* to commemorate a deceased family member.

**Veronensibus:** dative plural: *the people of the city of Verona*. Verona was (and is) a city in northern Italy, about one hundred miles east of Milan. Pliny identifies the people of Verona as **nostris**, *our*, because he, too, as a native of the town of Comum, had been raised in northern Italy. There still exist in Verona the well-preserved remains of a Roman amphitheater, but we do not know if Maximus's gladiatorial exhibition took place there.

**amaris:** The present (passive) tense denotes a duration of time: *you are and have been loved.*

**Inde ... habuisti:** *From that place (city), you had a wife.* Pliny means that Maximus had a wife from Verona, or, less literally, found a wife in Verona.

**memoriae:** dative case; indirect object of **debebatur**.

**opus aliquod:** *some public structure.* Maximus might have commissioned a permanent memorial but instead chose a gladiatorial spectacle. **Opus aliquod** and **spectaculum** are the subjects of **debebatur**.

**hoc:** refers specifically to **spectaculum**.

**quod ... funeri:** The antecedent of **quod** is **hoc**. As a verb for this relative clause, supply **debetur**: *To whose memory was owed either some public structure or a spectacle, and this especially, which particularly* (is owed) *to a funeral.* Pliny suggests that a gladiatorial spectacle was a particularly appropriate way of commemorating Maximus's wife because such spectacles had once been associated with funerals. (See the introduction to this letter.)

2 Praeterea tanto consensu rogabaris, ut negare non
constans, sed durum videretur. Illud quoque egregie,
10   quod tam facilis, tam liberalis in edendo fuisti. 3 Nam
per haec etiam magnus animus ostenditur. Vellem
Africanae, quas coëmeras plurimas, ad praefinitum
diem occurrissent. Sed, licet cessaverint illae
tempestate detentae, tu tamen meruisti ut acceptum
15   tibi fieret, quod, quo minus exhiberes, non per te stetit.
Vale.

---

2    **consensu:** Pliny implies that so many people in the town made the same
request: that Maximus honor his deceased wife with a display of gladiators.

**ut:** introduces a result clause with the subjunctive verb **videretur**.

**negare:** This infinitive is the subject of **videretur**.

**constans, durum:** These adjectives modify the infinitive and are therefore
neuter singular but may apply also to a person's character. A wealthy man who
continued to refuse to pay for public entertainments might be considered by
the townspeople not firm, but rude or harsh.

**Illud:** The pronoun refers to the following statement. Supply **fecisti**: *This also
you did admirably, the fact that* (**quod**) . . .

**edendo:** gerund, from **edere**.

3    **Vellem:** The subjunctive use is potential. The imperfect tense is used to denote a wish unfulfilled in present time. The opportunity for the event to take
place has passed: *I might have wished.* **Vellem** is followed by a noun (substantive) clause (which is not introduced by **ut**). The verb of the subordinate
noun clause, **occurrissent**, is an optative subjunctive: *Would that the African
animals had arrived!* The sentence can be translated *I might have wished that
the African animals had arrived,* or less literally (and without translating the
potentiality) *I wish that the African animals had arrived.*

**Africanae:** Supply **bestiae**, *beasts, animals*. The word **bestia** is feminine in
gender; the animals, however, were not necessarily all female. Large cats, such
as lions, were brought to Italy from Africa to be slaughtered by trained performers known as **venatores**, *hunters*. These performers were not technically
**gladiatores**, who were trained performers who fought other humans. The
wild beast "hunts" were different in origin from the gladiatorial exhibitions,

although they were often produced on the same days. Maximus evidently spent a great deal of money to sponsor his spectacle, because importing large cats was very expensive.

**plurimas:** literally *very many*. Translate *in very large numbers*.

**licet:** This present tense verb form introduces a concessive subjunctive clause. In this usage, **licet** may be translated as a conjunction: *although*.

**illae:** the African beasts.

**meruisti:** introduces an indirect command: **ut ... fieret**.

**acceptum ... fieret:** the passive form of the phrase **acceptum facere**. (**Fio, fieri** is used as the passive of **facio, facere**.) **Acceptum facere**, in reference to a debt or obligation, means *to make note* (**facere**—active voice) *as having been paid* (**acceptum**), that is, *to give credit for*. Here the expression means *(you have deserved) that credit be given* (**fieret**—passive voice) *to you* (for your promise to supply African beasts).

**quo minus:** often written as one word, **quominus**, means *that ... not*. Here: *that you did not produce the display*. **Quominus** introduces a subjunctive clause.

**non per te stetit:** literally *it did not stand through you*. Translate: *it was not your fault*.

# 18. Letter 7.5

L etter 7.5 is another letter addressed by Pliny to his young wife Calpurnia. In Letter 6.4, he recorded that she had traveled to Campania to recuperate from an illness, and that he, having remained in
Rome, was distressed by her absence and ill health. It is not known whether
she was still in Campania when he wrote the present letter or whether this
absence was a different occasion. It is noteworthy that Pliny chose to publish these letters and thus leave for posterity a portrait of himself as a loving
husband. Although we cannot know whether he was truly happy in his marriage—and whether Calpurnia was truly happy—he evidently considered
it important that his readers receive an image of him not only as a respected
public figure but also as an affectionate husband. Similarly in Letter 6.34,
he depicts Maximus as having been very fond of his wife. In Letter 3.16,
Section 10, he referred to the **concordia** of Arria the Elder's marriage, and
in Letter 4.19, Section 5 to the **concordia** of his own. Pliny's views on marriage may reflect those of his contemporaries.

---

## C. PLINIUS CALPURNIAE SUAE S.

1 Incredibile est quanto desiderio tui tenear. In causa
amor primum, deinde quod non consuevimus abesse.
Inde est, quod magnam noctium partem in imagine
5 tua vigil exigo; inde, quod interdiu, quibus horis te
visere solebam, ad diaetam tuam ipsi me, ut verissime
dicitur, pedes ducunt; quod denique aeger et maestus
ac similis excluso a vacuo limine recedo. Unum tempus
his tormentis caret, quo in foro et amicorum litibus
10 conteror. 2 Aestima tu, quae vita mea sit, cui requies in
labore, in miseria curisque solacium. Vale.

---

1   **tui:** objective genitive.

**tenear:** an indirect exclamation, which uses the same construction as an
indirect question and therefore requires a subjunctive.

**In causā:** Supply **est**, whose subject would be **amor**. Less literally *the reason is.*

**quod:** *because.* Here **quod** introduces a causal clause with an indicative verb.

**in imagine tua:** literally *on your image.* Pliny is awake at night, calling to mind an image of his wife.

**quibus horis:** ablative of time; literally *during which hours.* English uses a demonstrative adjective followed by the relative: *during those hours in which.*

**ipsi:** nominative masculine plural. Construe with **pedes**.

**ut verissime dicitur:** Pliny is commenting on the words that follow, **pedes ducunt**, and observing that the proverbial expression, that the feet lead of their own accord, is very true.

**similis excluso:** Pliny is here comparing himself to a figure common in Latin erotic poetry, the excluded lover. However, the situation in love poetry is quite different: The couple is not married (or not to one another). The woman loved by the man has ended their affair and refuses to let him into her home. He thus stands at her door, refused entrance and "excluded." In Pliny's situation, he is happily married, and his wife is temporarily away from home. The only similarity between Pliny and the excluded lover is the passion that they both express for the women they love. It is remarkable, in the history of Latin literature, that Pliny chose to use an image from erotic poetry to proclaim so publicly his feelings for his wife. In Letter 4.19, Section 4, Pliny notes that Calpurnia sings his poems (**versus**). We do not know the nature of these poems.

**Unum:** Translate as *only one.* Construe with **tempus**.

**quo:** ablative of time. The antecedent is **tempus**.

**in foro:** Pliny, as a lawyer and a public official, is referring specifically to the area of the Forum where the law courts and Senate house were located. Pliny's point is that he finds relief from his anguish caused by Calpurnia's absence in immersing himself in his work and in the anxiety and trouble that his work causes. (In contrast, in Letter 6.4, he complains that his work in Rome has kept him from traveling to Campania to be with Calpurnia.)

2   **sit:** subjunctive in an indirect question.

**cui:** The antecedent is an **ego**, which is implicit in the word **mea**. Supply **est** with **cui requies**. **Cui** is dative of possession.

**requies in labore, in miseria curisque solacium:** Note the chiastic arrangement of the words: noun, prepositional phrase, prepositional phrase, noun. This arrangement emphasizes the surprising conjunction of tranquility and work, anxiety and comfort.

# 19. Letter 7.19

I n Letter 7.19, Pliny records the serious illness of a woman named Fannia. She is also mentioned briefly in Letter 3.11, Section 3, Pliny's account of his assistance to the opponents of the emperor Domitian, and
in Letter 3.16, Section 2, where he acknowledges that she provided him
with information about the fortitude of Arria the Elder. Fannia was the
granddaughter of Arria the Elder and the daughter of Arria the Younger.
She was married to Helvidius the Elder, who had been an unrelenting critic
of the emperor Vespasian (69–79 CE), the father of the emperor Domitian.
He was twice sent into exile. During his second exile, in the mid-70s CE,
he was executed. After his death, his widow Fannia, who had accompanied
him in both his exiles, continued to support the imperial opponents. Her
stepson, Helvidius the Younger, was, like his father, critical of the imperial
regime; he was sentenced to execution in 93 CE. As noted in Letter 3.11,
Fannia and her mother, Arria the Younger, were at the same time sentenced
to exile. Pliny's letters have left for posterity vivid portraits of three generations of very resolute women.

The letter is addressed to a man named Priscus. We know nothing more
about him.

---

C. PLINIUS PRISCO SUO S.

1 Angit me Fanniae valetudo. Contraxit hanc dum
adsidet Iuniae virgini, sponte primum (est enim
adfinis), deinde etiam ex auctoritate pontificum. 2 Nam
5   virgines, cum vi morbi atrio Vestae coguntur excedere,
matronarum curae custodiaeque mandantur. Quo
munere Fannia dum sedulo fungitur, hoc discrimine
implicita est. 3 Insident febres, tussis increscit; summa
macies, summa defectio. Animus tantum et spiritus
10  viget Helvidio marito, Thrasea patre dignissimus;

1    **hanc:** refers to **valetudo**.

    **Iuniae** (or **Juniae**): Junia was a Vestal Virgin, and a relative of Fannia. She is otherwise unknown. She may have been related to Junius Arulenus Rusticus and Junius Mauricus, who are mentioned in Letter 3.11, Section 3, as having been punished in 93 CE for criticizing Domitian's regime.

    **virgini:** Supply **Vestali**. On Vestal Virgins, see also Letter 4.11.

    **pontificum:** The Vestal Virgins were under the superintendence of the state priests. See also Letter 4.11, Section 6.

2    **cum ... coguntur: cum** temporal with the indicative mood.

    **atrio:** ablative of place from which without the preposition (which is included in the compound verb **ex-cedere**). Although **atrium** was the designation for the central room in a Roman house, it is here used more broadly to mean the whole *house* or *residence*. The residence of the Vestal Virgins (who began their service at an age between six and ten years; see the introduction to Letter 4.11) was in the Roman Forum. Its remains are still visible today.

    **Vesta, -ae (f.):** the spirit or deity of hearth fires. The hearth fire in Roman homes was critical to the survival of residents because it cooked their food and kept them warm. The Vestal Virgins, on behalf of all residents of the state, were entrusted with performing the rites to honor Vesta.

    **curae custodiaeque:** datives.

    **Quo munere:** The ablative case is required by the verb **fungitur**. Translate the relative adjective **quo** as if it were a demonstrative such as **illo**. This use of the relative adjective at the beginning of a sentence is *resumptive*; the pronoun refers to something in the previous sentence and *resumes* the thought expressed in that sentence. The relative is used to link its sentence more closely with the preceding sentence.

    **dum:** When **dum** means *while*, the verb of its clause uses a present indicative tense where English uses a past tense.

3    **macies, defectio:** Supply **est**.

    **viget:** The verb is singular although there are two subjects, **animus et spiritus**, whose meanings are similar. These nouns are modified by one adjective, **dignissimus** (which governs the ablatives **Helvidio** and **Thraseā**).

    **Helvidio:** Helvidius the Elder, the husband of Fannia and the father of Helvidius the Younger. See the introduction to this letter.

    **Thrasea:** Thrasea Paetus, the father of Fannia and the husband of Arria the Younger. A critic of the emperor Nero (54 to 68 CE), he was sentenced to execution in 66 CE but chose to preempt execution by committing suicide. On the reasons for choosing suicide over execution, see the notes to Letter 3.16, Section 6.

reliqua labuntur, meque non metu tantum, verum
etiam dolore conficiunt. 4 Doleo enim feminam
maximam eripi oculis civitatis nescio an aliquid simile
visuris. Quae castitas illi, quae sanctitas, quanta
15   gravitas, quanta constantia! Bis maritum secuta in
exsilium est, tertio ipsa propter maritum relegata.
5 Nam, cum Senecio reus esset, quod de vita Helvidi
libros composuisset, rogatumque se a Fannia in
defensione dixisset, quaerente minaciter Mettio Caro
20   an rogasset, respondit:

---

**reliqua:** neuter plural nominative. Pliny means all the remaining parts of
Fannia, other than her mind and courage. He is referring to her body. He
states, at first (with **labuntur**), that all the remaining parts (her body) are
failing. Then (with **conficiunt**) he means that the remaining parts (her body)
consume him with fear and grief (because he can see that they are failing).

4   **Doleo:** here introducing an indirect statement.

**oculis civitatis:** *from the eyes of the state;* dative of separation (or reference).
Pliny means *from the people of the Roman state.*

**nescio an:** The phrase means literally *I do not know whether,* and it is sometimes
followed by an indirect question. Here, however, it can be translated as if an
adverb: (eyes) *perhaps not* (about to see). Compare Letter 4.11, Section 8.

**aliquid simile:** object of **visuris**. Although Pliny is implying that the Romans
will never again see *anyone* similar to Fannia, he uses a neuter pronoun, **aliquid**,
*anything.* The idiom is not uncommon in Latin. Compare the use of **nihil** in
Letter 5.16, Section 1.

**visuris:** future active participle modifying **oculis**: eyes *about to see, that will
in the future see.*

**illi:** dative of possession.

**propter maritum relegata:** Supply **est**. In 93 CE, about twenty years after
the execution of her husband, Fannia was relegated (banished) for reasons
explained in the following sentences.

A person condemned to **exsilium** suffered, in addition to exile, the loss
of citizenship and the confiscation of property. A person condemned to **rel-
egatio** did not lose citizenship or property. We do not know where Fannia
spent her years of banishment.

5   **Nam, cum Senecio reus esset:** Here begins a very long and complex sentence. Its main verb is **respondit**, the subject of which is Fannia. The situation being described is the Senate investigation in 93 CE of seven people accused of criticizing Domitian. For the names of the seven, see Letter 3.11, Section 3.

Readers may choose to draw a diagram of this complicated sentence. The first section is **cum ... dixisset**, which is subordinate to **respondit**. The **cum** clause contains two verbs, **esset** and **dixisset**, each in turn governing a subordinate clause. Subordinate to **esset** is the clause **quod ... composuisset**. Subordinate to **dixisset** is **rogatum ... defensione**. The enclitic **-que**, attached to **rogatum**, joins the two verbs in the **cum** clause, **esset** and **dixisset**.

**Nam:** This long sentence explains Pliny's words, in the previous sentence, that Fannia had been relegated because of her husband. She was tried for treason because she had encouraged the writing of a biography of her husband and preserved a copy even after the Senate had ordered copies to be destroyed.

**cum:** introducing two temporal clauses.

**Senecio:** nominative case. Herennius Senecio was one of the three opponents of Domitian whom Pliny, in Letter 3.11, Section 3, records were executed in 93 CE. He was charged with treason because he had written a biography of Helvidius the Elder (**vita Helvidi**), a critic of the imperial system.

**reus:** The trial of Senecio took place before the trial of Fannia. His testimony was then used at her trial.

**quod:** introducing a causal clause with **composuisset**. The subjunctive mood alerts the reader that Pliny is reporting a reason put forward by someone else.

**rogatumque ... dixisset:** the second clause of the **cum** construction. The subject is still Senecio. **Dixisset** introduces an indirect statement. The reflexive **se** is the accusative subject; **rogatum** (supply **esse**) is the infinitive predicate: *when he had said that he had been asked.*

**in defensione:** Translate with **dixisset**: *in* (his own) *defense.*

**quaerente:** Readers who have survived the **cum** construction are ready to tackle the main section of the sentence. The main verb is **respondit**. The topic now is Fannia's trial and her responses to questioning by a prosecutor.

**quaerente ... Caro:** ablative absolute. Mettius Carus was here interrogating Fannia: *with Carus inquiring,* or better: *when Carus inquired.* There are three indirect questions dependent on **quaerente**.

**Mettio Caro:** ablative case. Mettius Carus was a lead prosecutor in the case against Fannia, whose trial was held in the Senate.

**an rogasset: Rogasset** is a contracted form of **rogavisset**. The subject is Fannia. This is the first indirect question (hence the subjunctive mood) introduced by **quaerente**. Mettius Carus inquired of Fannia whether she had asked Senecio to write a biography of her husband, Helvidius the Elder.

"Rogavi," an commentarios scripturo dedisset: "Dedi,"
an sciente matre: "Nesciente"; postremo nullam
vocem cedentem periculo emisit. 6 Quin etiam
illos ipsos libros, quamquam ex necessitate et metu
25    temporum abolitos senatus consulto, publicatis bonis
servavit; habuit tulitque in exsilium exsilii causam.
7 Eadem quam iucunda, quam comis, quam denique
(quod paucis datum est) non minus amabilis quam
veneranda!

---

**"Rogavi":** Fannia replies, "Yes, I did ask." Pliny portrays Fannia as replying
very curtly and bravely to the prosecutor.

**an . . . dedisset:** the second indirect question introduced by the **quaerente**
of the ablative absolute. The subject is again Fannia.

**scripturo:** modifies an understood **Senecioni** (dative of indirect object). The
future active participle indicates purpose or intention: *to him (Senecio) about
to write*, or better: *to Senecio who was planning to write*.

**an sciente matre:** For the verb of this third indirect question introduced by
the **quaerente**, understand **dedisset**.

**sciente matre:** ablative of attendant circumstance: *with her mother knowing*.
Mettius inquired whether Fannia had given the notebooks to Senecio *with
her mother knowing*. Mettius was trying to ascertain not only whether Fannia's
activities were treasonous, but also whether her mother, Arria the Younger,
was involved. Ultimately her mother was also relegated, but we do not know
what charges were brought against her.

**"Nesciente":** *not knowing*; another ablative of attendant circumstance.
Fannia's reply (as reported by Pliny) is again just one word.

**postremo . . . emisit:** Fannia did not yield to the impending danger of criminal conviction and uttered no word (**vocem**, *voice*) that would incriminate
others. **Cedentem** modifies **vocem**, although the thought is that Fannia did
not yield to danger.

6    **libros:** Helvidius's notebooks and Senecio's biography of him. **Libros** is the
object of **servavit**.

**quamquam:** Translate with **abolitos** (perfect passive participle of **abolere**),
which modifies **libros**. **Quamquam** is used here concessively with a participle rather than with a finite verb.

**ex:** translate as *through, as a result of*. Pliny was a member of that very Senate which decreed that books by and about Helvidius the Elder be burned. Now, after the death of the emperor Domitian, he attributes the actions of himself and his fellow senators to the pressure and fear of those times. He is implying that all senators felt that their lives were in danger if they did anything that displeased Domitian.

**necessitate:** *pressure*.

**consulto:** ablative of means. **Senatus** is genitive. The two words are often written as one, **senatusconsultum**, *decree of the Senate*, in which case the **senatus** part remains always in the genitive, while the **consultum** part declines.

**publicatis bonis:** an ablative absolute with a concessive meaning: *although her property had been confiscated*. Although Pliny writes in Sections 4 and 10 (and also in Letter 3.11, Section 3) that Fannia had been relegated, a sentence that usually did not involve confiscation of property, he here reports that she *did* lose property. It is not possible to solve the discrepancy.

**servavit:** The subject is Fannia. The object is **libros**. The decree of the Senate had ordered that the books be burned, but Fannia had managed to save some copies and to take them into exile with her.

**exsilii causam:** in apposition to **libros**. Fannia took into exile the cause of her (sentence of) exile. Again there is a vagueness about whether Fannia was exiled or relegated.

7    **Eadem:** nominative singular = **Fannia**.

**quam iucunda:** Translate **quam** as *how*. Supply **est**. So far in the letter, Fannia appears formidable in her defiance of authority. Pliny now tries to soften her image by describing her as a pleasant and affable person.

**quod:** *what* (quality), (a quality) *which*, in reference to the following adjectives, **amabilis**, **veneranda**.

**non minus . . . quam:** *no less . . . than*.

**veneranda:** a gerundive modifying **eadem**.

30   Eritne quam postea uxoribus nostris ostentare
     possimus? erit a qua viri quoque fortitudinis exempla
     sumamus? quam sic cernentes audientesque miremur,
     ut illas quae leguntur? 8 Ac mihi domus ipsa nutare
     convulsaque sedibus suis ruitura supra videtur, licet
35   adhuc posteros habeat. Quantis enim virtutibus
     quantisque factis adsequentur, ut haec non novissima
     occiderit?

---

**Eritne quam: -Ne** is the enclitic particle attached to the end of a word to indicate a question. *Will there be* (supply *any other woman*) *whom . . . ?* **Quam,** *whom*, is the direct object of **ostentare.**

**possimus:** subjunctive in a relative clause of characteristic.

**erit a qua:** a second question, although not signaled by the enclitic particle **-ne.** *Will there be* (supply *any other woman*) *from whom . . . ?*

**viri:** nominative plural: *we men.*

**exempla:** The use of real people as models for behavior was a cornerstone of Roman moral education. From childhood, Romans were advised to pattern their behavior after that of people, living or historical, who embodied the virtues valued by Roman society. Pliny's teacher Quintilian wrote: "However much the Greeks excel in moral precepts, so much do the Romans excel in real examples, which is a far greater thing" (*Institutio Oratoria* 12.2.30).

**sumamus:** subjunctive in a relative clause of characteristic.

**quam:** a third question, although not signaled by an introductory **eritne:** (Will there be any other woman) *whom . . . ?*

**sic cernentes audientesque:** nominative plural present participles, modifying the understood subject (*we*) of **miremur.** Pliny means that Fannia is a living legend, a live model. Residents of Rome can see her and hear her in person but also admire her just like those women who, being now dead, are only read about. One example of a heroic woman of the past would be Fannia's grandmother, Arria the Elder. The set of virtues admired in women was not the same as that admired in men. Consider the behavior of Pliny's wife, Calpurnia (Letter 4.19), and of Minicia (Letter 5.16).

**miremur:** subjunctive in a relative clause of characteristic.

**ut illas:** Understand **miremur:** *as we admire those* (women).

**leguntur:** Pliny means *read about*, not *read* (in the sense of *Hemingway is read*).

8   **mihi:** Construe with **videtur**, whose subject is **domus**.

**supra:** Translate this adverb with **ruitura** (future active participle).

**licet:** This present tense verb form introduces a concessive subjunctive clause. In this usage, **licet** may be translated as a conjunction: *although*.

**licet ... habeat:** Pliny is concerned that the house (family line) of Helvidius is on the verge of collapse. He reminds himself and his readers that the house still has descendants, but he is not optimistic about the future. Fannia had no birth children and was therefore the last direct descendant of Arria the Elder, Arria the Younger, and their husbands, Caecina Paetus and Thrasea Paetus. Fannia's husband, Helvidius the Elder, had one son by a previous marriage, Helvidius the Younger, but he had been executed in 93 CE. At his death, he left one son and two daughters, all still young children. Not many years after the execution, however, in Letter 4.21 (not included in this volume), Pliny reports the deaths of the two daughters, both in childbirth, and laments that the son is now the last surviving member of his family.

**adsequentur:** The subject is the descendants referred to in the previous sentence.

**ut:** introducing a result clause.

**haec:** nominative feminine singular; Fannia.

**non:** Construe with **occiderit**.

**novissima:** *the last* of her family and of her family tradition. (On the meaning of **novissima**, compare Letter 6.16, Section 20, and Letter 6.20, Section 15.) Pliny conflates two concerns in this sentence: that the families of Helvidius and Fannia may physically die out, and that the family members who are now alive may not possess the qualities necessary to sustain the family tradition of courageous political action. We do not know what happened to the son of Helvidius the Younger, that is, whether he produced children and whether he was politically active.

9 Me quidem illud etiam adfligit et torquet, quod
matrem eius, illam (nihil possum inlustrius dicere)
40  tantae feminae matrem, rursus videor amittere,
quam haec, ut reddit ac refert nobis, sic auferet secum
meque et novo pariter et rescisso vulnere adficiet.
10 Utramque colui, utramque dilexi; utram magis,
nescio, nec discerni volebant. Habuerunt officia mea
45  in secundis, habuerunt in adversis. Ego solacium
relegatarum, ego ultor reversarum; non feci tamen
paria atque eo magis hanc cupio servari, ut mihi
solvendi tempora supersint. 11 In his eram curis, cum
scriberem ad te; quas si deus aliquis in gaudium
50  verterit, de metu non querar. Vale.

---

9    **quod:** *the fact that.* Construe with **videor.**

**matrem eius, illam ... matrem:** *her* (Fannia's) *mother, that* (famous) *mother.*
Both appearances of **matrem** refer to Arria the Younger. The demonstrative
**ille** often means not just *that one,* but *that famous one.* Compare Letter 3.16,
Sections 2 and 13.

**inlustrius:** comparative degree, neuter singular accusative. When Pliny
writes that he can say nothing *more praiseworthy,* he is praising Arria the
Younger for raising so admirable a daughter.

**tantae feminae:** genitive; refers to Fannia.

**quam:** The antecedent is **matrem** (Arria the Younger); **quam** is the object of
**reddit, refert,** and **auferet.** Note that **auferet** is future indicative.

**haec:** Fannia, the subject of **reddit, refert,** and **auferet.** Pliny implies that
Fannia is so similar to her mother that she seems to bring her back to life.

**ut ... sic:** *just as ... so thus.*

**secum:** = **cum se.** The preposition **cum,** which usually precedes the word it
governs, is joined enclitically to personal pronouns.

   Just as Fannia has brought her mother back to life, so thus she will take
her *with her,* if she dies.

**et ... et:** *both ... and.*

**rescisso:** perfect passive participle of **rescindere.**

**10**  **utram magis:** Supply **dilexi**. Note the difference in meaning between **utramque** and **utram**.

**discerni:** Fannia and Arria never wished for Pliny to make a distinction between them regarding whom he loved more.

**officia:** *services*. Pliny states that the two women had his help.

**in secundis, in adversis:** Pliny is speaking of times or circumstances.

**Ego:** Supply **eram**.

**solacium:** We do not know what solace Pliny provided to the women during the time that they were banished from Rome.

**relegatarum, reversarum:** feminine plural genitive of the perfect participles of **relegare** and **revertor**. The participles refer to Fannia and Arria the Younger. As noted above, Fannia and her mother were punished with relegation in 93 CE but returned to Rome after the death of Domitian in 96 CE.

**ultor:** After the death of Domitian in 96 CE, Pliny attempted to prosecute the man principally responsible for the executions and relegations in 93 CE.

**paria:** neuter plural accusative. Pliny admits that his **officia** to the women were not equal to those that they did for him. We do not know what their **officia** to him were. Perhaps their family helped him advance in his career.

**eo magis:** *by this* (much) ... *more, for this* (reason) ... *more*. Translate with **cupio**, which introduces an accusative-infinitive construction, **hanc ... servari**. **Hanc** refers to Fannia.

**ut:** introduces a purpose clause.

**solvendi:** gerund in the genitive case.

**tempora:** Translate as singular: *time*, or as plural: *opportunities*. Pliny is hoping that Fannia will live many more years so that he will have more time and therefore more opportunities to pay his debts to her, that is, to give her as much help as her family gave to him. We do not know when Fannia died or whether she died of the illness mentioned in this letter.

**11**  **in:** *in the midst of.*

**eram, scriberem:** Latin uses the imperfect tense to acknowledge that the recipient of the letter will be reading it after the author has written it. English uses the present tense to convey the situation of the author as he or she is writing the letter. On the epistolary imperfect, see Letter 6.4, Section 2.

**quas:** The antecedent is **curis**.

**si:** introduces a future more vivid condition, with a future perfect indicative in the protasis and a future indicative in the apodosis.

# 20. Letter 8.5

In Letter 8.5, Pliny reports the death of the wife of Macrinus, a man to whom Pliny addresses several letters, but whose identity is not secure. Like Letters 4.19, 6.4, 6.34, and 7.5, this letter provides us with a glimpse into the nature of Roman marriages, at least from a man's point of view. It is curious that Pliny does not provide the wife's name.

The letter is addressed to Rosanius Geminus, a younger friend to whom Pliny addresses several letters.

---

C. PLINIUS GEMINO SUO S.

1 Grave vulnus Macrinus noster accepit. Amisit uxorem singularis exempli, etiam si olim fuisset. Vixit cum hac triginta novem annis sine iurgio, sine offensa.

5  Quam illa reverentiam marito suo praestitit, cum ipsa summam mereretur! quot quantasque virtutes, ex diversis aetatibus sumptas, collegit et miscuit! 2 Habet quidem Macrinus grande solacium, quod tantum bonum tam diu tenuit; sed hinc magis exacerbatur,

10  quod amisit. Nam fruendis voluptatibus crescit carendi dolor. 3 Ero ergo suspensus pro homine amicissimo, dum admittere avocamenta et cicatricem pati possit, quam nihil aeque ac necessitas ipsa et dies longa et satietas doloris inducit. Vale.

---

1    **noster:** *our friend.* Latin sometimes gives the possessive adjective the additional meaning of *dear friend.* Compare Letter 3.11, Section 1.

**singularis exempli:** genitive of quality (or description). On the Roman penchant for **exempla**, see Letter 7.19, Section 7.

**olim:** Pliny's point is that Macrinus's wife would have been considered an exceptional model even if she had lived in a previous era. The Romans typically believed that previous eras were more virtuous than their own.

**fuisset:** pluperfect subjunctive in a past contrary to fact condition.

**annis:** The ablative case is occasionally used, instead of the accusative, to express duration of time. Compare Letter 4.13, Section 1.

**Quam:** feminine accusative singular, of the interrogative adjective **qui, quae, quod**, used here as an exclamatory. Translate with **reverentiam**: *What respect!*

**illa, ipsa:** nominative feminine singular.

**cum:** Translate here as *while*. This concessive construction takes the subjunctive mood.

**summam:** modifies an understood **reverentiam**.

**sumptas:** perfect passive participle, modifying **virtutes**.

**collegit et miscuit:** Macrinus's wife may have been about fifty-five years old at the time of her death, if she had married Macrinus when she was about fifteen years old. Pliny's point is that she had continued to cultivate virtues throughout her life and had acquired virtues appropriate to her age as she—and the marriage—matured. In Letter 5.16, Section 2, in which Pliny reports the death of Minicia Marcella, he praises this young girl as having the wisdom and seriousness of an older woman, but also the sweetness and modesty of a girl. Minicia, who was about to be married at the age of twelve years, deserved special commendation because she already displayed the virtues of a much older woman.

2   **quod:** The word occurs twice in this sentence, introducing first **tenuit** and then **amisit**. Translate as *because*.

**amisit:** Understand **tantum bonum** as the object. The neuter accusative **bonum** is here used as a substantive: *a boon, a good thing*.

**fruendis:** gerundive of **fruor**. Translate as *enjoyed*. Here the gerundive has no implication of obligation or futurity. The ablative case expresses cause. The sorrow of losing a person increases when one has enjoyed many pleasures with that person.

**carendi:** gerund; objective genitive.

3   **dum:** *until*. This use of **dum** requires the subjunctive.

**quam:** modifies **cicatricem**. Compare Pliny's comments in Letter 5.16, Sections 10 and 11, about how time heals wounds.

**ac:** *as*.

**dies:** *time*. Compare Letter 5.16, Section 11, for Pliny's observations about alleviating grief.

# 21. Letter 8.10

I n Letter 8.10, Pliny reports to his wife's grandfather, Calpurnius Fabatus, that she has suffered a miscarriage. The miscarriage was certainly
an emotional and physical trauma for Calpurnia. The Romans believed
that the purpose of marriage was to produce a new generation of family
members, and young brides were expected to fulfill the duty of bearing children soon after they were married. As noted in the introduction to Letter
4.19, many children died before they were even five years old, and therefore
a wife was expected to have many pregnancies to ensure that at least one
or two of the children survived to adulthood.

Calpurnia's miscarriage was also a bitter disappointment for Pliny, who,
though married three times, still had no children. As the sole survivor of his
family, he was acutely aware of his failure to reproduce his family line. Still,
despite his own grief, he had to write this letter to console his grandfather-
in-law, for whom the news would be distressing. Calpurnius Fabatus had
no other descendants of child-bearing age and was depending on his granddaughter to perpetuate the family line. He had had two adult children, a
son (Calpurnia's father, now deceased) and a daughter (Calpurnia's aunt,
who had played a major role in raising her; see Letter 4.19) who seems not
to have had any surviving children. In this letter, Pliny seems to anticipate
that the grandfather will be angry. Did he regret marrying his granddaughter to a man who had not, in two previous marriages, produced children?

---

### C. PLINIUS FABATO PROSOCERO SUO S.

1 Quo magis cupis ex nobis pronepotes videre, hoc
tristior audies neptem tuam abortum fecisse, dum se
praegnantem esse puellariter nescit, ac per hoc
5  quaedam custodienda praegnantibus omittit, facit
omittenda. Quem errorem magnis documentis
expiavit, in summum periculum adducta.

---

1    **Quo magis . . . hoc tristior:** a correlative construction with an ablative of
degree of difference: *by what* (amount) *more . . . by this* (amount) *sadder.*

**ex nobis:** Pliny means *from me and Calpurnia.*

**tristior:** *sadder.* Latin often uses an adjective (here modifying the understood subject of **audies**) where English would use an adverb (*more sadly*).

**audies:** future indicative; introduces an accusative-infinitive construction in indirect statement: **neptem . . . fecisse**.

**abortum:** Here the word means *miscarriage,* not *abortion.* In contrast, in Letter 4.11, Section 6, where Pliny is determined to depict Domitian as a villain, his use of the word **abortus** is designed to prompt readers to recall the unsubstantiated rumor that Domitian had forced his niece to have an abortion.

**dum:** When **dum** means *while,* the verb it introduces uses a present indicative tense where English would use a past tense.

**puellariter:** Pliny attributes Calpurnia's miscarriage to her being young and inexperienced. She was probably still a teenager at the time of her pregnancy because girls were often married for the first time in their early teens. Minicia, of Letter 5.16, was engaged to be married when she was twelve years old. Miscarriages were unfortunately not infrequent in the ancient world, probably because of poor nutrition and medical care, especially among the lower classes. Yet even a privileged girl like Calpurnia, from a wealthy family, might experience medical problems.

**quaedam:** accusative neuter plural, object of **omittit**.

**praegnantibus:** dative of agent with the gerundive **custodienda**, which modifes **quaedam**.

**facit omittenda:** With this phrase, supply **quaedam praegnantibus**. **Omittenda** is a gerundive modifying **quaedam**.

**in summum periculum:** Calpurnia almost died as a result of the miscarriage.

**adducta:** perfect passive participle, modifying the subject of **expiavit**.

2 Igitur, ut necesse est graviter accipias senectutem
tuam quasi paratis posteris destitutam, sic debes agere
10   dis gratias, quod ita tibi in praesentia pronepotes
negaverunt, ut servarent neptem, illos reddituri,
quorum nobis spem certiorem haec ipsa quamquam
parum prospere explorata fecunditas facit. 3 Isdem
nunc ego te quibus ipsum me hortor, moneo, confirmo.
15   Neque enim ardentius tu pronepotes quam ego liberos
cupio, quibus videor a meo tuoque latere pronum ad
honores iter et audita latius nomina et non subitas
imagines relicturus. Nascantur modo et hunc nostrum
dolorem gaudio mutent. Vale.

---

2    **ut ... sic:** *while ... yet.* This construction uses the indicative mood.

**accipias:** The subjunctive is required after **necesse est**, although there is no
introductory conjunction. **Accipias** is then followed by an accusative-infinitive
construction. Understand **esse** with **destitutam** to form the infinitive.

**quasi paratis posteris:** literally *already prepared posterity.* Pliny means that
a next generation was already "in the works" because a child had been con-
ceived and Calpurnia was pregnant. Translate *a next generation already on its
way.* The ablative is of separation.

**dis:** = **deis.**

**negaverunt, servarent:** The understood subject is **dei.**

**ut:** introduces a purpose clause.

**illos:** The antecedent is **pronepotes.**

**reddituri:** modifying the understood **dei.**

**quorum:** The antecedent is **illos. Quorum** is an objective genitive dependent
on **spem.**

**spem:** direct object of **facit.**

**certiorem:** modifies **spem**: (makes hope) *more certain.*

**haec ipsa ... fecunditas:** Construe together as the subject of **facit.**

**quamquam . . . explorata:** literally *although ascertained too little happily.* **Quamquam** is used here concessively with the perfect passive participle rather than with a finite verb. Compare Letter 7.19, Section 6.

**parum prospere:** Pliny here uses the rhetorical figure *litotes.* By *too little happily,* he means *very unhappily.* Compare Letter 6.20.17.

**explorata:** modifies **fecunditas.** Pliny's point is that Calpurnia's pregnancy made the expectation of great-grandchildren more certain because it proved that she was able to bear children, although her fertility was ascertained unhappily by her miscarriage.

3   **Isdem:** *with the same (thoughts).* Followed by the relative **quibus:** *with which.*

**hortor, moneo, confirmo:** Construe with both **te** and **ipsum me** as the direct objects.

**tu:** Supply **cupis.**

**quibus:** dative of indirect object with the future active participle **relicturus;** the antecedent is **liberos.**

**videor . . . relicturus:** Construe these two words together: *I seem about to leave (to bequeath).* Less literally: *it seems that I will leave (bequeath).*

**a meo tuoque latere:** *from my side and from your side.* **Latere** here means *family* or *lineage.* Pliny is suggesting that the hoped-for descendants, coming from two illustrious families, will enjoy successful political careers, particularly because he will bequeath to them easy access, well-known family names, and famous ancestors.

**pronum ad honores iter et audita latius nomina:** Note the arrangement of the words. The two adjective-noun combinations enclose the phrase and adverb that expand their meaning.

**imagines:** Elite Roman families often displayed in their homes images of their famous ancestors. By *not sudden images,* Pliny means that his house can boast that it has images of illustrious ancestors who lived a long time ago and thus that his family has been distinguished for many generations.

**Nascantur, mutent:** hortatory subjunctives. The subject is an understood **liberi.**

**hunc nostrum dolorem:** literally *this our grief;* less literally *this grief of ours.*

# 22. Letter 8.16

Letter 8.16 is addressed to Plinius Paternus, who was also the addressee of Letter 1.21. The topic of both letters is slavery. Although this man has the same **nomen** as Pliny, we have no evidence that they were related. Another letter concerning slaves is Letter 3.14, about the attack on Larcius Macedo. There Pliny describes the murder of a slave owner by some of his slaves. Although Pliny admits that Macedo had been a cruel master, he expresses no sympathy for the slaves. His lack of compassion for the slaves in that letter is quite different from the thoughts he expresses here. Keep in mind that Pliny selected and edited the letters that he published. It is intriguing that he chose to publish two letters that portray him as holding contrasting opinions about slaves.

---

### C. PLINIUS PATERNO SUO S.

1 Confecerunt me infirmitates meorum, mortes etiam, et quidem iuvenum. Solacia duo nequaquam paria tanto dolori, solacia tamen: unum facilitas
5   manumittendi (videor enim non omnino immaturos perdidisse, quos iam liberos perdidi), alterum, quod permitto servis quoque quasi testamenta facere, eaque ut legitima custodio.

---

1    **meorum:** *my* (slaves). The adjective **meus** (here the genitive plural **meorum**), when used without a noun, can mean *a member of the household*. Here Pliny is referring specifically to his slaves. Compare Letter 9.36, Section 4.

**iuvenum:** genitive plural: *of young* (slaves).

**Solacia duo:** Supply **mihi sunt**; dative of possession.

**unum:** Supply **est**. The second **solacium** is introduced later in the sentence by **alterum**.

**facilitas:** Pliny's use of the word **facilitas** is ambiguous. He may mean the *ease* of the legal process of manumission, or (more likely) his own *willingness* to manumit some of his slaves. The slaves whom Pliny manumitted were probably household slaves who attended to his personal needs and were therefore well known to him. It is less likely that he would be concerned about the health of slaves who worked on the several farms he owned because he would rarely know any of them personally.

**manumittendi:** gerund. The verb **manumittere** is composed of **manus** and **mittere. Manus** means *hand* but also, by extension, *power* or *control*. To *manumit* is to send someone out of one's control, that is, to free her or him. Some Roman slave owners were very cruel to their slaves. (Consider Letter 3.14.). On the other hand, in comparison with other slave-owning societies, the Romans manumitted a relatively large number of slaves. The hope of manumission was the carrot for slaves; dreadful physical abuse was the stick. A slave owner could manumit slaves when he was alive or leave instructions in his will that they be freed upon his death. The advantage of the latter choice was that the owner continued to benefit from the use of the slaves. The disadvantage was to his heirs, who inherited less property, since slaves were considered valuable property.

**non omnino:** Construe with **immaturos**: *not entirely prematurely*. Pliny consoles himself with the thought that, although the slaves die while still young, they die as free persons (**liberos**), that is, having been manumitted.

**immaturos:** Latin often uses an adjective (here, *them premature*) where English would prefer an adverb (*them prematurely*). Compare Letter 5.16, Section 1.

**eaque:** accusative neuter plural; refers to **testamenta**.

**ut legitima:** *as if legal*. The wills would not, however, have been considered legal by a court, for reasons explained below.

2 Mandant rogantque, quod visum; pareo ut iussus.
10  Dividunt, donant, relinquunt dumtaxat intra domum;
     nam servis res publica quaedam et quasi civitas domus
     est. 3 Sed, quamquam his solaciis adquiescam, debilitor
     et frangor eadem illa humanitate, quae me, ut hoc
     ipsum permitterem, induxit. Non ideo tamen velim
15  durior fieri. Nec ignoro alios eius modi casus nihil
     amplius vocare quam damnum, eoque sibi magnos
     homines et sapientes videri. Qui an magni sapientesque
     sint, nescio; homines non sunt.

---

2  **quod visum:** Supply **est**: *what seems best* (to them). The passive voice of **videre** can mean *to seem best* or *to seem right*.

**res publica, civitas:** Slaves had the legal status of property, like a donkey or a shovel. Therefore they could not legally be citizens of any political unit. Pliny represents the **domus**, *household*, as their **res publica** or **civitas**. (Nor could slaves form legal marriages or claim their own offspring as their legal children. The children, like their parents, belonged to the owner and could be sold, like cattle or furniture, at any time.)

   Being themselves property, they could not legally own property. Any items that they might have in their possession, such as clothing, tools, or trinkets given to them by the family that owned them, or items that they found, legally belonged to their owner. At any time, but especially upon the death of a slave, her/his owner could claim these items. Pliny allowed his slaves to consider such items as their property and to bequeath them to other slaves in the household, but only within the household (**domus**). He may have appeared more generous than other slave owners, but, in reality, since the items never left his household, he remained the legal owner of them.

**domus:** the subject of **est**. **Res publica** and **civitas** are predicate nouns.

3  **quamquam:** Note Pliny's use of the subjunctive, **adquiescam**, here. Although the indicative with **quamquam** was more common in earlier writers, by Pliny's time, the subjunctive was also regularly used. The subjunctive may provide an element of potentiality to the statement, *although I may find comfort*, where an indicative would be a simple statement of fact, *although I find comfort*.

**ut ... permitterem:** noun (substantive) clause of result.

**velim:** potential subjunctive.

**Nec ignoro:** *Nor am I unaware* = *I know*, followed by an indirect statement construction whose accusative subject is **alios**.

**eius modi:** Construe with **casus** (which is the direct object of **vocare**).

**damnum:** a financial loss. Pliny contrasts himself with those slave owners who consider the death of a slave to be only a financial loss, that is, a loss of property.

**eoque:** *and* (**-que**) *for this reason*.

**sibi . . . videri:** literally *seem to themselves*; less literally *regard themselves as*. Compare the uses of **sapiens** in Letter 5.16, Section 8, and **sapientem** and **sapienti** in Letter 3.11, Section 5.

**videri:** the second infinitive of the indirect statement construction. The accusative subject is still **alios**. **Magnos homines et sapientes** are predicate nouns and adjectives. **Sapientes** may here mean simply *wise men*, or more specifically *philosophers*.

**Qui:** the subject of **sint**. Translate as *they*. This is another example of the *resumptive* use of the relative pronoun. Compare Letter 3.11, Section 8. Pliny, as often, uses the relative pronoun instead of a demonstrative pronoun such as **illi**.

**an:** *whether*; introduces the indirect question of which **sint** is the verb. The subjunctive clause is dependent on **nescio**.

**homines:** Pliny means that these men do not possess the qualities that define human and humane behavior.

4 Hominis est enim adfici dolore, sentire, resistere
tamen et solacia admittere, non solaciis non egere.
5 Verum de his plura fortasse quam debui, sed pauciora
quam volui. Est enim quaedam etiam dolendi voluptas,
praesertim si in amici sinu defleas, apud quem lacrimis
tuis vel laus sit parata vel venia. Vale.

---

4      **Hominis:** predicate genitive: *it is* (the characteristic) *of a man.*

**non solaciis non egere:** The Stoic philosophers believed that people should
endure the loss of a loved one without grieving. In contrast, in Letter 5.16,
Sections 10 and 11 (in which Pliny reports the untimely death of Minicia
Marcella), he urges his addressee to offer **solacium** to Minicia's father (who
was a student of Stoicism) and not to expect him to react to his daughter's
death without grieving.

5      **de his plura:** Supply **scripsi. Plura** is neuter plural accusative: *more* (things).

**dolendi:** gerund.

**si . . . defleas:** The verb is present subjunctive in the protasis of a future less
vivid condition. The apodosis **est,** however, is indicative, making the statement about the pleasure of grieving more emphatic and unequivocal. The
construction is a "mixed condition."

**lacrimis:** dative.

**sit parata:** relative clause of characteristic. Translate **sit** as a present subjunctive, and **parata** as a predicate adjective with **laus** and **venia,** rather than as
the participial element of a perfect passive verb: *is furnished, is readily offered.*

This plaque was found in the tomb of the Statilius family, constructed
in the late first century BCE or early first century CE in the outskirts of
Rome. Several niches (**columbaria**) inside the tomb held the ashes of
slaves and freedpersons who had worked for the family. The inscription
on this plaque announces that the remains are those of Nothus, a secretary. **Librarius a manu** means "scribe by hand." Translate as "(Here
rest the remains) of Nothus the secretary." The rest of the inscription is
in elegiac couplets. The plaque now resides in the National Roman Museum at the Baths of Diocletian; a copy of the inscription is included in
the *Corpus Inscriptionum Latinarum* (CIL vi. 6314). (Public Domain)

> Non optata tibi coniunx monimenta locavit
>     ultima in aeternis sedibus ut maneant
> spe frustra gavisa Nothi quem prima ferentem
>     aetatis Pluton invidus eripuit.
> Hunc etiam flevit quaequalis turba et honorem
>     supremum digne funeris inposuit.

Your wife has placed (here) your memorial, though (one) not
desired (**optata**) by you / so that your final remains (**ultima**)
may rest in eternal surroundings, / (your wife) having in vain
taken pleasure (**gavisa**) in the promise (**spe:** that is, in the hope
that she and her husband would live long and happily) of Nothus,
whom, while he was enjoying (**ferentem**) the prime (moments) /
of life, jealous Pluton (= Pluto) snatched (him) away. / A coequal
(that is, people of similar status) crowd also wept for him and /
fittingly bestowed the final honor of a funeral ceremony.

# 23. Letter 9.6

I n this letter, Pliny proclaims his disdain for chariot races. Few residents
of Rome, however, shared his attitude. Chariot races were among the
most popular and most enduring spectator events throughout the Roman Empire. (In Letter 6.34, Pliny briefly mentions two other forms of
spectator entertainments: gladiatorial combats and animal "hunts.") In
Rome, races took place in the Circus Maximus ("The Very Great Racetrack"). By the imperial period, the Circus Maximus could accommodate
about 250,000 spectators (a piece of information provided by Pliny the
Younger's uncle, Pliny the Elder: *Natural History* 36.102). The races were
called the **Ludi Circenses** ("Racetrack Entertainments") and were funded by the state. The satiric poet Juvenal, who lived about the same time
as Pliny, complained in his *Satire* 10.81 that his fellow Romans no longer
participated as voters in the elections that determined political affairs and
now cared only about **panem et circenses**, "bread and circuses," that is,
handouts of food and free entertainments.

There were four chariot-racing companies (**factiones**; singular **factio**)
in Rome, each represented by a color: Red, White, Blue, and Green. For a
fee, the **factiones** supplied horses, chariots, and even drivers to the government officials who produced the races. Many of the drivers were slaves or
former slaves and, during the races, each wore a tunic dyed in the color of
the **factio** for which he worked, just as today members of sports teams wear
shirts in the team colors.

The letter is addressed to Calvisius Rufus, who was, like Pliny, a native
of the northern Italian town of Comum (modern Como). Pliny reports
that he has been in Rome, peacefully engaged in literary activities, while
others have flocked to the chariot races. Such events, he asserts, hold no
attraction for him.

---

## C. PLINIUS CALVISIO SUO S.

1 Omne hoc tempus inter pugillares ac libellos
iucundissima quiete transmisi. "Quem ad modum"
inquis "in urbe potuisti?" Circenses erant, quo genere
spectaculi ne levissime quidem teneor. Nihil novum,
nihil varium, nihil quod non semel spectasse sufficiat.

1    **Omne hoc tempus:** Chariot races were not produced every day, or even every month. They were special events. During the month of September, however, there were about two weeks of races.

**pugillares:** See Letter 1.6, Section 1.

**iucundissima quiete:** ablative of manner without the preposition **cum.**

**Quem ad modum:** often written as one word: **quemadmodum:** *in what manner? how?*

**inquis:** *you say, exclaim.* Pliny imagines that the addressee of the letter, Calvisius, is asking the question. Compare the use of **inquis** in Letter 1.6, Section 1.

**in urbe:** *in Rome.* On the use of **urbs** to designate specifically Rome, compare Letters 4.13, Section 1, and 10.96, Section 4.

**Circenses = Ludi Circenses:** *Racetrack Entertainments.* The Latin word **circus** means *circle,* but the racetrack was, like modern racetracks, oval.

**quo genere:** ablative of means, *by which type;* less literally *a type* (of spectacle) *by which.*

**levissime:** superlative adverb.

**Nihil novum:** Supply **est:** *there is.* In his disdain for entertainments popular with the masses, Pliny may be modeling his remarks on those of Cicero who, in a letter composed about 150 years earlier, had written dismissively about an extravagant display of spectacular entertainments: **Neque nos ... quicquam novi vidimus**—"Nor did we see anything new" (*Ad familiares* 7.1.3).

**non:** Construe with **sufficiat.**

**spectasse:** a contracted (syncopated) perfect active infinitive form of **spectare.** The full form is **spectavisse.**

**sufficiat:** relative clause of characteristic introduced by **quod,** whose antecedent is the neuter **nihil.**

2 Quo magis miror tot milia virorum tam pueriliter
identidem cupere currentes equos, insistentes curribus
homines videre. Si tamen aut velocitate equorum

10    aut hominum arte traherentur, esset ratio non nulla;
nunc favent panno, pannum amant, et, si in ipso
cursu medioque certamine hic color illuc, ille huc
transferatur, studium favorque transibit, et repente
agitatores illos, equos illos, quos procul noscitant,

15    quorum clamitant nomina, relinquent.

---

2    **miror:** introducing an accusative-infinitive construction.

**tot milia ... cupere: Tot milia** is the accusative subject of **cupere**, which is the infinitive verb of the indirect statement.

**virorum:** partitive genitive.

**equos:** There were usually four horses in a chariot. Sometimes, however, there were only two horses or, on rare occasions, as many as eight.

**insistentes:** present active participle of **insistere** (which takes the dative case). The chariot drivers stood as they drove. Note the arrangement of the words; the noun and its modifying adjective enclose the dative.

**videre:** the complementary infinitive after **cupere**. It has two objects, **equos** and **homines**. Note the arrangement of the words; the two infinitives enclose the two objects and their modifiers.

**Si ... nulla:** a present contrary to fact condition, requiring the imperfect subjunctive.

**velocitate ... arte:** Note the chiastic (ABBA) word order: ablative genitive, genitive ablative.

**non nulla:** literally *not no*. Translate as *some*. The expression is an example of the rhetorical figure *litotes*, by which the writer emphasizes something by denying its opposite. Compare Letter 3.11, Section 5, and Letter 6.20, Section 17.

**panno:** *piece of cloth*. Pliny means the colored tunic that the chariot drivers wore. Again note the chiastic (ABBA) word order: verb noun, noun verb.

**ille:** modifies an understood **color**.

**transferatur:** Pliny imagines a situation where two drivers might miraculously, in the middle of a race, exchange colored tunics, as if they had transferred to one another's **factio**. The verb is present subjunctive in the protasis of a future less vivid condition. However, the apodosis of the condition, whose verbs, **transibit** and **relinquent**, are future indicative, is future more vivid. The construction is a "mixed condition." The indicative in the apodosis makes emphatic the certainty of the result. Pliny is certain that the spectators will move their support.

**studium favorque:** *enthusiasm and applause.* Although there are two nouns as the subject, the predicate, **transibit**, is singular, perhaps because the two nouns are so similar in meaning that they seem to express just one idea. They might be translated as *enthusiastic applause* (adj. + noun). This use of two nouns instead of a single modified noun is a figure known as *hendiadys*.

**agitatores, equos:** the objects of **relinquent**, whose subject is an understood **tot milia virorum**.

**Noscitant** and **clamitant** are frequentative verbs, formed from **noscere** and **clamare**. They denote that the action occurred frequently or repeatedly. Compare Letter 4.19, Section 3.

The point of this sentence is that the spectators are fickle and will abandon their support even of drivers and horses whom they know so well that they can recognize them at a distance. Pliny is suggesting that the spectators were fans of a particular **factio**, rather than of a particular driver or horse, and that they would cheer for a different driver if the drivers changed **factiones** and colored tunics. While it is true that many Roman spectators were fanatically devoted to a particular **factio**, some individual drivers acquired large followings of fans. The poet Martial, who lived about the same time as Pliny, wrote about a very popular driver named Scorpus, whom he describes as "the pride of the noisy Circus, the darling of Rome" (*Epigram* 10.53). Scorpus died at the young age of twenty-six years, probably in an accident on the track. Chariot driving was a very dangerous activity.

3 Tanta gratia, tanta auctoritas in una vilissima tunica,
mitto apud vulgus, quod vilius tunica, sed apud
quosdam graves homines; quos ego cum recordor in re
inani, frigida, adsidua, tam insatiabiliter desidere, capio
20   aliquam voluptatem, quod hac voluptate non capior.
4 Ac per hos dies libentissime otium meum in litteris
colloco, quos alii otiosissimis occupationibus perdunt.
Vale.

---

3   **gratia:** Supply **est**.

**tunicā:** *tunic,* the garment dyed in one of the four colors of the racing **factio-nes** and worn by the chariot drivers.

**mitto apud vulgus: Mittere** here means *to pass over, omit.* Translate *say nothing about* (the influence of tunics) *among the rabble* (or *I won't mention . . .*). Compare Letter 3.11, Section 6.

**quod vilius:** Supply **est**. The antecedent of **quod** is **vulgus**. Note the social snobbery of Pliny's description of the majority of spectators. Pliny expects the **vulgus** to behave childishly (**pueriliter** in Section 2), but he is appalled that his social peers, **quosdam graves homines**, would exhibit the same unrefined behavior.

**tunicā:** ablative of comparison with **vilius**, which is the neuter singular comparative adjective of **vilis**.

**quos:** The antecedent is **homines**. This is another example of the *resumptive* use of the relative pronoun. Compare Letter 3.11, Section 8. Pliny often uses a relative pronoun where an English speaker would expect a demonstrative pronoun, such as **illos**. Construe **quos** with the **cum** temporal clause, where it serves as the accusative subject of the infinitive **desidere**. The indirect statement is introduced by **recordor**. Consider the word order **cum ego recordor quos (= illos) desidere**. On **cum** with the indicative, see Letter 7.19, Section 2.

**re:** here denotes the activity of watching chariot races. Translate as *activity*.

**desidere:** Pliny's use of this verb is pejorative. He means not just that the men sit at the races but that, as they *sink* insatiably in their seats, they *sink* in his opinion of them.

**capio . . . capior:** In the first instance, translate the verb as *take*; in the second, as *taken in,* that is, *captivated*. Also, **voluptatem** means a smug, self-satisfied pleasure, while **voluptate** means the pleasure of watching races. Note the chiastic (ABBA) word order.

On the popularity of chariot races, the satiric poet Juvenal wrote **totam hodie Romam Circus capit**: *Today the racetrack takes in all of Rome* (*Satire* 11.197). The verb **capit** has two meanings here: the Circus provides seating for everybody in Rome, and the Circus captures the attention of everybody in Rome.

4    **quos:** The antecedent is **dies**.

**otiosissimis:** superlative of **otiosus**: *idle*. Note the clever wordplay. Pliny writes that he is spending his *idle time* in literary activities, while other men (those at the chariot races) are wasting their days in *very idle* activities. He contrasts himself, and his admirable (as he thinks) use of his idle time (**otium**), with other men who (he judges) waste these days. **Otiosissimis occupationibus** is an oxymoron because *idleness* and *activity* are opposite and contradictory concepts.

In several letters, Pliny is eager to present himself as a man dedicated to literary endeavors and scornful of activities that did not (he believed) involve intellectual stimulation. Consider Letter 1.6 (about hunting) and Letter 1.15, Section 2 (about dinner party entertainment). In Letters 4.6 and 9.36, moreover, he portrays himself as someone more concerned about writing than about managing his estates.

This is a photo of a mosaic housed in the Museum of Gallo-Roman Civilization in Lyon, in east-central France. The mosaic depicts a chariot race on a racetrack similar to the Circus Maximus in Rome. The chariot drivers were usually slaves or freedmen to whom the faction owners might give a small percentage of the prize winnings. (Creative Commons 2.0)

# 24. Letter 9.12

The addressee of Letter 9.12 was a wealthy landowner of equestrian rank named Terentius Iunior. (For the definition of **eques**, see the note on Letter 3.14, Section 7.) In the letter, the childless Pliny offers Iunior advice on raising his son. He begins by relating an anecdote about a man who, according to Pliny, was too strict.

---

## C. PLINIUS IUNIORI SUO S.

1 Castigabat quidam filium suum quod paulo sumptuosius equos et canes emeret. Huic ego iuvene digresso: "Heus tu, numquamne fecisti quod a patre corripi posset? 'Fecisti?' dico? Non interdum facis quod
5 filius tuus, si repente pater ille, tu filius, pari gravitate reprehendat? Non omnes homines aliquo errore ducuntur? Non hic in illo sibi, in hoc alius indulget?" 2 Haec tibi admonitus immodicae severitatis exemplo, pro amore mutuo scripsi, ne quando tu quoque filium
10 tuum acerbius duriusque tractares. Cogita et illum puerum esse et te fuisse, atque ita hoc, quod es pater, utere, ut memineris et hominem esse te et hominis patrem. Vale.

---

1    **quidam:** Pliny does not divulge the name of the father in this anecdote. Perhaps he omitted the name in the published version of the letter in order not to embarrass the man.

**sumptuosius:** comparative adverb formed from the adjective **sumptuosus**. Here the comparative means *too extravagantly*, not *more extravagantly*.

**emeret:** subjunctive mood after **quod** because Pliny is reporting the reason given by the father, not supplying his own reason. Contrast Letter 1.11, Section 2.

**Huic ego:** Supply **dixi**.

**iuvene digresso:** ablative absolute.

**Heus tu:** Pliny here begins a direct quotation that extends to **indulget**.

**numquamne:** -**Ne** is an enclitic particle.

**quod:** Translate as *(something) which*. **Quod** here introduces a relative clause of characteristic, which requires a subjunctive mood.

**patre:** Translate as *by* (your) *father*.

**'Fecisti' dico?:** *Do I say "Have you done"?*

**Non interdum facis:** *Do you not sometimes do?* Pliny gently reminds the man that, even as an adult, he sometimes does things that his son could rebuke.

**pater ille, tu filius:** Supply **esset** for a present contrary to fact condition: *if he were the father and you the son.*

**reprehendat:** The subjunctive is required because the verb is used in a relative clause of characteristic. The tense is present because the introductory verb, **facis**, is present tense (primary sequence).

**hic ... alius:** *this man in that way, another man in this way.* Note the chiastic (ABBA) word order: **hic in illo ... in hoc alius.** The reflexive pronoun **sibi** is the dative with **indulget.** Construe **sibi** with both **hic** and **alius**.

2    **Haec tibi:** Construe with **scripsi.**

**immodicae severitatis:** Pliny thought that the father's verbal chastisement was excessively harsh. It would be interesting to know whether the father also imposed a punishment.

**ne:** introduces a negative purpose clause requiring a subjunctive mood. **Tractares**, the verb governed by **ne**, is in the imperfect subjunctive because the main verb of the sentence, **scripsi**, is perfect indicative, a secondary tense. Pliny uses the perfect tense to acknowledge that the recipient of the letter will be reading it after he has written it. This use is called epistolary. English uses the present tense to convey the temporal point of view of the author as (when) he or she is writing the letter. Compare Letter 10.17, Section 4.

**acerbius duriusque:** The comparative here means *too harshly.*

**Cogita:** present imperative introducing an indirect statement.

**et ... et:** *both ... and.*

**te fuisse:** Understand **puerum**: *that you were* (once) *a boy.*

**ita:** Translate with **utere.**

**hoc, quod:** *this, the fact that.* **Hoc** is ablative case with **utor.**

**utere:** second singular present imperative of the deponent verb **utor.**

**ut memineris:** Following **ita, ut** introduces a result clause. **Memineris** is a perfect active subjunctive, but it is translated as present tense. The verb is defective and has only perfect system forms. It is followed by an accusative-infinitive construction in indirect statement.

# 25. Letter 9.36

I n this letter, Pliny describes how he spends a typical summer day on his
estate in Tuscany. The addressee is Gnaeus Pedanius Fuscus, a young
man who was at the beginning of his senatorial career. Pliny is careful to portray himself as being ardently engaged in literary activities. He
stresses his fondness for such activities also in Letter 1.6 (in preference
to hunting) and in Letter 9.6 (in preference to watching chariot races). In
contrast, he gives only a brief and dismissive reference, at the end of the
letter, to his involvement in the agricultural activities on the estate, the
very activities that provided him with income. Either he was a very careless landowner or, more likely, he deliberately de-emphasized his interest
in the running of the estate in order to impress Fuscus with his dedication
to literary pursuits.

---

C. PLINIUS FUSCO SUO S.

1 Quaeris, quem ad modum in Tuscis diem aestate
disponam. Evigilo cum libuit, plerumque circa horam
primam, saepe ante, tardius raro. Clausae fenestrae
manent. 2 Mire enim silentio et tenebris, ab iis quae
avocant abductus, et liber et mihi relictus, non oculos
animo, sed animum oculis sequor, qui eadem quae
mens vident, quotiens non vident alia.

---

1    **quem ad modum:** often written as one word: **quemadmodum**: *in what manner? how?* See Letter 9.6, Section 1. These words here introduce an indirect
question.

**Tuscis:** Supply **agris**, *my Tuscan fields* or *estate.* In Letter 4.6, Section 1, Pliny
lamented that his Tuscan estate had been struck by a hailstorm that damaged the crops. Pliny's considerable wealth was derived mainly from land
ownership, and he regularly visited his several estates to make sure that they
were being managed profitably. He also used his visits to rest from his hectic
schedule in Rome.

**circa horam primam:** *around the first hour.* The first hour began at sunrise;
the twelfth ended at sunset. The Romans divided the daylight period into
twelve units, or **horae.** Because the amount of daylight was greater in the

summer and less in the winter, the length of each hour varied during the year. A **hora** at the winter solstice would be about forty-five minutes, at the summer solstice, about seventy-five minutes. On Roman hours, see also Letter 6.16, Section 4, and Letter 6.20, Section 6.

2   **Mire ... alia:** The subject of this long and complex sentence is an understood **ego**, and the predicate is **sequor**. The understood **ego** is modified by **abductus** (participle), **līber** (adjective), and **relictus** (participle).

**ab iis:** Construe with **abductus**. **Iis** is neuter plural, *from those things.*

**qui:** The antecedent is **oculis**. **Qui** is the subject of **vident** (whose object is **eadem**).

**quae mens:** Supply **videt**. The antecedent of **quae** is **eadem**. (Both are neuter plural accusative.) **Mens** and **animus** are here used synonymously.

**quotiens non vident alia:** *whenever they* (the eyes) *do not see other things.* In the darkness of the shuttered bedroom, the eyes do not see other things and thus can focus on forming images of what the mind "sees." Pliny follows his mind (his thoughts) that, in the darkness, directs his eyes to form images. In contrast, when the room is lit, the eyes direct what the mind thinks about.

Cogito, si quid in manibus, cogito ad verbum scribenti
10    emendantique similis, nunc pauciora, nunc plura, ut
vel difficile vel facile componi tenerive potuerunt.
Notarium voco et, die admisso, quae formaveram dicto.
Abit rursusque revocatur rursusque dimittitur. 3 Ubi
hora quarta vel quinta (neque enim certum
15    dimensumque tempus), ut dies suasit, in xystum me
vel cryptoporticum confero, reliqua meditor et dicto.
Vehiculum ascendo. Ibi quoque idem quod ambulans
aut iacens; durat intentio mutatione ipsa refecta.
Paulum redormio, dein ambulo, mox orationem
20    Graecam Latinamve clare et intente non tam vocis
causa quam stomachi lego; pariter tamen et illa
firmatur.

---

**Cogito:** Pliny means that he mulls over or reflects upon literary projects he is currently working on and continues the process of composition. The verb is repeated for emphasis.

**si:** Supply **habeo.**

**quid:** used instead of **aliquid** because the clause is introduced by **si.**

**in manibus:** *in hands.* English uses the phrases *on hand* or *in progress.*

**ad verbum:** *word by word.* Construe with **scribenti.**

**scribenti, emendanti:** These present participles are in the dative case because they are governed by **similis.** Pliny states that, as he cogitates in the dark bedroom, he is similar to someone writing and amending, although he is not actually writing.

**similis:** nominative masculine singular, modifying the understood subject (**ego**) of **cogito.**

**pauciora, plura:** Construe with **cogito.** Both adjectives are neuter plural accusative. They modify an understood *things,* that is, *literary passages.*

**ut:** *as.*

**difficile, facile:** adverbs.

**potuerunt:** perfect indicative. The subject is an understood *things* or *literary passages.*

**teneri:** *held* (in memory). Pliny is composing in his head, not writing down the passages. Note the enclitic **-ve**.

**die:** *daylight.* Compare Letter 6.20, Section 18. (In the following sentence, **dies** means *day* or *weather.*)

**dicto:** Understand **ea,** *those things,* as the object of **dicto**. The antecedent of **quae** is this understood **ea**.

**revocatur, dimittitur:** Pliny keeps his secretary very busy.

3    **Ubi:** Supply **est**.

**me:** the object of **confero**.

**ascendo:** This verb can be used with or without the preposition **in** or **ad**. Compare Letter 3.16, Section 8, and Letter 6.16, Section 5.

**Ibi quoque idem:** Supply **facio** here and **feci** with the **quod** clause. **Idem**, a neuter singular accusative, is the antecedent of **quod**.

**mutatione ipsa:** ablative of means. Pliny is referring to the change of position, from lying in bed or on a couch to sitting in a carriage. Note the arrangement of the words; the noun and modifier in the nominative case (**intentio . . . refecta**) enclose the noun and modifier in the ablative case.

**refecta:** perfect passive participle, nominative singular, modifying **intentio**.

**redormio:** Pliny probably takes a nap after lunch, or after the sixth hour, which began at the midpoint of the day (our *noon*).

**orationem Graecam:** As a well-educated Roman man, Pliny would have had a very good knowledge of Greek.

**Latinamve:** Note the enclitic **-ve**.

**clare, intente:** adverbs formed from adjectives.

**tam . . . quam:** correlative.

**vocis causā:** In the ablative case **causā** serves as a preposition governing the genitive case, and often (as here) it is postpositive, that is, it follows the word it governs.

**stomachi:** Construe also with **causā**. Reading aloud was thought to be beneficial for the digestive system.

**lego:** Here the word means *read aloud, recite.*

**et:** *also.*

**illa:** nominative case; a reference to **vocis**.

4 Iterum ambulo, ungor, exerceor, lavor. Cenanti mihi,
si cum uxore vel paucis, liber legitur; post cenam
25   comoedus aut lyristes; mox cum meis ambulo,
quorum in numero sunt eruditi. Ita variis sermonibus
vespera extenditur, et quamquam longissimus dies
cito conditur. 5 Non numquam ex hoc ordine aliqua
mutantur. Nam, si diu iacui vel ambulavi, post somnum
30   demum lectionemque, non vehiculo, sed, quod
brevius, quia velocius, equo gestor. Interveniunt amici
ex proximis oppidis, partemque diei ad se trahunt
interdumque lasso mihi opportuna interpellatione
subveniunt.

---

4      **ungor:** passive voice: *I am rubbed with oil*. A slave applied the oil while mas-
saging Pliny's body. The oil and the accumulated dirt were later scraped off
as part of the bathing process.

**exerceor:** another passive form. However, it is difficult to comprehend the
meaning of the passive, that is, how Pliny is exercised by slaves. Perhaps Pliny
is describing the process of the slaves helping him with the exercise equipment. Or **exerceor** may be used as a middle voice, in a reflexive sense: *I exercise myself.*

**lavor:** In Letter 3.14, Section 2, Pliny writes about a man who was being
bathed (passive voice: **lavabatur**) by his slaves. However, the passive form
may represent a middle voice, to convey a reflexive sense: *I bathe myself.*

**legitur:** Again the verb means *read aloud* (here by a slave).

**comoedus aut lyristes:** Supply **est**. In Letter 1.15, Section 2, Pliny tells a
friend that, if he had accepted his dinner invitation, Pliny would have provided for entertainment a **comoedus** or a **lector** or a **lyristes**. However, the
friend preferred vulgar entertainers from Gades and the richer food at someone else's house.

**cum meis:** *with my (people)*; less literally, *with members of my household*. A
Latin word for household was **domus**. See Letter 8.16, Section 2: **nam servis
res publica quaedam ... domus est**. Pliny would include in his definition of
*household* anyone living under the same roof and therefore family members,
both nuclear and extended, friends, freed persons, and slaves.

**quorum in numero:** *in the number of whom;* less literally *among whom.*

**eruditi:** Treat **eruditi** as a substantive: *educated men.*

**quamquam:** here modifying **longissimus**: *although very long.*

5    **Non numquam:** an example of the rhetorical figure *litotes,* by which the writer emphasizes one thing by denying its opposite. Compare Letter 3.11, Section 5.

**quod:** Supply **est**. The antecedent of **quod** is the activity of being carried by a horse. Supply **est** also with **quia velocius**.

**partemque diei ad se trahunt:** *and they draw part of the day to themselves.* Pliny means that they take up, or occupy, part of his day.

**lasso mihi:** dative with the verb **subveniunt**.

35  6 Venor aliquando, sed non sine pugillaribus, ut
quamvis nihil ceperim, non nihil referam. Datur et
colonis, ut videtur ipsis, non satis temporis, quorum
mihi agrestes querellae litteras nostras et haec urbana
opera commendant. Vale.

---

6  **Venor:** present indicative of the deponent verb **venari**. On Pliny's hunting experience, see Letter 1.6.

**ut:** introduces a purpose clause.

**quamvis:** a concessive clause requiring a subjunctive verb.

**non nihil referam:** Pliny brings back ("bags") a literary composition rather than an animal. Compare Letter 1.6, Section 1.

**Datur:** Supply **tempus** as the subject. Pliny also (**et**) gives time to the **colonis**, but they think that it is not enough: **non satis temporis**.

**colonis:** These people are the tenant farmers or sharecroppers who lease land on the estate from Pliny. They pay a rental fee for their use of the land or give Pliny a percentage of their harvest, which he then sells for his own profit. (In addition, part of the land on Pliny's estates was under his direct management and worked by his own slaves.)

Pliny's wealth was generated to a great extent by the land leases on his several estates. It is perhaps disappointing to modern readers that Pliny seems so scornful of these people whose hard labor provided him with so comfortable a life. However, his attitude was probably prevalent among people of his social class.

**ut:** *as.*

**ipsis:** dative case; the peasant farmers.

**temporis:** partitive genitive.

**quorum:** *whose.* The antecedent is **colonis**.

**mihi:** Construe with **commendant**.

**agrestes:** This word means both *agricultural* and *boorish*. In contrast, **urbana** means both *urban* and *refined*. Pliny dismisses farmworkers as uncouth and inferior to people of his own class.

**querellae:** subject of **commendant**. In Letter 4.6, Section 1, Pliny reported that hail had damaged the crops on his Tuscan estate. He could absorb the consequent loss of income, but tenant farmers, who lived at subsistence level, might be devastated by such a loss. Perhaps one complaint that the peasants on his estate had was that he was charging too much for land leases.

**litteras nostras:** *our literary pursuits.* Pliny claims that the irksome task of listening to the complaints of his **coloni** makes him appreciate even more the pleasures of literary pursuits and urban activities.

# 26. Letter 10.17

P liny had a successful career as a lawyer, senator, and public official. Over the years, he was selected to the positions of quaestor, tribune, praetor, augur, and finally, in 100 CE, to the prestigious position of consul. (On Pliny's career, see "The Life of Pliny" in the introduction to this book.) He was also chosen twice to serve as a minister of treasuries. In this latter role, he seems to have acquitted himself well and to have indicated that he was skillful in financial management. (His interest and expertise in the area of financial administration may indicate that his apparent indifference in Letter 9.36 to agricultural matters at his Tuscan villa is merely a literary pose.) About ten years after Pliny served as consul, the emperor Trajan appointed him to be his legate, or representative, in the province of Bithynia-Pontus, an area that is now northern Turkey. (See Map 3.) It is not possible to establish a precise date for his appointment; it was probably around 110 CE. The assignment was not an easy one. The province was prosperous, but it was plagued by financial corruption among civic officials. Pliny's assignment was to travel through the province, examine the financial records of each city, uncover misappropriation of funds, and reorganize public finance systems. He was also empowered to hear and decide on legal cases that required a judgment by a Roman official rather than a local magistrate.

The letters in Book 10 are letters that Pliny wrote to Trajan, and Trajan's replies. In Letter 10.17, addressed to Trajan, Pliny informs the emperor that he has reached the province after a sea voyage from Italy to Asia Minor. In his salutation, Pliny addresses Trajan as **imperator**. During the republican period, this title was given to very successful military commanders. During the imperial period, the title was restricted to the emperor. The English word *emperor* derives from the Latin **imperator**.

---

## C. PLINIUS TRAIANO IMPERATORI

1 Sicut saluberrimam navigationem, domine, usque
Ephesum expertus ita inde, postquam vehiculis iter
facere coepi, gravissimis aestibus atque etiam febriculis
5   vexatus Pergami substiti.

1    **Sicut:** Construe with **saluberrimam**.

**saluberrimam:** Pliny is reporting that he was not ill during the lengthy sea voyage from Italy to Asia Minor. The voyage probably lasted three or four weeks, although the ship undoubtedly stopped at several ports along the way to pick up supplies.

**domine:** vocative case. The word **dominus**, *master* or *my lord*, had been used even before the imperial period as a polite form of address from inferiors to superiors. By the time of Domitian and Trajan, it was becoming a regular title for the emperor. It was also the term used in reference to a slave owner; see Letter 3.14, Section 1.

**usque:** Motion toward a town (here, Ephesus) is expressed by the accusative case without the preposition **ad**.

**Ephesum:** Pliny disembarked at Ephesus, a large city on the west coast of Asia Minor. The extensive remains of the ancient city are in Izmir Province, Turkey.

**expertus** and **vexatus:** These words are the understood subject of **substiti**.

**vehiculis:** ablative of means.

**Pergami:** locative case. Pergamum was a town about eighty miles north of Ephesus.

**substiti:** perfect indicative of **subsistere**.

2 Rursus, cum transissem in orarias naviculas,
contrariis ventis retentus, aliquanto tardius quam
speraveram, id est XV kal. Octobres, Bithyniam intravi.
Non possum tamen de mora queri, cum mihi
10 contigerit, quod erat auspicatissimum, natalem tuum
in provincia celebrare. 3 Nunc rei publicae Prusensium
impendia, reditus, debitores excutio; quod ex ipso
tractatu magis ac magis necessarium intellego. Multae
enim pecuniae variis ex causis a privatis detinentur;
15 praeterea quaedam minime legitimis sumptibus
erogantur. 4 Haec tibi, domine, in ipso ingressu meo
scripsi.

---

2    **Rursus:** In Letter 10.15 (not included in this volume), Pliny reports that, during the voyage across the Mediterranean, he had been delayed **contrariis ventis** off the coast of Greece.

**transissem:** pluperfect active subjunctive in a **cum**-temporal clause. Troubled by the oppressive heat and having developed a fever, Pliny decided to abandon the overland road trip and to sail to his province.

**in orarias naviculas:** Pliny had sailed from Italy in a seagoing vessel but now boarded a smaller ship that stayed in the coastal waters.

**aliquanto:** ablative of degree of difference with the comparative **tardius**.

**id est:** *that is.*

**XV kal. Octobres:** *fifteen days before the October Kalends.* **kal.** = **Kalendas**. This temporal expression is regularly placed in the accusative case. (Pliny has chosen to omit the words **dies**, *days*, and **ante**, *before*.) **Octobres** is an adjective modifying **Kalendas**. The Kalends (**Kalendae**) were the first day of the month. Fifteen days before the Kalends of October was, according to the Roman method of calculating, in our terms, *September 17.* See Letter 6.16, Section 4, for another example of Roman dating. (On the Roman custom of counting days inclusively, see the note on Letter 6.16, Section 20.)

**contigerit:** perfect subjunctive in a **cum**-causal clause. The subject of **contigerit** is the infinitive **celebrare**. Literally *since to celebrate befell to me* or, less literally, *since it befell me to celebrate.* Pliny means that he had the good fortune to celebrate.

**quod:** *which.* Pliny means the opportunity to celebrate the emperor's birthday. Trajan's birthday was September 18 or XIIII (or XIV) kal. Octobres.

3 **Prusensium:** masculine and feminine genitive plural, the inhabitants of Prusa, a city in the western part of the province of Bithynia.

**quod:** the *resumptive* use of the relative pronoun. Compare Letter 3.11, Section 8. Pliny here uses the relative pronoun where an English speaker would expect a demonstrative pronoun, such as **id** (*this*). **Quod** refers to the examination of the city finances.

**ex ipso tractatu:** *from this very process* (of examining).

**intellego:** introduces an indirect statement in which **quod** is the accusative subject and the infinitive **esse** is understood: *I understand which (this) (to be) necessary.*

**pecuniae:** Translate as *sums of money.*

**quaedam:** feminine plural nominative. Supply **pecuniae**.

4 **ingressu:** Pliny means at the very beginning of his term of office.

**scripsi:** Pliny uses the perfect tense to acknowledge that the recipient of the letter will be reading it after he has written it. English, in contrast, uses the present tense to convey the temporal point of view of the author as (when) he or she is writing the letter. Compare Letter 9.12, Section 2.

# 27. Letter 10.33

I n the ancient world, the necessity of using wood-burning stoves, hearths, oil lamps, candles, and lanterns for cooking, heating, and lighting made fires an ever-present threat. In Letter 10.33, Pliny consults with Trajan about establishing a unit of firemen in Nicomedia, the capital city of the province of Bithynia. (See Map 3.) Such units existed in Rome and other cities in the western part of the Roman Empire. In imperial Rome, seven thousand men served in the capacity of firefighters.

Like many of the letters in Book 10, this letter reveals that Pliny worked diligently to identify and address the problems of the residents of his province. Not all governors were so conscientious. (See "The Letters of Pliny" in the introduction.)

---

### C. PLINIUS TRAIANO IMPERATORI

1 Cum diversam partem provinciae circumirem, Nicomediae vastissimum incendium multas privatorum domos et duo publica opera, quamquam via

5 interiacente, Gerusian et Iseon absumpsit. 2 Est autem latius sparsum, primum violentia venti, deinde inertia hominum, quos satis constat otiosos et immobiles tanti mali spectatores perstitisse; et alioqui nullus usquam in publico sipo, nulla hama, nullum denique

10 instrumentum ad incendia compescenda. Et haec quidem, ut iam praecepi, parabuntur.

---

1 **circumirem:** It was Pliny's responsibility, as Trajan's legate, to travel around the province, and both to investigate the financial management of each area and to decide on legal cases that involved Roman, not just local, laws.

**Nicomediae:** locative case.

**domōs:** accusative plural of the feminine gender noun **domus** (hence **multas**). The noun has both second and fourth declension forms. The alternative accusative plural form is **domūs**.

**duo publica opera:** The two public buildings were a **Gerusia** (or **Gerousia**) and an **Iseon** (temple of Isis). A **Gerusia** was a building in which members of the city's elite met. Isis was a goddess whose worship had originated in Egypt but had become very popular throughout the Empire.

**quamquam via interiacente:** ablative absolute. The fire had spread although a road lay between the buildings. **Quamquam** indicates that the ablative absolute has a concessive meaning. Compare Letter 6.16, Section 12.

**Gerusian:** The -**an** ending is a Greek accusative ending, the equivalent of a Latin -**am** accusative ending. The language of the people of the eastern part of the Roman Empire was Greek.

**Iseon:** The -**on** ending is a Greek accusative ending, the equivalent of a Latin -**um** accusative ending.

2   **Est ... sparsum:** Understand **incendium** as the subject.

**latius:** comparative form of the adverb.

**quos:** The antecedent is **hominum**. In its own clause, **quos** is the accusative subject of the infinitive predicate **perstitisse**, in an indirect statement construction that is introduced by **satis constat**.

**satis:** Translate with **constat**: *it is generally agreed*.

**tanti mali:** objective genitive with **spectatores**.

**spectatores:** *as spectators* (rather than helping to fight the fire).

**nullus:** modifies **sipo**.

**in publico:** *in a public area*. Supply **erat**. See Letter 3.14, Section 6.

**ad incendia compescenda:** literally *for fires to be controlled*; less literally *for controlling fires*. The **ad** introduces a construction expressing purpose. **Compescenda** is a gerundive, in the accusative neuter plural.

**haec:** *these things*. Pliny means the tools for fighting fires.

3 Tu, domine, dispice an instituendum putes collegium
fabrorum dumtaxat hominum CL. Ego attendam, ne
quis nisi faber recipiatur neve iure concesso in aliud
15    utatur; nec erit difficile custodire tam paucos.

---

3    **putes:** subjunctive in the indirect question introduced by **an**.

**instituendum:** Supply **esse**. The construction is an indirect statement after
**putes**. The accusative subject is **collegium**; the infinitive predicate is the
understood **esse**, which, with the gerundive **instituendum**, forms a passive
(second) periphrastic construction: literally *is to be established*, less literally
*should be established*.

**collegium:** an association of people who have the same occupation or who
share a common interest.

**hominum:** in apposition to **fabrorum**.

**CL:** The Roman numeral for 150.

**ne:** introducing a negative purpose clause.

**quis:** instead of **aliquis**, after the negative implication of **ne**.

**faber:** Here the word refers specifically to an approved fireman.

**neve:** **-Ve** is an enclitic, *or*, with the **ne** introducing the negative purpose
clause (**ne -ve**).

**iure concesso:** ablative case required by **utatur**. **Ius** here means *privilege*. The
*privilege* that would be granted to the firemen would be to assemble in order
to prepare for firefighting. Pliny assures Trajan that he will not allow them to
assemble for any other purpose. The reasons for the restrictions on assembly
are discussed in Letter 10.34.

**in aliud:** *for another purpose.*

**utatur:** The subject is **faber**.

This bust of Trajan (emperor 98–117 CE) was discovered in the Baths of Caracalla (built in the early third century CE) in Rome. Many Roman emperors, beginning with Augustus and including Trajan, built public baths that also served as cultural centers and were often richly decorated with sculptures and other works of art. The bust is now located in the Ny Carlsberg Glyptotek, an art museum in Copenhagen, Denmark. (© Creative Commons 2.0/Carole Raddato)

# 28. Letter 10.34

Letter 10.34 is the emperor Trajan's response to Pliny's request in Letter 10.33 to establish a unit of firemen in Nicomedia. The request was made in the aftermath of a devastating fire during which city residents stood by and watched buildings burn. Pliny thought that it would be beneficial to have an association or **collegium** of men who would have the responsibility and equipment to fight fires. His idea seems sensible. He needed, however, to obtain Trajan's approval because the emperor, like his predecessors, was suspicious of assemblies of lower-class people. Although **collegia** were allowed in Rome and elsewhere in Italy, they were strictly regulated in terms of membership and activities. There existed among the upper class, who held the positions of power in the state, an anxiety that the **collegia**, whose members were largely lower class, might engage in political activities that would threaten to destabilize the state. There was fear that even associations founded for professional, social, or religious purposes might have secret agendas to promote political unrest. Because there had been several occasions of fierce riots in Bithynia before Pliny's arrival, Trajan had forbidden the existence there of associations of all types. Pliny's request in Letter 10.33 was thus a request for an exception to Trajan's mandate.

---

TRAIANUS PLINIO
1 Tibi quidem secundum exempla complurium
in mentem venit posse collegium fabrorum apud
Nicomedenses constitui. Sed meminerimus provinciam
5 istam et praecipue eam civitatem eius modi factionibus
esse vexatam.

---

1 **Tibi ... in mentem vēnit:** literally *(It) came to you into the mind;* less literally *(It) came into your mind.* **Vēnit** is perfect indicative. The subject of **vēnit** (the *it*) is the accusative-infinitive clause **posse collegium ... constitui.** Literally *an association to be able to be organized,* or less literally *that an association could be organized.*

**secundum exempla complurium:** *in accordance with the examples of several* (other cities). To take Rome as an example, there was an organization of about seven thousand firefighters in that city.

**Nicomedenses, -ium (m. pl.):** *residents of Nicomedia.*

**meminerimus:** first person plural, perfect active subjunctive of the defective verb **memini**, whose forms are perfect system but whose meanings are present system. The subjunctive is a hortatory subjunctive, which introduces an indirect statement construction.

**factionibus:** In Letter 9.6, the word **factio** was applied specifically to a company that produced chariot races. Here the word is used more generally to mean an association of people who gather together because they share an interest or goal. The interest might originally have been a common profession. However, Trajan reminds Pliny that factions at Nicomedia had sometimes engaged in violent rivalries with one another or sometimes incited riots in protest of government policies.

Quodcumque nomen ex quacumque causa dederimus
iis, qui in idem contracti fuerint, hetaeriae eaeque brevi
fient. 2 Satius itaque est comparari ea, quae ad
10  coërcendos ignes auxilio esse possint, admonerique
dominos praediorum, ut et ipsi inhibeant, ac, si res
poposcerit, adcursu populi ad hoc uti.

---

**Quodcumque nomen:** the object of **dederimus** (which is a future perfect indicative).

**in idem:** *for the same* (purpose).

**contracti fuerint:** future perfect indicative.

**hetaeriae eaeque brevi fient:** *They will become* **hetaeriae,** *and they will become these* (**eae** = **hetaeriae**) *in a short period of time.* **Eaeque = eae** + the enclitic **que**. **Hetaeria** is a Greek word. (The language of Pliny's province was Greek.) Its meaning was similar to that of the Latin **collegium**. However, Trajan's words suggest that in the Greek-speaking regions of the Roman empire, clubs or associations were more likely to engage in civil disorder than in the Latin-speaking regions.

**brevi:** adverb: *shortly* or *in a short period of time.*

2    **Satius ... est:** *It is preferable.* The subject is the accusative-infinitive construction **comparari ea,** *those things to be provided;* less literally *that those things be provided.* **Ea** refers to the firefighting equipment.

**ad coërcendos ignes:** literally *for fires to be controlled;* less literally *for controlling fires.* The **ad** introduces a construction expressing purpose. **Coërcendos** is a gerundive, in the accusative masculine plural.

**auxilio:** dative of purpose.

**possint:** present subjunctive in a relative clause of characteristic.

**admonerique dominos:** another accusative-infinitive subject of **satius est**.

**ut:** introduces an indirect command.

**inhibeant:** *use* (them), that is, the firefighting tools that Trajan recommends be made available.

**res:** *the situation.*

**adcursu:** The ablative case is required with **uti**.

**ad hoc:** *for this purpose,* i.e., for helping to fight the fire.

**uti:** This infinitive is parallel in use to **admoneri**. Both infinitives have **domi-nos** as their accusative subject. *It is preferable (1) that the owners be warned, and (2) that they use the crowd.* Clearly Trajan's suspicion of **collegia** was a greater concern to him than the problem of urban fires.

# 29. Letter 10.96

I n the decades after the death of Jesus, his disciples traveled extensively throughout the Roman Empire, disseminating information about him and trying to make converts to their religion. Letters 10.96 and 10.97 contain the earliest non-Christian literary evidence about the nature and growth of Christianity in the Greek-speaking regions of the Empire and about the responses of Roman officials to this new religion. These letters have been the subject of extensive discussion among scholars. In Letter 10.96, Pliny requests guidance from Emperor Trajan about adjudicating cases of people who have been accused of being Christians. There is no evidence in this letter of a persecution of Christians by the Roman state. The accusations were made by local residents. In the Roman world, there was no regular police force to arrest criminals and no public prosecutor's office. It was therefore customary for private individuals to report suspected wrongdoing to government officials.

We do not know the reasons for which people brought to Pliny accusations against their Christian fellow townspeople. We do know, however, that the people of the province of Bithynia-Pontus were a contentious lot and that conflicts between factions and associations were not uncommon. We also know that local residents frequently brought to the court of the Roman governor disputes that were motivated by personal enmity rather than a real concern about wrongdoing. It is possible that the accusations against Christians were prompted by factors not directly connected to religion. Nonetheless, as Letter 10.34 reveals, Roman officials were very concerned about the existence of factions and associations, especially those that seemed to encourage subversive actions that threatened the stability of the Roman state. The Christians appeared to fall into this category because they insulted the Roman gods by declaring that there was only one true god—their god. This attitude was incomprehensible to people whose religions were polytheistic, as most religions of the Mediterranean area were. The Romans were tolerant of other religions as long as the worshippers did not deny the validity of the gods who had protected and enriched the Roman state for centuries. The Romans countenanced Jews, although they were monotheistic, because Jews did not seek to persuade others to join them. The Christians, however, were eager to make converts. The Romans worried that the contempt that the Christians expressed for their gods would cause the gods to destroy the entire state. To act as the Christians did, and to encourage others to do so, was, in the eyes of Roman officials, tantamount to endangering the state. A resolution to the situation was not possible. The monotheistic Christians could not acknowledge the existence of other gods, and Roman officials could not allow the presumed treasonous activity of denying the existence of their gods.

---

## C. PLINIUS TRAIANO IMPERATORI

1 Sollemne est mihi, domine, omnia, de quibus dubito, ad te referre. Quis enim potest melius vel cunctationem meam regere vel ignorantiam instruere? Cognitionibus
5   de Christianis interfui numquam. Ideo nescio quid et quatenus aut puniri soleat aut quaeri. 2 Nec mediocriter haesitavi, sitne aliquod discrimen aetatum, an quamlibet teneri nihil a robustioribus differant;

---

1   **Cognitionibus de Christianis interfui numquam:** Pliny's words indicate that there had previously been investigations of Christians, but it is not known whether he means in Rome or in this province. **Cognitionibus** is dative (after **interfui**); **Christianis** is ablative.

   **quid ... quaeri:** Pliny is concerned with learning what the precedents are for dealing with accusations against Christians. **Quid** is the subject of **soleat**. Construe as **quid soleat aut puniri aut quaeri, et quatenus**.

   **soleat:** present subjunctive in an indirect question.

2   **sitne:** The -**ne** is the enclitic particle introducing a question. Translate as *whether.* Here there is a series of questions, phrased as alternatives. The *or whether* part of each alternative question is introduced by **an**. The subjunctive verbs in the series can be explained as being indirect questions after **haesitavi**. Even as direct questions, however, they would probably be deliberative subjunctives: *should there be some distinction for ages?*

   **discrimen aetatum:** *distinction for ages.* **Aetatum** is an objective genitive. Pliny wonders whether he should judge children less harshly than adults.

   **quamlibet teneri:** nominative plural, the subject of **differant**. Translate as *the young, however young.*

   **nihil:** adverbial: *not at all.*

detur paenitentiae venia, an ei, qui omnino Christianus
10  fuit, desisse non prosit; nomen ipsum, si flagitiis careat,
an flagitia cohaerentia nomini puniantur. Interim, <in>
iis, qui ad me tamquam Christiani deferebantur, hunc
sum secutus modum. 3 Interrogavi ipsos an essent
Christiani. Confitentes iterum ac tertio interrogavi
15  supplicium minatus. Perseverantes duci iussi. Neque
enim dubitabam, qualecumque esset, quod faterentur,
pertinaciam certe et inflexibilem obstinationem debere
puniri.

**detur:** There is no enclitic -**ne** attached to **detur**. However, English would repeat the *whether.*

**paenitentiae:** dative singular.

**ei:** dative singular. Construe with **prosit**, whose subject is the infinitive **desisse**. Pliny wonders whether pardon should be denied to a person who now declares that he has renounced Christianity.

**desisse:** syncopated perfect active infinitive of **desinere** (rather than **desiisse**).

**nomen ipsum:** Supply **puniatur(ne)**, *whether the title itself should be punished.* By **nomen**, Pliny means identification as belonging to an association of people who worshipped Christ. As Letter 10.34 reveals, Trajan had forbidden the formation of **collegia** in Pliny's province, even for the beneficial purpose of fighting fires. In professing to be a Christian, a person admitted to being a member of a forbidden association and therefore subject to punishment under Trajan's mandate. Pliny was concerned, however, about punishing someone who had committed no **flagitia**.

**si:** *even if.*

**careat:** The subject is **nomen**, which here implies *the mere title* or *designation* (of being Christian). **Careat** is a present subjunctive in a future less vivid protasis.

**cohaerentia:** present participle, neuter nominative plural. The Christians were accused by their enemies of engaging in cannibalism and incest. The charges of depraved behavior may have arisen from erroneous interpretations of the Eucharist and the Christians' use of the terms *brother* and *sister* in reference to one another.

**\<in\>:** Translate **in** as *among*. Chevron brackets are used to indicate that a word printed in the text does not appear in the manuscripts. Editors have concluded that Pliny's original letter contained that word, but it was omitted in error by the people who later copied the letter. Contrast the use of square brackets in Letter 4.13, Section 8.

**iis:** ablative plural; an alternative form for **eis**.

**deferebantur:** The verb **deferre** means *to bring* but in some circumstances has the connotation of *to accuse*. Pliny had not planned to arrest Christians. The charges against them were brought before Pliny by private individuals, residents of the province, who may have complained that the Christians formed a **collegium** in violation of Trajan's mandate and, moreover, that the **collegium** engaged in criminal activities.

3    **an essent:** indirect question.

**Confitentes:** present participle, accusative plural, object of **interrogavi**. The present participle of deponent verbs is active in form and meaning.

**minatus:** The perfect participle of deponent verbs is passive in form but active in meaning.

**Perseverantes:** present participle, accusative plural, object of **iussi**. Some of the people who were brought before Pliny either denied that they were Christians or said that they had already renounced their Christianity. Others, however, continued to say that they were Christians, even when Pliny gave them three chances to deny it (and thereby escape punishment). By **perseverantes**, Pliny is referring to the people who persisted in admitting that they were Christians. He does not, however, report that they had committed any **flagitia**. Pliny thus seems to have punished them for refusing to renounce the title of Christian and refusing to discontinue their participation in the kind of association that was forbidden by Trajan's mandate.

**duci:** *to be led away*, that is, to be taken away for punishment, probably a painful execution.

**dubitabam:** Here the verb is followed by an accusative-infinitive construction: **pertinaciam . . . debere puniri**. Elsewhere the verb is sometimes followed by **quin** + the subjunctive.

**esset, faterentur:** Subordinate clauses in indirect statements, such as **pertinaciam . . . debere puniri**, use the subjunctive mood. Pliny gives his reason for sending for punishment those who persisted in admitting that they were Christians. Regardless of what they were admitting (however benign the goals of their **collegium** might be), their obstinacy (in continuing to admit that they were members of a **collegium**) ought to be punished. To Pliny, they appeared to be willfully defying the emperor's edict.

4 Fuerunt alii similis amentiae, quos, quia cives
20    Romani erant, adnotavi in urbem remittendos. Mox
      ipso tractatu, ut fieri solet, diffundente se crimine
      plures species inciderunt. 5 Propositus est libellus sine
      auctore multorum nomina continens. Qui negabant
      esse se Christianos aut fuisse, cum praeeunte me
25    deos appellarent, et imagini tuae, quam propter hoc
      iusseram cum simulacris numinum adferri, ture ac vino
      supplicarent, praeterea male dicerent Christo, quorum
      nihil posse cogi dicuntur,

---

4     **similis amentiae:** genitive of quality (description).

      **quos . . . remittendos:** Supply **esse**. This clause serves as the indirect state-
      ment construction after **adnotavi**. **Remittendos (esse)** is a passive (second)
      periphrastic and thus expresses obligation. Literally *whom I noted down to be
      remanded*; less literally *whom I noted down should be remanded*.

      **in urbem:** By **urbs**, Pliny means Rome. On the use of **urbs** to designate spe-
      cifically Rome, compare Letter 4.13, Section 1. A Roman governor could
      exact capital punishment on non-Roman defendants in his province. If, how-
      ever, the defendant was a Roman citizen, the governor was required to send
      him to Rome for trial.

      **ipso tractatu:** *by the process itself*, or *because of the investigation itself*. Compare
      the phrase **ex ipso tractatu** in Letter 10.17, Section 3.

      **diffundente se:** **Diffundente** is a present participle modifying **crimine**,
      which here means *accusation*. **Se** is a reflexive pronoun, object of **diffundente**.
      English would not use a reflexive pronoun here. The Latin use, however, effec-
      tively depicts how the occurrence of accusations seemed to gain momentum
      and spread, with no encouragement from Pliny, but simply because it became
      known that he had held one investigation. People began to submit to his office
      accusations, some of them perhaps motivated by personal animosity, not by
      concern for the welfare of the community.

      **plures species:** *more forms* (of accusations) *occurred*. There occurred a greater
      variety of accusations. Pliny now found himself in the situation where he was
      required to hold many investigations.

5     **sine auctore:** *anonymously*.

      **Qui:** Translate as *those who*.

**cum:** *when*. This conjunction introduces several temporal clauses, the first of whose verbs is **appellarent**. The subject of these verbs can be translated as *they*, but syntactically the subject is the clause **qui . . . fuisse**: *when those who denied . . . that they had been Christians called upon the gods . . .*

**praeeunte me:** ablative absolute or attendant circumstance: *with me leading the way*. The accused were asked to repeat after Pliny an invocation to the Roman gods.

**deos:** Pliny means the gods worshipped by the Romans.

**imagini tuae:** dative with **supplicarent** (which is subjunctive in the **cum**-temporal clause).

**propter hoc:** *for this purpose*. Pliny had ordered a statue of Trajan, as well as statues of the Roman gods, to be brought to the investigations for the purpose of testing the defendants' religious commitments. To Pliny, paying reverence to Trajan was not an act of worship but rather a declaration of loyalty to the Roman state. The Christians, however, considered a prayer on behalf of Trajan to be an instance of praying to a false god. They believed that they could not participate in the ritual of the Roman state without offending their god.

**cum simulacris numinum:** This **cum** serves as a preposition: *along with statues of the* (Roman) *gods*.

**ture ac vino:** ablatives of means. Incense and wine were regularly used in the supplication of gods.

**male dicerent:** *they cursed* (another subjunctive in the **cum**-temporal clause). Literally *they spoke malevolently to*, hence the dative **Christo**.

**Christo: Christus** (the nominative form) is a title, not a name. It is the Latin transliteration of the Greek word **Christos**, which is, in turn, a translation of the Hebrew word that means "the anointed one," "the Messiah." After his death, Jesus of Nazareth was referred to by early Christians in the Greek-speaking part of the Roman Empire as the **Christos**, the Anointed One, the prophesied Messiah. Thus Jesus Christ means Jesus the Anointed One.

**quorum nihil:** *none of which things*.

**dicuntur:** The subject is found in the subsequent clause: *those who are truly Christians*. The Christians were said to be able to be forced (supply **facere**, *to do*) none of these things, that is, denouncing Christ and praying to the Roman gods.

qui sunt re vera Christiani, dimittendos esse putavi.

30   6 Alii ab indice nominati esse se Christianos dixerunt
et mox negaverunt; fuisse quidem, sed desisse, quidam
ante triennium, quidam ante plures annos, non nemo
etiam ante viginti. <Hi> quoque omnes et imaginem
tuam deorumque simulacra venerati sunt et Christo
35   male dixerunt. 7 Adfirmabant autem hanc fuisse
summam vel culpae suae vel erroris, quod essent soliti
stato die ante lucem convenire, carmenque Christo
quasi deo dicere secum invicem, seque sacramento
non in scelus aliquod obstringere, sed ne furta, ne
40   latrocinia, ne adulteria committerent, ne fidem
fallerent, ne depositum appellati abnegarent.

---

**re vera:** *truly.*

**dimittendos esse:** A passive (second) periphrastic in an indirect statement.
Supply **eos** as the accusative subject. Literally: *them to be dismissed.* Less literally: *that they should be dismissed.*

**putavi:** This is, finally, the main verb of the long sentence: *I thought that those*
(supply **eos**) *who* (**qui**, the very first word of the sentence) *denied... should be
dismissed.*

6   **ab indice:** Although, as mentioned in the introduction above, it was customary for private individuals, rather than a public prosecutor, to make a case for
prosecution, Pliny was now dealing with accusations made anonymously.

**dixerunt:** introduces three infinitives in indirect statements: **esse, fuisse,
desisse.** However, construe **negaverunt** only with **esse**. (Or translate simply
as *they denied it.*) On the form **desisse**, see the note in Section 2.

**et:** Here **et** has an adversative use: *and yet* or *but.* Compare Letter 3.16,
Section 9.

**ante triennium:** prior to (or before) the three-year period that included the
day on which they were interrogated. Translate as *three years earlier.*

**<Hi>:** On the use of chevron brackets, see the note in Section 2.

**et ... et:** *both ... and.*

7    **Adfirmabant** is the main verb of this long sentence. It is followed immediately by an accusative and infinitive in indirect statement: **hanc fuisse summam**. This construction is, in turn, followed by the subordinate clause: **quod essent soliti**.

**quod:** *the fact that.*

**essent soliti:** pluperfect subjunctive. **Solere** is a semi-deponent verb. In the perfect system, its forms are passive, but the meanings are active. The subjunctive is required because of the subordinate clause in the indirect statement after **adfirmabant**. The complementary infinitives after **essent soliti** are **convenire, dicere,** and **obstringere**.

**stato:** perfect passive participle of **sistere**. The participle means *appointed, fixed.*

**secum invicem:** *with one another, each in turn.* The defendants seem to be referring to antiphonal chanting.

**se:** Translate this reflexive pronoun as the direct object of **obstringere**.

**sacramento:** ablative of means.

**in scelus aliquod:** *for some wickedness.* The defendants admitted that they had sworn an oath, but not an oath to commit crimes. They denied that they were a gang of criminals.

**ne:** introduces several negative indirect commands (**committerent, fallerent, abnegarent**). The indirect command construction is dependent on the idea of *vowing* contained in the phrase **se sacramento obstringere**. **Ne** is repeated three times with **committerent**, which has three objects: **furta, latrocinia,** and **adulteria**. The defendants bound themselves by an oath that they would not commit criminal or immoral activities.

**depositum:** a *deposit* in the sense of money given to a friend for safekeeping. In the ancient world, there were no formal banks. People without secure residences therefore had to entrust their money to private individuals.

**appellati:** nominative plural, perfect passive participle: *having been called upon,* that is, to return the deposit. **Abnegarent** here means to deny that they had ever received the deposit.

Quibus peractis morem sibi discedendi fuisse
rursusque coeundi ad capiendum cibum, promiscuum
tamen et innoxium; quod ipsum facere desisse post
45    edictum meum, quo secundum mandata tua hetaerias
esse vetueram. 8 Quo magis necessarium credidi ex
duabus ancillis, quae ministrae dicebantur, quid esset
veri, et per tormenta quaerere. Nihil aliud inveni quam
superstitionem pravam immodicam.

---

**Quibus peractis:** The main verb of the sentence is **adfirmabant**, understood
from the beginning of the previous sentence. The understood **adfirmabant**
introduces the indirect statement **morem . . . fuisse**.

   **Quibus peractis:** an ablative absolute, belonging within the indirect
statement **morem . . . fuisse**. Translate the *resumptive* relative pronoun
**quibus** as if it were the demonstrative pronoun **eis**. Pliny is referring to the
antiphonal chanting and the swearing of oaths. (On this use of the relative
pronoun, see Letter 3.14, Section 4.)

**sibi:** dative of possession.

**discedendi, coeundi:** gerunds used as appositional genitives with **morem**.

**ad capiendum cibum:** ad + gerundive and noun to express purpose. Literally
*for food to be eaten*; less literally *to eat food*.

**promiscuum . . . et innoxium:** These adjectives modify **cibum**. The defendants
were eager to refute any charges of cannibalism. See the note in Section 2. The
meal they refer to was not the Eucharist, but a simple evening meal shared by
the congregation. It was a common feature of **collegia**, whatever the shared
interests of their members, to assemble on a regular basis for a meal. However
innocent these assemblies were, they roused the suspicions of Roman officials,
particularly if any money was collected. The participants may have intended
the money to cover the expenses of the meal, but Roman officials worried about
the accumulation of a treasury to fund attacks on the state.

**quod ipsum facere:** Construe this phrase with **desisse**. **Quod ipsum** is the
object of **facere**. Translate the *resumptive* relative pronoun **quod** as if it were
the demonstrative pronoun **id**.

**desisse:** infinitive in an indirect statement introduced by an understood
**adfirmabant**. Supply **se** as the accusative subject of **desisse**. On the form
**desisse**, see the note in Section 2.

**quo:** The antecedent is **edictum**.

**secundum mandata tua:** Trajan had issued instructions to Pliny (and undoubtedly to other governors) to prohibit the existence of **hetaeriae** (or **collegia**) in his province. The prohibition applied to a wide variety of associations, not just Christians. See Letter 10.34.

8    **magis:** Translate as *even more, all the more.*

**credidi:** introduces an indirect statement. Supply an **esse: quaerere (esse) necessarium**, *I believed to seek out* (to be) *even more necessary*, or, less literally, *I believed that it was even more necessary to seek out.*

**ex duabus ancillis, quae ministrae dicebantur:** Pliny writes that the two **ancillae** (*female slaves*) were called **ministrae**, which is the Latin word for *servants*. Since his province was in the Greek-speaking part of the Roman Empire, the local people who brought the two women to him presumably used a Greek word to describe them. The Greek word was probably **diakonissa**, the feminine form of **diakonos**. In ancient Greek, those words meant *servant* or *attendant*. Then, when Pliny was composing his letter to Trajan, he translated that Greek word into a Latin word with a similar meaning: **ministra**. However, later in Christian usage, the terms **diakonissa** and **diakonos** came to mean a person who holds an office in the church and thus *serves* the congregation. (From the Greek, there evolved the English words *deaconess* and *deacon*.) Some scholars have maintained that the two **ancillae** were described to Pliny as **diakonissai** not because they were slaves but because they were church officials. It is more likely, however, that the two women were simply slaves belonging to the church and that when the local people used the term **diakonissai**, they meant only *servants*. Pliny interrogated the **ancillae** because, as slaves attending to the needs of the church leaders, they would have seen and heard everything that happened in the church. Indeed, they may not have been Christians themselves and, if not, they may have been expected to provide unbiased information. Since they were slaves, Pliny could torture them to provide information.

**quid esset veri:** an indirect question (after **quaerere**) and therefore requiring a subjunctive verb. **Veri** is a partitive genitive. Pliny wanted to learn whether the accounts of the defendants about the activities of the Christians were truthful.

**per tormenta:** It was customary in the ancient Roman world to torture slaves while they were being interrogated. The Romans, like the Greeks, believed that slaves would tell the truth only under torture. We do not know if the two **ancillae** survived the torture.

**superstitionem:** This word was pejorative and was used by Roman authors to designate religious practices that were not Roman.

50    Ideo, dilata cognitione, ad consulendum te decucurri.
      9 Visa est enim mihi res digna consultatione, maxime
      propter periclitantium numerum. Multi enim omnis
      aetatis, omnis ordinis, utriusque sexus etiam vocantur
      in periculum et vocabuntur. Neque civitates tantum,
55    sed vicos etiam atque agros superstitionis istius
      contagio pervagata est; quae videtur sisti et corrigi
      posse. 10 Certe satis constat prope iam desolata templa
      coepisse celebrari, et sacra sollemnia diu intermissa
      repeti, passimque venire <carnem> victimarum, cuius
60    adhuc rarissimus emptor inveniebatur. Ex quo facile
      est opinari, quae turba hominum emendari possit, si sit
      paenitentiae locus.

---

**Ideo:** Pliny was hesitant to execute people simply because they were superstitious. He had discovered no threats to public security. The issue was whether
their assembly to practice their superstitious rites should be construed as a
**collegium** and therefore prohibited, in accordance with Trajan's mandate.

**dilata cognitione:** ablative absolute.

**ad consulendum te: ad** + gerundive and pronoun to express purpose.
Literally *to you to be consulted*; less literally *to consult you*.

9    **Visa est:** The subject is **res**.

     **digna:** predicative adjective modifying **res**. **Digna** governs the ablative
     **consultatione**.

     **periclitantium:** genitive plural of the present participle, which for deponent
     verbs has an active form and an active meaning.

     **Multi . . . vocabuntur:** Pliny's words offer insight into how rapidly interest
     in Christianity had spread in Asia Minor.

     **Neque . . . tantum:** *not . . . only.*

     **quae:** = **contagio**.

     **sisti, corrigi:** infinitives complementary to **posse**.

10   **satis:** Translate with **constat**: *it is generally agreed.* **Constat** introduces an
     indirect statement; its infinitive verb is **coepisse**. There are three accusative
     subjects with **coepisse: templa, sollemnia**, and **<carnem>**.

**prope:** Translate with **desolata**.

**coepisse:** perfect active infinitive: *have begun.* (On this defective verb, see Letter 3.11, Section 8.) It is followed by several complementary infinitives, two (**celebrari, repeti**) in the passive voice.

**celebrari:** Pliny adds some new information to his account of the situation in his province. He states that as interest in Christianity has spread, participation in the rites of the Roman religion has waned. In addition, the purchase of the meat of animals killed during the sacrifices of the Roman and other religions has declined. Christians were, by the rules of their own religion, forbidden to eat the meat of sacrificial animals because they would be indirectly participating in a false religion. Pliny's words perhaps provide some clues to the reasons why people in the province might have disliked the Christians and asked that he investigate them. Non-Christians may have feared the obliteration of their ancestral customs. More importantly, they may have resented their Christian neighbors because they seemed to engage defiantly in behavior that would offend the Roman gods and thus cause them to punish the entire state. And the meat sellers may have harbored personal resentment against the Christians for a decline in their sales. Several decades earlier, silversmiths in Ephesus had complained that the preaching of Paul had convinced people to stop purchasing silver images of the Greek/Roman goddess Artemis (Acts 19:23–41).

**venire:** *to be on sale.* The first person form of this verb is **veneo** (not **venio, venire**). The verb is formed from a contraction of two words, **venum + ire,** *to go for sale.* For the cognate adjective **venalis**, see Letter 1.21, Section 2.

Despite Pliny's optimistic report that the local religions were regaining ground lost to Christianity, the reality was that Christianity continued to make converts and eventually became the dominant religion of the area.

**<carnem>:** This word does not appear in the manuscripts, but many editors believe that Pliny's original letter contained the word and that it was omitted in error by the people who later copied the letter.

**cuius:** The antecedent is **carnem**. In its clause, **cuius** is an objective genitive with **emptor**.

**possit:** present subjunctive in an indirect question. The clause is also part of a future less vivid condition, of which **si . . . locus** is the protasis, hence the present subjunctive **sit**.

**paenitentiae locus:** *an opportunity for repentance.* Cf. Section 2: **paenitentiae venia**. Pliny's focus here is on persuading people who had adopted the new **superstitio** to abandon Christianity and to return to reverence for the Roman gods. If he were successful, Pliny would both eradicate what he considered to be a **collegium** and, at the same time, eliminate the threat of angering the Roman gods.

# 30. Letter 10.97

In Letter 10.97, which is Trajan's reply to Pliny's request for advice, the emperor makes two recommendations: that Pliny not hunt down the Christians in his province and that he not tolerate anonymous informers. This response is in keeping with the long-standing practice of Roman officials to let residents of a province deal with disputes they had among themselves. The practice had not, however, worked well in other situations in Bithynia-Pontus, a province where factional disagreements were frequent, disruptive, and sometimes violent. As governor, Pliny had, on several occasions, found himself in a quandary over how to maintain law and order without becoming too involved in local politics. In addition, the people who had accused the Christians of wrongdoing had probably pointed out that the Christians were flouting Trajan's own injunction against **collegia**, that they were endangering the Roman state by encouraging others to scorn the Roman gods, and that their crimes were therefore not local but of concern to the whole Empire. The Roman legal system encouraged anyone who felt that the law had been broken to lay information openly before local magistrates or the governor. Anonymous denunciation was a different matter. It was regarded as a practice engaged in by a despotic ruler. The emperor Domitian, for example, was criticized for his use of secret informers. Trajan, who strove to acquire a reputation as a just and benevolent emperor, opposed anonymous denunciation because he thought it would reflect adversely on his reign. In writing to Trajan for advice, Pliny may have been hoping for a statement of procedures to be followed in every situation. Trajan, however, preferred to recommend action on a case-by-case basis, keeping local conditions in mind. He was not prepared to put in writing a fixed policy for universal application.

We do not know how long it took Pliny's letter to reach Trajan, and Trajan's reply to reach Pliny.

---

## TRAIANUS PLINIO

1 Actum quem debuisti, mi Secunde, in excutiendis causis eorum, qui Christiani ad te delati fuerant, secutus es. Neque enim in universum aliquid, quod
5 quasi certam formam habeat, constitui potest.

1    **Actum:** *the procedure;* direct object of **secutus es.**

**mi:** vocative singular of **meus.**

**Secunde:** Trajan addresses Pliny not by his **nomen gentilicium, Plinius,** but
by his **cognomen, Secundus.** On Roman naming practices, see "The Life of
Pliny" in the introduction.

**in excutiendis causis eorum: in** + gerundive and noun. Literally *in the cases
to be investigated of those* (people); less literally *in investigating the cases of those*
(people).

**Christiani:** Translate *as being Christians.*

**delati fuerant:** The verb **deferre** means *to bring* but in some circumstances
has the connotation of *to accuse, to bring for investigation.* Compare Letter
10.96, Section 2.

**in universum:** *in* (regard to) *the whole,* that is, *as a universally applicable rule.*
Trajan was reluctant to transmit to Pliny a guideline that could be construed
as having a form that was fixed and unvarying (**certam formam**) and applicable to situations in any region of the Empire (**in universum**).

**aliquid:** the subject of **potest.**

**quod:** The antecedent is **aliquid.**

**habeat:** subjunctive in a relative clause of characteristic.

2 Conquirendi non sunt; si deferantur et arguantur, puniendi sunt, ita tamen, ut, qui negaverit se Christianum esse idque re ipsa manifestum fecerit, id est, supplicando dis nostris, quamvis suspectus in praeteritum, veniam ex paenitentia impetret. Sine auctore vero propositi libelli <in> nullo crimine locum habere debent. Nam et pessimi exempli nec nostri saeculi est.

―――――――――

2    **Conquirendi non sunt:** passive (second) periphrastic. The subject of the construction is *they*, that is, the people who are suspected of being Christians.

**deferantur et arguantur:** present subjunctives in the protasis of a future less vivid condition. However, the verb in the apodosis, **puniendi sunt,** is present indicative, thus creating a mixed condition. Using the indicative in the apodosis makes the statement more forceful.

Trajan advises that, although people suspected to be Christians must not be hunted down by Pliny, they must be punished if they are reported and proved to be Christians. His advice has puzzled readers ever since. Pliny had asked Trajan directly, in Letter 10.96, Section 2, whether people should be punished for being Christians, even if they have not committed any of the atrocious crimes attributed to Christians (**flagitia cohaerentia nomini**). At that point in the letter, he seems to have had reservations about punishing people whose only offense was belonging to the kind of association that was forbidden by Trajan's mandate. However, Pliny also reveals in Section 3 of that letter that he had already punished (probably with execution) people who continued to profess to be Christians and that he had done so because they were obstinate. He does not report that they had committed any crimes beyond refusing to renounce Christianity. It thus seems that he punished them not for **flagitia** but for refusing to give up their participation in an association or **collegium**. Trajan does not directly address Pliny's question of whether to punish people who had not committed atrocious crimes. It is clear, however, that he believed that membership in an association that was deemed to constitute a threat to the security of the Roman state was a sufficient reason to warrant punishment.

**ut:** introduces a result clause whose verb is the subjunctive **impetret** (the final word in this long sentence).

**se Christianum esse:** an indirect statement after the verb **negaverit**.

**id ... manifestum:** By **id** Trajan means the assertion that she or he is not Christian.

**re ipsa:** *by deed itself, in very deed.*

**id est:** *that is.*

**supplicando:** gerund, ablative of means. Note that Trajan requires that the accused persons supplicate only the statues of the gods, not his image. In Letter 10.96, Pliny revealed that he had required that the accused also supplicate an image of Trajan and curse Christ.

**quamvis suspectus:** *although having been suspected.* **Suspectus** modifies the *he* implied in **qui negaverit.**

**veniam ex paenitentia impetret:** The subject of **impetret** is the *he* implied in **qui negaverit.** Compare **detur paenitentiae venia** in Letter 10.96, Section 2. Trajan here answers Pliny's question about whether those people who were once Christian, but demonstrate that they no longer are, should receive pardon. Trajan recommends mercy for those people who will recognize the validity of the Roman gods and thus show their loyalty to the Roman state.

**<in> nullo crimine:** The word in chevron brackets does not appear in the manuscripts, but many editors believe that Pliny's original letter contained the word and that it was omitted in error by the people who later copied the letter.

**crimine:** *criminal investigation.*

**pessimi ... est:** The subject of **est** is the use of anonymous accusations. The first genitive, **exempli**, is a genitive of quality (description); the second, **saeculi**, is a possessive genitive. Literally: (The use of anonymous accusations) *is of the worst example and is not of our era.* Less literally: (The use) *creates the worst example and does not belong in our era.* Trajan took pride in having returned fairness and openness to Roman life after the reign of Domitian.

# Appendix of Inscriptions

Our information about the life of Pliny the Younger comes primarily from his letters and his one preserved speech, the *Panegyricus*. We do, however, also have inscriptional evidence about his family, career, and benefactions to his hometown of Comum.

Inscriptions (Latin *in* + *scriptum* = "written on") are words that have been written on or carved into durable material such as stone or metal. The study of inscriptions is known as epigraphy (Greek *epi* + *graphein* = "to write on"). The largest collection of Latin inscriptions is the multi-volume *Corpus Inscriptionum Latinarum* (CIL). Another collection, which contains many of the same inscriptions as CIL, is *Inscriptiones Latinae Selectae* (ILS).

Unfortunately none of the inscriptions documenting Pliny's life have survived completely intact over the almost two thousand years since his death. A fragment of one inscription has been preserved in the wall of a courtyard of the church of St. Ambrose in Milan. The entire inscription had presumably been installed in Comum in the early second century CE. Pliny himself may have commissioned it to be placed in one of the public buildings whose construction he funded or to be attached to his tombstone. Or the people of Comum may have commissioned the inscription to commemorate the achievements and generosity of their distinguished fellow townsman.

During the Middle Ages, the inscription was moved (for reasons unknown) to the church in Milan. At some point in time, it was broken into pieces, and today only one piece remains (CIL v. 5262 = ILS 2927). Fortunately, however, the inscription was copied in a fifteenth century manuscript and a large amount of its content is thus available to us. Three other inscriptions, also fragmentary, provide some information about Pliny (CIL v. 5263, v. 5667, xi. 5272). Much of the information duplicates that from CIL v. 5262 (ILS 2927), but, in some cases, it is additional and supplements our knowledge about Pliny.

Here is the text of the fragment now in Milan.

C PLINIUS L F
AUGUR LEGAT PRO PR
CONSULARI POTESTA
IMP CAESAR NERVA
CURATOR ALVEI TI
PRAEF AERARI SAT
QUAESTOR IMP

Inscriptions are difficult to read for several reasons. One is that the people who composed the texts used many abbreviations. In addition, they often did not use space breaks between words. In the passages below, the words have been spelled out in full for the convenience of modern readers, but the use of an abbreviation in the inscription is made apparent by the use of round brackets. For example, the first line of the first passage of the original inscription reads as C. PLINIUS L. F. The letters C, L, and F are abbreviations. The letters within the round brackets indicate what words the abbreviations represent: C(AIUS) PLINIUS L(UCI) F(ILIUS).

Another reason for the difficulty presented to readers by inscriptions is that many inscriptions are fragmentary, that is, the stone was damaged or broken, and therefore some or many of the letters or words are illegible or missing. Epigraphers who interpret inscriptions attempt to restore the illegible or missing letters and words, and thus reconstruct the message of the inscription. The letters and words they supply are placed within square brackets. For example, in the first line of the first passage below, the words [SECUNDUS CO(N)S(UL)] have been supplied both because they appear in the other three inscriptions and because it seems certain that Pliny would want to have included his full name and a reference to his position as consul. Within the square brackets, the letters (N) and (UL) appear in round brackets, indicating that, in the other inscriptions, the word CONSUL was abbreviated as COS. In some places, the damage to the inscription is such that epigraphers have not been able to propose a restoration, that is, have not been able to conjecture what the lost or illegible letters may have been. In these cases, a lacuna has been indicated by the use of an ellipsis (. . .).

The inscription lists the record of Pliny's accomplishments in descending order, beginning with the most prestigious, the consulship, and ending with minor appointments that he held at the start of his career in public office: the military tribuneship and membership on a board of ten.

# Latin Text of CIL v. 5262 (ILS 2927)

C(AIUS) PLINIUS L(UCI) F(ILIUS) OUF(ENTINA TRIBU)
  CAECILIUS [SECUNDUS CO(N)S(UL)]

AUGUR LEGAT(US) PRO PR(AETORE) PROVINCIAE
  PON[TI ET BITHYNIAE PRO]

CONSULARI POTESTA[TE] IN EAM PROVINCIAM E[X
  SENATUS CONSULTO AB]

IMP(ERATORE) CAESAR(E) NERVA TRAIANO
  AUG(USTO) GERMAN[ICO DACICO P(ATER)
  P(ATRIAE) MISSUS]

CURATOR ALVEI TIBERIS ET RIPARUM ET
  [CLOACARUM URBIS]

PRAEF(ECTUS) AERARI SATURNI PRAEF(ECTUS)
  AERARI MIL[ITARIS PR(AETOR) TRIB(UNUS) PLEBIS]

QUAESTOR IMP(ERATORIS) SEVIR EQUITUM
  [ROMANORUM]

TRIB(UNUS) MILIT(UM) LEG(IONIS) [III] GALLICA[E IN
  PROVINCIA SYRIA X VIR STLI]

TIB(US) IUDICAND(IS) THERM[AS EX HS . . .] ADIECTIS
  IN

ORNATUM HS $\overline{\text{CCC}}$ [. . . ET EO AMP] LIUS IN TUTELA[M]

HS $\overline{\text{CC}}$ T(ESTAMENTO) F(IERI) I(USSIT) [ITEM IN
  ALIMENTA] LIBERTOR(UM) SUORUM HOMIN(UM)
  C]

HS |$\overline{\text{XVIII}}$| $\overline{\text{LXVI}}$ DCLXVI REI [P(UBLICAE) LEGAVIT
  QUORUM IN]CREMENT(A) POSTEA AD EPULUM

[PL]EB(IS) URBAN(AE) VOLUIT PERTIN[ERE ITEM VIVU]
  S DEDIT IN ALIMENT(A) PUEROR(UM)

ET PUELLAR(UM) PLEB(I) URBAN(AE) HS [$\overline{\text{D}}$ ITEM
  BYBLIOTHECAM HS ? ET] IN TUTELAM BYBLIOTHE

CAE HS $\overline{\text{C}}$

# TRANSLATION

Gaius Plinius Caecilius Secundus, son of Lucius, of the tribe Oufentina,[1] consul;[2] augur; legate of praetorian rank with proconsular power[3] for the province of Pontus and Bithynia, sent into that province in accordance with a decree of the Senate, by the emperor Nerva[4] Trajan Augustus Germanicus[5] Dacicus,[6] father of the fatherland;[7] curator[8] of the bed and banks of the Tiber and of the sewers of the city; prefect of the treasury of Saturn;[9] prefect of the military treasury;[10] praetor; tribune of the plebs; quaestor of the emperor; member of the board of six men for Roman equestrians;[11] military tribune of the Third Gallic legion in the province Syria; member of the board of ten

---

1    A tribe (Latin: *tribus*) was a voting unit of one of the electoral and legislative assemblies (the *Comitia Tributa*) of ancient Rome. Enrollment in one of these tribes entitled a man to cast a vote. (Women did not have the right to vote.) Distribution into tribes was based on geographic location, not family ancestry.

2    For information about the role of consul and of other offices held by Pliny, see the Vocabulary and the Subject Index.

3    proconsular power: Pliny was granted the type of authority granted to a consul, but only within the province assigned to him. In his province, he served "as a (Latin: *pro*) consul."

4    Trajan's adoption by the previous emperor, Nerva, is indicated by the use of his name.

5    Germanicus: This word is a title added to Trajan's name to commemorate his military successes in Germany.

6    Dacicus: This word is a title added to Trajan's name to commemorate his military successes in Dacia.

7    *pater patriae*: "father of the fatherland." During the republican period, this honorific title was awarded by the Senate to men who had performed outstanding service to Rome. During the imperial period, the Senate reserved the title for emperors.

8    *curator*: The curator (superintendent) of the Tiber River occupied a position of considerable responsibility because flooding of the river, with the consequent damage to structures, was a frequent problem in Rome.

9    the treasury of Saturn (Latin: *aerarium Saturni*): The treasury and financial accounts of the Roman people were kept in the Temple of Saturn in the Roman Forum.

10   the military treasury (Latin: *aerarium militare*): The military treasury, which was established by the emperor Augustus and supported by several kinds of taxes, funded the retirement benefits of military veterans.

11   *sevir*: A sevir was a member of a board of six men (Latin: *sex viri*). We do not know what the specific duties were of the board for Roman equestrians. On the meaning of *eques* (equestrian), see the Vocabulary and the Subject Index.

men for judicial matters.[12] In his will he ordered the construction of baths at a cost of . . . sesterces. . . with 300,000 sesterces[13] added for outfitting them . . . and further 200,000 sesterces for their maintenance. Also he bequeathed to his hometown 1,866,666 sesterces, for the support of 100 of his freedmen, the interest on which he wished afterward to be applied to an annual banquet for the people of the town. Also, while alive, he gave 500,000 sesterces for the support of boys and girls of the townspeople.[14] Also he gave a library and 100,000 sesterces for the maintenance of the library.[15]

---

12  *Xvir:* A decemvir (abbreviated as Xvir) was a member of a board of ten men (*decem viri*). X is the Roman numeral for 10. The board on which Pliny served was charged with judging lawsuits. The men who served on this board were usually at the beginning of their public careers.

13  A *sestertius* was a Roman coin, for which the English translation is sesterce. In inscriptions, the symbol designating the word sesterius is HS. It is placed in front of the Roman numeral indicating the number of sesterces in question. Compare the use of the symbol $ to designate the English word dollar. Thus HS C signifies 100 sesterces. In inscriptions, for large sums, the Roman numerals were not all written. A form of abbreviation was used instead. When a horizontal line or bar was inscribed above a Roman numeral, that number was multiplied by 1000. When a horizontal bar was inscribed above and two vertical bars on each side of the number, the number was multiplied by 100,000.

Thus HS C = 100 sesterces
HS $\overline{C}$ = 100,000 sesterces
HS $|\overline{C}|$ = 10,000,000 sesterces

Therefore in the inscription above, in line 12, HS $|\overline{XVIII}|$ $\overline{LXVI}$ DCLXVI = 18 x 100,000 (= 1,800,000), 66 x 1000 (= 66,000) and 666, for a grand total of 1,866,666 sesterces.

It is not possible to determine the value of a sesterce relative to modern money or prices because the differences between ancient and modern economies are significant. A few examples provide some perspective on the value and purchasing power of a sesterce and on the magnitude both of Pliny's wealth and of his generosity as it is recorded in the inscription. During Pliny's lifetime, the emperor Domitian raised the annual salary of a rank-and-file soldier from 900 sesterces to 1200 sesterces. From records found at Pompeii, we know that one sesterce would purchase four pounds of bread, which would provide a daily ration of food for two adults in an era when wheat was the mainstay of the average diet. In Letter 3.19 (not in this volume), Pliny contemplates purchasing an agricultural estate that is for sale for 3,000,000 sesterces (a price he considers a "bargain"). In Letter 6.3 (not in this volume), he writes that he had bestowed upon an old family servant a small farm that cost 100,000 sesterces.

14  500,000 sesterces for the support of boys and girls of the townspeople: Pliny mentions this philanthropy in Letters 1.8.10 and 7.18.2 (not in this volume).

15  library: In Letter 1.8 (not in this volume), Pliny tells a friend that he has given a speech in Comum at the dedication of the library. In Letter 5.7.3 (not in this volume), he mentions a gift to the community of 1,600,000 sesterces.

# Latin Text of CIL v. 5263, CIL v. 5667, and CIL xi. 5272

The following fragments contain information similar to that found in CIL v. 5262. The translation and notes provided for CIL v. 5262 can be used when reading these fragments.

## CIL v. 5263

This fragment is embedded in the wall of the Como Cathedral. Because it is a dedicatory inscription, set up to honor Pliny, his name and the offices he held appear in the dative case.

C(AIO) PLINIO L(UCI) F(ILIO)

OUF(ENTINA) CAECILIO

SECUNDO CO(N)S(ULI)

AUG(URI) CUR(ATORI) ALVEI TIBER(IS)

ET RIP[AR(UM) ET CLOAC]A[(RUM)] URB(IS)

## CIL v. 5667

This inscription records the gratitude of the people of Vercellae (modern Fecchio), a town southwest of Comum. Pliny may have owned an estate there and been a benefactor of the town. The inscription now resides in a museum in Milan. The final line provides information not available in the other inscriptions: that Pliny had been a *flamen*, that is, that he had belonged to an order of men selected to oversee the performance of the worship of the deified emperor Titus (Domitian's older brother and predecessor as emperor).

C(AIO) PLINI[O L(UCI) F(ILIO)]

OUF(ENTINA) CAEC[ILIO]

SECUNDO. [CO](N)S(ULI)

AUGUR(I) CUR(ATORI) ALV(EI) TIB(ERIS)

E[T RI]P(ARUM) ET CLOAC(ARUM) URB(IS)

P[RAEF(ECTO) A]ER(ARII) SAT(URNI) PRAEF(ECTO)

AER(ARII) MIL[IT(ARIS)] Q(UAESTORI) IMP(ERATORIS)

SEVIR(O) EQ(UITUM) R(OMANOUM) TR(IBUNO) M[I] L(ITUM)

LEG(IONIS) III GALL(ICAE) XVIRO

STL(ITIBUS) IUD(ICANDIS) FL(AMINI) DIVI T(ITI) AUG(USTI) VERCELLENS[ES]

# CIL xi. 5272

This inscription is from Hispellum (modern Spello), a town in Umbria. We do not know what Pliny's connection to the town was.

[C(AIUS) PLINIUS L(UCI) F(ILIUS) OUF(ENTINA) CAECILIUS SECUNDUS CO(N)S(UL) AUGUR]

[XVIRO STLIT(IBUS) IUDICAND(IS) TRI(BUNUS) MIL(ITUM) LEG(IONIS) III GALLI]CA[E]

[SEVIR EQ(UITUM) R(OMANORUM) QUAESTOR IMPERATORI]S TRIB(UNUS) PLEBIS PR(AETOR)

[PRAEF(ECTUS) AER(ARII) MILIT(ARIS) PRAEF(ECTUS) AER(ARII) SATURNI CUR(ATOR) ALVEI] TIBERIS EX S(ENATUS) C(ONSULTO) PRO

[CONSULARI POTESTATE LEGATUS PR(O) PR(AETORE) PROVINCIAE PONTI] ET BITHYNIAE ET LEGATUS

[IN EAM AB IMP(ERATORE) CAES(ARE) NERVA TRAIANO AUG(USTO) MISSUS TESTAME]NTO [FIERI] IUSSIT.

For additional information about the inscriptions, see Géza Alföldy, *Städte, Eliten und Gesellschaft in der Gallia Cisalpina* (Stuttgart, 1999), pp. 221–244 and Tafel VI.

# Genealogy Chart I

## The Family of Pliny

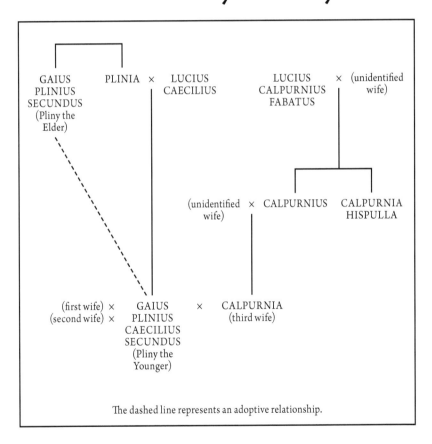

The dashed line represents an adoptive relationship.

# Genealogy Chart 2

## The Family of Arria

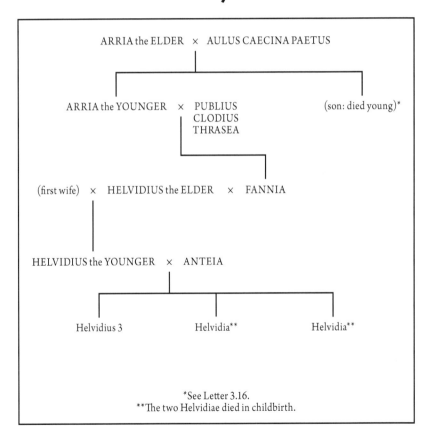

ARRIA the ELDER × AULUS CAECINA PAETUS

ARRIA the YOUNGER × PUBLIUS CLODIUS THRASEA          (son: died young)*

(first wife) × HELVIDIUS the ELDER × FANNIA

HELVIDIUS the YOUNGER × ANTEIA

Helvidius 3          Helvidia**          Helvidia**

*See Letter 3.16.
**The two Helvidiae died in childbirth.

# Glossary of Proper Names

Note these abbreviations.

**C.**    abbreviation for the praenomen **Gaius**

**Cn.**    abbreviation for the praenomen **Gnaeus**

**L.**    abbreviation for the praenomen **Lucius**

---

**Acilius:** addressee of Letter 3.14

**Aefulanus Marcellinus:** addressee of Letter 5.16; otherwise unknown to us.

**Arria the Elder:** the mother of Arria the Younger.

**Arria the Younger:** the mother of Fannia.

**Artemidorus:** Stoic philosopher from Syria; student and son-in-law of Musonius Rufus.

**Arulenus Rusticus:** See **Junius Arulenus Rusticus**.

**Bithynia-Pontus:** a province in northern Asia Minor (now northern Turkey), sometimes referred to simply as Bithynia. Pliny was sent there as Trajan's legate around 110 CE (Letters 10.17, 10.33, 10.34, 10.96, 10.97). The province was formed after the Romans, in the first century BCE, took control of two former kingdoms, Bithynia and Pontus.

**Caecina Paetus:** the husband of Arria the Elder, the father of Arria the Younger.

**Caesar:** All emperors after Augustus assumed his family name, Caesar, as a title.

**Calpurnia:** addressee of Letters 6.4 and 7.5; Pliny's third wife.

**Calpurnia Hispulla:** addressee of Letter 4.19; paternal aunt of Pliny's wife, Calpurnia.

**L. Calpurnius Fabatus:** addressee of Letter 8.10; paternal grandfather of Pliny's wife, Calpurnia.

**Calvisius Rufus:** addressee of Letter 9.6; like Pliny, a native of the northern Italian town of Comum (modern Como).

**Campania:** a region of Italy, south of Rome, that included Mount Vesuvius and the cities of Naples, Misenum, Stabiae, and Pompeii.

**Capri:** an island in the southern part of the Bay of Naples; known in Latin as **Capreae, -ārum (f. pl.)**. See Map 2.

**Claudius:** Roman emperor from 41 to 54 CE.

**Clodius Thrasea:** See **Thrasea Paetus**.

**Comum:** Pliny's hometown in northern Italy, about twenty-five miles north of modern Milan. See Map 1.

**Cornelia:** senior Vestal Virgin, **Virgo Vestalis Maxima**, in the 80s CE.

**C. Cornelius Minicianus:** addressee of Letter 4.11; a wealthy **eques** and, like Pliny, a native of the Transpadane region of Italy.

**Cornelius Tacitus:** addressee of Letters 1.6, 4.13, 6.16, and 6.20. He is the well-known historian of early imperial Rome.

**Diana:** Roman goddess of hunting.

**Domitian:** Roman emperor from 81 to 96 CE; known in Latin as **Domitianus**.

**Ephesus:** A large city on the west coast of Asia Minor. The extensive remains of the ancient city are in Izmir Province, Turkey. See Map 3.

**Fabatus:** See **Calpurnius Fabatus**.

**Fabius Justus:** addressee of Letter 1.11. He was, like Pliny, a senator.

**Fannia:** the daughter of Arria the Younger; the granddaughter of Arria the Elder; the wife of Helvidius the Elder; and the stepmother of Helvidius the Younger. She was condemned to exile in 93 CE.

**Formiae:** a town on the west coast of Italy, about halfway between Rome and Naples. See Map 2.

**Fuscus:** See **Pedanius Fuscus**.

**Geminus:** See **Rosanius Geminus**.

**Gratilla:** the wife of Arulenus Rusticus, one of the three friends of Pliny sentenced to death in 93 CE.

**Helvidius the Elder:** the husband of Fannia, and the father of Helvidius the Younger. He was executed in the mid-70s CE.

**Helvidius the Younger:** stepson of Fannia; like Pliny, a senator and lawyer. He was one of the three friends of Pliny sentenced to death in 93 CE.

**Herculaneum:** One of the towns buried by the eruption of Mount Vesuvius in 79 CE. It is about five miles west of Vesuvius. See Map 2.

**Herennius Senecio:** like Pliny, a senator and lawyer. He came to Rome from Spain. A critic of Domitian, he was one of the three friends of Pliny sentenced to death in 93 CE.

**Hispania:** Hispania was the Roman name for the Iberian peninsula (and thus included both modern Spain and Portugal). The Romans divided it into several provinces.

**Hispulla:** See **Calpurnia Hispulla**.

**Illyricum:** Roman territory on the eastern Adriatic coast. The southern part of Illyricum was the province of Dalmatia. See Map 1.

**Iunia:** See **Junia**.

**Iunior:** See **Terentius Iunior**.

**Julia:** niece of the emperor Domitian.

**Julius Genitor:** addressee of Letter 3.11; a teacher of rhetoric and a friend of Pliny.

**Julius Naso:** addressee of Letter 4.6; a young man aspiring to a senatorial career.

**Junia:** a Vestal Virgin, and a relative of Fannia. She is otherwise unknown. She may have been related to **Junius Arulenus Rusticus** and **Junius Mauricus**.

**Junius Arulenus Rusticus:** consul in 92 CE; he was one of the three friends of Pliny sentenced to death in 93 CE.

**Junius Mauricus:** the brother of Rusticus; exiled in 93 CE.

**Larcius Macedo:** a wealthy freedman whose identity is known only from Letter 3.14.

**Laurentinum:** Pliny's estate at Laurentum, a town on the coastline, about sixteen miles southwest of Rome. See Map 2.

**Livy:** a Roman historian (known in Latin as **Titus Livius**) who wrote a history of Rome. He lived from about 60 BCE to 17 CE.

**Macrinus:** His grief at his wife's death is described by Pliny in Letter 8.5.

**Maecilius** (or perhaps **Metilius**) **Nepos:** addressee of Letter 3.16. A man of senatorial rank, he is otherwise unknown to us.

**Mauricus:** See **Junius Mauricus**.

**Maximus:** addressee of Letter 6.34.

**Mediolanum:** city in northern Italy, now Milan. See Map 1.

**Mettius Carus:** a lead prosecutor in the case against Fannia that Pliny reports in Letter 7.19.

**Minerva:** Roman goddess of intellectual endeavors.

**Minicia Marcella:** daughter of Pliny's friend, Minicius Fundanus.

**Minicius Fundanus:** friend of Pliny and father of Minicia Marcella.

**Misenum:** a port town at the northwest end of the Bay of Naples, about twelve miles from the city of Naples. See Map 2.

**Musonius Rufus:** an Italian Stoic philosopher; father-in-law of Artemidorus.

**Nepos:** See **Maecilius Nepos**.

**Nerva:** Roman emperor from 96 to 98 CE.

**Nicomedia:** the capital city of the Roman province of Bithynia. See Map 3.

**Paetus:** See **Caecina Paetus**.

**Panegyricus:** the title of the speech that Pliny delivered in the Senate as suffect consul in 100 CE. In the speech, he praised Trajan effusively.

**Paternus:** See **Plinius Paternus**.

**Cn. Pedanius Fuscus:** addressee of Letter 9.36; a young man who was at the beginning of his senatorial career.

**Pergamum:** a town about eighty miles north of Ephesus in Asia Minor. See Map 3.

**Plinia:** mother of Pliny the Younger, sister of Pliny the Elder.

**Plinius Paternus:** addressee of Letters 1.21 and 8.16. Despite his **nomen**, he does not seem to have been a relative of Pliny the Younger.

**Pliny the Elder:** known in Latin as **C. Plinius Secundus**; uncle of Pliny the Younger.

**Pliny the Younger:** known in Latin as **C. Plinius Caecilius Secundus**; the author of the letters.

**Pompeii:** one of the towns buried by the eruption of Mount Vesuvius in 79 CE. It is about six miles southeast of Vesuvius; known in Latin as **Pompēiī, -ōrum (m. pl.).** See Map 2.

**Pomponianus:** a resident of the area close to Mount Vesuvius.

**Priscus:** addressee of 7.19; otherwise unknown to us.

**Prusa:** a city in the western part of the province of Bithynia. See Map 3.

**Rectina:** a resident of the area close to Mount Vesuvius; wife of Tascius.

**Rome:** the capital city of the Roman Empire, situated on the Tiber River; known in Latin as **Roma.** See Map 2.

**Rosanius Geminus:** addressee of Letter 8.5; a young friend of Pliny.

**Rusticus:** See **Junius Arulenus Rusticus**.

**Scribonianus:** Camillus Scribonianus was the commander of two legions in the Roman territory of Illyricum. He was the instigator of a failed plot to overthrow the emperor Claudius in 42 CE.

**Senecio:** See **Herennius Senecio**.

**Septicius:** addressee of Letter 1.1.

**C. Septicius Clarus:** addressee of Letter 1.15. (He may be the same person as the above.)

**Stabiae:** a town on the coast of the Bay of Naples, about ten miles south of Mount Vesuvius, now known as Castellamare; known in Latin as **Stabiae, -ārum (f. pl.).** See Map 2.

**Statoria Marcella:** wife of Minicius Fundanus, mother of Minicia Marcella.

**Syria:** a Roman province; it covered a larger area than the modern country.

**Tacitus:** See **Cornelius Tacitus**.

**Tascius:** husband of Rectina; a resident of the area close to Mount Vesuvius.

**Terentius Iunior:** addressee of Letter 9.12; a wealthy landowner of equestrian rank (**eques**).

**Thrasea Paetus:** the father of Fannia and the husband of Arria the Younger. A critic of the emperor Nero (54 to 68 CE), he was sentenced to execution in 66 CE, but he chose to preempt execution by committing suicide.

**Titus Livius:** See **Livy**.

**Trajan:** Roman emperor from 97 to 117 CE; addressee of Letters 10.17, 10.33, 10.34, 10.96, and 10.97; known in Latin as **Trajanus**.

**Verona:** a city in northern Italy, about 100 miles east of Milan. See Map 1.

**Vesta:** the spirit or deity of hearth fires. The Vestal Virgins, on behalf of all residents of the state, were entrusted with performing the rites to honor Vesta.

**Vesuvius:** volcanic mountain about six miles east of Naples, and about eighteen miles east of Misenum. See Map 2.

# Vocabulary

## A

**ā, ab:** (+ abl.) from, away from; by

**abdō, -ere, -didī, -ditum:** to hide, conceal

**abdūcō, -ere, -duxī, -ductum:** to separate, remove

**abeō, -īre, -īvī, -itum:** to move away, go away

**ābiciō, -ere, -iēcī, -iectum:** to throw

**abnegō, -āre, -āvī, -ātum:** to deny, refuse

**aboleō, -ēre, -ēvī, -itum:** to destroy

**abōminor, -ārī, -ātus sum (dep. verb):** to detest, dread

**abortus, -ūs (m.):** miscarriage; abortion; **abortum facere:** to suffer a miscarriage.

**abrumpō, -ere, -rūpī, -ruptum:** to break off

**abscondō, -ere, -con(di)dī, -conditum:** to hide, conceal

**absens, -tis:** absent

**absentia, -ae (f.):** absence

**absolvō, -ere, -solvī, -solūtum:** to finish, complete

**absum, abesse, afuī, afutūrus:** to be away, absent, apart

**absūmō, -ere, -mpsī, -mptum:** to destroy

**abundantia, -ae (f.):** abundance

**ac = atque**

**accēdō, -ere, -cessī, -cessum:** (+ dat., acc., or **ad** + acc.) to add; to approach

**acceptum, -ī (n.):** credit. See **facere acceptum.**

**accidō, -ere, -cidī:** to happen

**accipiō, -ere, -cēpī, -ceptum:** to accept, receive; to learn

**accubō, -āre, -āvī, -ātum:** to lie down, recline at dinner

**ācer, ācris, ācre:** ardent, vehement

**acerbus, -a, -um:** bitter, untimely; harsh, severe. **Acerbius** is the comparative form of the adverb.

**actus, -ūs (m.):** procedure

**acūmen, -inis (n.):** astuteness, judgment

**ad:** (+ acc.) at, near; to, toward

**adcursus, -ūs (m.):** a running toward; a gathering crowd (of people who have run to watch)

**addō, -ere, -idī, -itum:** to add; **addere gradum:** to hurry

**addūcō, -ere, -duxī, -ductum:** to bring along; to draw, lead; to influence, induce

**adeō (adv.):** what is more; so much, to such a degree

**adeō, -īre, -īvī, -itum:** to approach

**adfectus, -ūs (m.):** affection, fondness, tenderness

**adferō, -ferre, attulī, allātum:** to bring

**adficiō, -ere, -fēcī, -fectum:** to affect, afflict

**adfīnis, -e:** related, kin

**adfirmō, -āre, -āvī, -ātum:** to assert, declare

**adflīgō, -ere, -xī, -ctum:** to distress

**adhibeō, -ēre, -uī, -itum:** to offer

**adhortor, -ārī, -hortātus sum (dep. verb):** to encourage, cheer

**adhūc (adv.):** still, as yet; until now

**adiciō, -ere, -iēcī, -iectum:** to apply to, add

**admīrātiō, -ōnis (f.):** admiration

**admittō, -ere, -mīsī, -missum:** to receive, welcome; to admit, allow

**admoneō, -ēre, -uī, -itum:** to alert, warn

**admoveō, -ēre, -mōvī, -mōtum:** to apply, offer

**adnotō, -āre, -āvī, -ātum:** to observe, notice; to note down, mark

**adparātus, -a, -um:** splendid, elaborate, sumptuous

**adparō, -āre, -āvī, -ātum:** to furnish, add

**adpropinquō, -āre, -āvī, -ātum:** to approach

**adquiēscō, -ere, -quēvī, -quētum:** (+ abl.) to assent to, find comfort in

**adsectātor, -ōris (m.):** follower, disciple; suitor

**adsensus, -ūs (m.):** applause, approval

**adsequor, -ī, -secūtus sum (dep. verb):** to make secure, certain

**adsideō, -ēre, -sēdī, -sessum:** (+ dat.) to sit near; to take care of, nurse

**adsiduus, -a, -um:** incessant

**adspiciō, -ere, -spexī, -spectum:** to examine, investigate

**adsum, -esse, -fuī, -futūrus:** to be present

**adsūmō, -ere, -sumpsī, -sumptum:** to choose, select

**adsurgō, -ere, -surrexī, -surrectum:** to stand up

**adulterium, -ī (n.):** adultery

**adventō, -āre, -āvī, -ātum:** to advance, draw near

**adversus (prep.):** (+ acc.) against

**adversus, -a, -um:** opposite; adverse, unfavorable

**aeger, -gra, -grum:** dejected, troubled

**aegrē (adv.):** with difficulty; reluctantly

**aegrōtō, -āre, -āvī, -ātum:** to be ill

**aequē (adv.):** equally; **aequē ac:** as equally as

**aes aliēnum (n.):** debt; **aes, aeris
(n.):** copper or bronze coin;
**aliēnus, -a, -um:** belonging to
someone else

**aestās, -ātis (f.):** summer, summer
heat

**aestimō, -āre, -āvī, -ātum:** to
judge, evaluate

**aestuō, -āre, -āvī, -ātum:** to burn,
be inflamed

**aestus, -ūs (m.):** heat

**aetās, -ātis (f.):** age; stage of life

**aeternitās, -ātis (f.):** immortality,
eternity

**aeternus, -a, -um:** eternal

**Africānus, -a, -um:** African

**ager, -rī (m.):** agricultural field;
farm area

**agitātiō, -ōnis (f.):** action,
activity

**agitātor, -ōris (m.):** chariot driver

**agitō, -āre, -āvī, -ātum:** to stir,
move

**agmen, -inis (n.):** throng

**agō, -ere, ēgī, actum:** to do;
to play the role of; to speak
in court; to live (*x* years); to
move; **grātiās agere:** to give
thanks

**agrestis, -e:** rural, agricultural;
boorish, uncouth; as a
substantive: **agrestis, -is (m.
and f.):** fieldworker, peasant

**āiō (defect. verb):** to say, state

**Albānus, -a, -um:** pertaining to
the area of the Alban Hills and
Lake Alba, about twelve miles
southeast of Rome. (See Map 2.)

**aliās (adv.):** at another time

**alibī (adv.):** elsewhere, at another
place

**alica (= halica), -ae (f.):** wheat,
spelt (a type of Italian grain)

**aliēnus, -a, -um:** belonging to
someone else

**aliōquī (adv.):** in other respects;
otherwise

**aliquandō (adv.):** sometimes

**aliquantum, -ī (n.):** a considerable
amount

**aliquī, aliqua, aliquod (adj.):**
some

**aliquis, aliqua, aliquid (indef.
pron.):** someone, something

**alius, -a, -ud:** other

**alius . . . alius:** one . . . another;
some . . . other

**alter, -tera, -terum:** one of two,
the other, the second

**altus, -a, -um:** deep; high; **in
altum:** high, on high

**amābilis, -e:** lovable, inspiring
affection

**amans, -antis:** (+ gen.) loving

**amanter (adv.):** lovingly,
affectionately

**ambitus, -ūs (m.):** corruption,
bribery

**ambulō, -āre, -āvī, -ātum:** to walk

**ambūrō, -ere, -ussī, -ustum:** to
burn, scorch

**ambustus, -a, -um:** burned

**āmentia, -ae (f.):** madness, folly

**amīcus, -ī (m.):** friend; also an
adjective and in the superlative
degree: **amīcissimus, -a,-um:**
very dear

**amita, -ae (f.):** (paternal) aunt

āmittō, -ere, -mīsī, -missum: to lose

amō, -āre, -āvī, -ātum: to love

amoenitās, -ātis (f.): beauty

amor, -ōris (m.): love

amplector, amplectī, amplexus sum (dep. verb): to take hold of

amplitūdō, -inis (f.): width, size

amplus, -a, -um: great, abundant

an (conj.): whether; or

ancilla, -ae (f.): maidservant, female slave

angō, -ere, -nxī, -nctum: to trouble, distress, grieve

angustus, -a, -um: narrow

anīlis, -e: elderly, of an elderly woman

anima, -ae (f.): breath

animal, -ālis (n.): animal

animus, -ī (m.): mind; resolve, initiative; intent; character

annus, -ī (m.): year

ante: (+ acc.) before, in front of

ante (adv.): before

anxius, -a, -um: anxious, troubling

aper, -prī (m.): wild boar

apertus, -a, -um: open; in apertum: into the open

appāreō, -ēre, -uī: to appear, become visible

appellō, -āre, -āvī, -ātum: to invoke, call upon

aptō, -āre, -āvī, -ātum: to prepare, make ready

apud: (+ acc.) at, near; among; at the home of; in the presence of; in the case of

aqua, -ae (f.): water

arbitror, -ārī, -ātus sum (dep. verb): to consider, believe

arbor, -oris (f.): tree

ardens, -entis: ardent, passionate. The superlative degree of the adverb is ardentissimē.

ardeō, -ēre, arsī, arsum: to burn, be on fire

ārea, -ae (f.): courtyard; yard, backyard

arguō, -ere, -uī, -ūtum: to prove guilty

arma, -ōrum (n. pl.): weapons, arms

ars, artis (f.): liberal art; skill

artifex, -ficis (m.): master of an art or skill; musician

artus, -a, -um: tight, close

as, assis (m.): a copper Roman coin of the smallest denomination, i.e., of as little value as a penny

ascendō, -ere, -endī, -ensum: to ascend, board; to climb up

aspernor, -ārī, -ātus sum (dep. verb): to reject

at (conj.): but; at least

āter, -tra, -trum: black, dark

atque (conj.): and moreover

ātrium, -ī (n.): central room in a Roman house

atrōx, -ōcis: horrible, atrocious

attendō, -ere, -dī, -tum: to pay attention, take care

attentē (adv.): attentively, carefully

attonitus, -a, -um: terrified, stunned

auctor, -ōris (m.): model, advisor; author

auctōritās, -ātis (f.): bidding, command, authority; influence, importance

audiō, -īre, -īvī, -ītum: to hear, listen to

auferō, auferre, abstulī, ablātum: to carry away, remove

augeō, -ēre, auxī, auctum: to increase, magnify

augur, -uris (m.): one of a group, or collegium, of Roman officials who observed and interpreted omens and signs in nature for the purpose of providing political and military advice

auguror, augurārī, augurātus sum (dep. verb): to interpret omens, predict

auris, -is (f.): ear

auspicātus, -a, -um: lucky, fortunate, auspicious

aut: or; aut ... aut = either ... or

autem (adv.): moreover; however

auxilium, -ī (n.): help, assistance

aversor, -ārī, aversātus sum (dep. verb): to turn away from, shrink back from

avia, -ae (f.): grandmother

avidus, -a, -um: eager

āvocāmentum, -ī (n.): distraction

āvocō, -āre, -āvī, -ātum: to call away, distract

avunculus, -ī (m.): maternal uncle

avus, -ī (m.): grandfather

## B

balineum, -ī (n.): bathing room, bath facility

beātus, -a, -um: blessed, fortunate

bene (adv.): well

benignitās, -ātis (f.): kindness, generosity

benignus, -a, -um: kind, generous

bētāceus, -ī (m.): beet

bīnī, -ae, -a (pl.): two each; two at a time

bis (adv.): twice

blandior, -īrī, blandītus sum (dep. verb): to flatter, coax

bonum, -ī (n.): a good, a blessing; in the plural, bona: goods, property

brevī (adv.): shortly, in a short time

brevis, -e: brief, short

bulbus, -ī (m.): onion

## C

calceō, -āre, -āvī, -ātum: to put on shoes

calidus, -a, -um: hot

cālīgō, -inis (f.): fog, smoke, cloud

campus, -ī (m.): field

candidus, -a, -um: white

canis, -is (m.): dog

cantō, -āre, -āvī, -ātum: to sing

capiō, -ere, cēpī, captum: to catch, capture; to take

caput, -itis (n.): head

careō, -ēre, -uī: (+ abl.) to be deprived; to be free of, be without

cāritās, -ātis (f.): affection, love, fondness

**carmen, -inis (n.):** a set of words, liturgy, chant

**carnifex, -icis (m.):** butcher, executioner

**carō, carnis (f.):** flesh, meat

**cārus, -a, -um:** dear, loved

**castīgātōrius, -a, -um:** reproving, chastising

**castīgō, -āre, -āvī, -ātum:** to chastise, reprove

**castitās, -ātis (f.):** chastity, virtuousness

**castus, -a, -um:** chaste, pure

**cāsus, -ūs (m.):** disaster, catastrophe; downfall, falling; misfortune

**cathedra, -ae (f.):** chair

**causa, -ae (f.):** cause, reason; legal case. In the ablative case, **causā,** *because of, for the sake of,* serves as a preposition governing the genitive case and often follows the word it governs.

**cēdō, -ere, cessī, cessum:** to shrink from, withdraw from; to yield to

**celebrō, -āre, -āvī, -ātum:** to make famous; to celebrate; to visit frequently or in great numbers; to crowd

**cēna, -ae (f.):** dinner

**cēnō, -āre, -āvī, -ātum:** to dine

**cēra, -ae (f.):** wax, wax writing tablet

**cernō, -ere, crēvī, crētum:** to see

**certāmen, -inis (n.):** competition

**certātim (adv.):** in rivalry, eagerly

**certē (adv.):** certainly, surely

**certus, -a, -um:** definite, undeniable, sure; fixed, unvarying

**cervīcal, -ālis (n.):** pillow

**cervīx, -īcis (f.):** neck

**cessō, -āre, -āvī, -ātum:** to delay, postpone; to be late

**cēterus, -a, -um:** the other, the rest of

**charta, -ae (f.):** papyrus

**Christiānus, -ī (m.), Christiāna, -ae (f.):** Christian

**cibus, -ī (m.):** food

**cicātrix, -īcis (f.):** wound, scar

**cingō, -ere, cinxī, cinctum:** to encircle

**cinis, -eris (m.):** ash

**circā:** (+ acc.) near, around

**Circēnsēs, -ium (m. pl.):** racetrack entertainments

**circumagō, -ere, -ēgī, -actum:** to bend around, curve

**circumeō, -īre, -īvī, -itum:** to travel around, tour

**circumferō, -ferre, -tulī, -lātum:** to proclaim, spread around

**circumiaceō, -ēre:** to lie near, be situated around

**circumsistō, -ere, -stetī:** to surround

**circumspiciō, -ere, -spexī, -spectum:** to look, seek out

**cithara, -ae (f.):** lyre

**citō (adv.):** quickly

**cīvis, -is (m. and f.):** citizen

**cīvitās, -ātis (f.):** state, commonwealth; community; city

**clādēs, -is (f.):** destruction

**clāmitō, -āre, -āvī, -ātum:** to keep shouting

**clāmor, -ōris (m.):** outcry, shouting

**clāritās, -ātis (f.):** brightness, clearness

**clārus, -a, -um:** clear, illustrious, renowned

**classis, -is (f.):** fleet, navy

**claudō, -ere, clausī, clausum:** to shut, close

**clēmenter (adv.):** gently

**cochlea, -ae (f.):** snail

**cōdicillī, -ōrum (m. pl.):** note, message (sing. in English)

**coëmō, -ere, -ēmī, -emptum:** to buy, purchase

**coeō, -īre, -īvī:** to meet, assemble

**–, –, coepī, coeptum:** I began. This defective verb occurs only in the perfect system.

**coërceō, -ēre, -cuī, -citum:** to control, suppress

**cōgitātiō, -ōnis (f.):** thought, meditation

**cōgitō, -āre, -āvī, -ātum:** to think, reflect upon

**cognitiō, -ōnis (f.):** legal inquiry

**cognoscō, -ere, -nōvī, -nōtum:** to learn; in the perfect tenses: to have learned, and therefore, to know

**cōgō, -ere, coēgī, coactum:** to urge; to force

**cohaereō, -ēre, -haesī:** to adhere

**cohibeō, -ēre, -uī, -itum:** hold, hold back, repress

**collātiō, -ōnis (f.):** contribution; comparison

**collēgium, -ī (n.):** an association of people who have the same occupation or who share a common interest

**colligō, -ere, -lēgī, -lectum:** to gather, collect; to understand

**collocō, -āre, -āvī, -ātum:** to place, employ

**colō, -ere, coluī, cultum:** to love, cherish

**colōnus, -ī (m.):** farmer, peasant

**color, -ōris (m.):** color

**cōmis, -e:** affable

**comitor, -ārī, -ātus sum (dep. verb):** to follow, accompany

**commendō, -āre, -āvī, -ātum:** to recommend, make agreeable

**commentārius, -ī (m.):** notebook, diary

**committō, -ere, -mīsī, -missum:** to allow (something) to happen; to commit, be guilty of

**commodus, -a, -um:** comfortable

**commoror, -ārī, -ātus sum (dep. verb):** to linger

**commūnis, -e:** common

**cōmoedus, -ī (m.):** comic actor

**comparō, -āre, -āvī, -ātum (1):** to provide

**comparō, -āre, -āvī, -ātus (2):** to compare

**compescō, -ere, -uī:** to suppress, control

**complector, complectī, -plexus sum (dep. verb):** to embrace

**complūrēs, -ium:** several, many

**compōnō, -ere, -posuī, -positum:** to compose

**comprehendō, -ere, -hendī, -hensum:** to capture

**computō, -āre, -āvī, -ātum:** to reckon, add up

**concēdō, -ere, -cessī, -cessum:** to grant, allow

**concĭdō, -ere, -cĭdī:** to fall

**concipiō, -ere, -cēpī, -ceptum:** to undertake

**concordia, -ae (f.):** harmony

**concubīna, -ae (f.):** concubine, a woman, usually a slave or perhaps a former slave (freedwoman), who served her master's sexual demands

**concupiscō, -ere, -cupīvī, -cupītum:** to long for

**concurrō, -ere, -currī, -cursum:** run up together

**condiciō, -ōnis (f.):** condition

**condō, -ere, -didī, -ditum:** to compose, write; to lay, put to rest

**condūcō, -ere, -duxī, -ductum:** to rent, hire

**conferō, -ferre, -tulī, collātum:** to bring together, collect; to transfer, move

**conficiō, -ere, -fēcī, -fectum:** to consume; to distress

**confirmō, -āre, -āvī, -ātum:** to confirm; to cheer, encourage

**confiteor, -ērī, -fessus sum (dep. verb):** to reveal; to confess

**confluō, -ere, -fluxī:** to flow, flock

**coniunx, -iugis (m. and f.):** spouse, husband, wife

**conquīrō, -ere, -sīvī, -sītum:** to seek out, search for

**consensus, -ūs (m.):** agreement, unanimity

**consentiō, -īre, -sensī, -sensum:** to agree, concur, plan together

**consīdō, -ere, -sēdī, -sessum:** sit down

**consilium, -ī (n.):** suggestion, advice; plan

**consistō, -ere, -stitī:** to stop, halt

**consōlātiō, -ōnis (f.):** consolation, consoling

**consōlor, -ārī, -ātus sum (dep. verb):** to comfort

**conspiciō, -ere, -spexī, -spectum:** to look at, view

**conspicuus, -a, -um:** visible

**conspīrō, -āre, -āvī, -ātum:** to agree, concur, plan together

**constans, -antis:** firm, resolute

**constantia, -ae (f.):** firmness of mind, resolve

**constituō, -ere, -uī, -ūtum:** to organize; to determine, establish

**constō, -stāre, -stitī:** to be consistent, correspond; **constat:** it is known, agreed

**constringō, -ere, -strinxī, -strictum:** to tie

**consuescō, -ere, -ēvī, -ētum:** to become accustomed to

**consul, -ulis (m.):** consul. During the republican period, consuls were the highest-ranking elected Roman magistrates. During the imperial period, when the emperor became the supreme authority, the power of the consuls was considerably

diminished. Their term of
service, moreover, was often
reduced from one year to two
months. A consul serving for
two months was called a **consul
suffectus**, or suffect consul.

**consulāris, -e:** of consular rank,
consular (someone who has
served as a consul)

**consulō, -ere, -luī, -ltum:** to
consider, take measures for; to
consult, ask the advice of; to
have regard for (+ dat.)

**consultātiō, -ōnis (f.):**
consultation

**consultō, -āre, -āvī, -ātum:** to
discuss

**consultum, -ī (n.):** decree.
**Senatus consultum:** a
decree passed in the Roman
Senate. The two words were
often written as one word,
**senatusconsultum**, *decree of
the Senate*. In this case, **senatus**
remained always in the genitive
case, while **consultum** could
be declined.

**contactus, -ūs (m.):** touch,
contamination

**contāgiō, -ōnis (f.):** infection,
contagion

**contemnō, -ere, -psī, -ptum:** to
scorn

**contemptus, -ūs (m.):** contempt,
disdain

**conterō, -ere, -trīvī, -trītum:** to
wear out, exhaust

**contexō, -ere, -texuī, -textum:** to
weave, compose

**contineō, -ere, -tinuī, -tentum:**
to control, restrain; to contain

**contingō, -ere, -tigī, -tactum:** to
happen, befall

**contrā:** (+ acc.) against

**contrā (adv.):** on the other hand,
in response

**contrahō, -ere, -traxī, -tractum:**
to draw together, arrange; to
incur; to contract (a disease)

**contrārius, -a, -um:** opposite,
opposing

**contubernium, -ī (n.):** dwelling,
home

**contumēlia, -ae (f.):** injury, insult,
outrage

**contundō, -ere, -tudī, -tūsum:** to
crush

**convellō, -ere, -vellī (-vulsī),
-vulsum:** to tear away, pluck,
wrench

**conveniō, -īre, -vēnī, -ventum:** to
come; to meet, assemble

**convertō, -tere, -tī, -sum:** to turn
around

**convocō, -āre, -āvī, -ātum:** to
convoke, call together

**cōpia, -ae (f.):** abundance, throng;
opportunity

**corpus, -oris (n.):** body

**corpusculum, -ī (n.):** little body

**corrigō, -ere, -rexī, -rectum:** to
correct, reform

**corripiō, -ere, -ripuī, -reptum:**
chide, reproach, criticize

**corrumpō, -ere, -rūpī, -ruptum:**
to ruin, spoil

**corruō, -ere, -ruī, -rutum:** to fall
down

**cotīdiē (adv.):** daily, every day

**crassus, -a, -um:** thick

**crēber, -bra, -brum:** frequent, numerous

**crēdō, -ere, -idī, -itum:** (+ dat.) to believe; to trust in, trust to, confirm

**crescō, -ere, crēvī, crētum:** to grow, increase

**crīmen, -inis (n.):** accusation, charge; criminal investigation

**crūdus, -a, -um:** raw, fresh

**cryptoporticus, -ūs (f.):** a covered walkway

**cubiculum, -ī (n.):** bedroom; chamber

**cucurbita, -ae (f.):** cucumber

**culpa, -ae (f.):** guilt, fault, error

**cum (temp. conj.):** when; **cum maximē:** when especially, precisely when

**cum (concess. conj.):** although; while

**cum (causal conj.):** because, since

**cum:** (prep. + abl.) with; sometimes follows the ablative: **mēcum**

**cum ... tum:** both ... and

**cumulō, -āre, -āvī, -ātum:** to heap, cover, load

**cunctātiō, -ōnis (f.):** hesitation, deliberation

**cunctor, -ārī, -ātus sum (dep. verb):** to hesitate

**cupiō, -ere, -īvī, -ītum:** to wish, desire

**cūr (interr. adv.):** why?

**cūra, -ae (f.):** concern, care; trouble; anxiety

**cūrātius (adv.):** more carefully

**cūrō, -āre, -āvī, -ātum:** to take care of; (with the acc. and gerundive) to cause something to be done, to order

**currō, -ere, cucurrī, cursum:** to run

**currus, -ūs (m.):** chariot

**cursus, -ūs (m.):** course; speed; race

**curvō, -āre, -āvī, -ātum:** to bend, curve

**custōdia, -ae (f.):** protection, guardianship

**custōdiō, -īre, -īvī, -ītum:** to watch, guard; to protect

**custōdīte (adv.):** guardedly, cautiously

## D

**damnō, -āre, -āvī, -ātum:** to condemn, declare guilty of

**damnum, -ī (n.):** loss

**dē:** (+ abl.) about, concerning

**dēbeō, -ēre, -uī, -itum:** to be obligated; ought, must, should; to owe

**dēbilitō, -āre, -āvī, -ātum:** to weaken

**dēbitor, -ōris (m.):** debtor

**dēcēdō, -ere, -cessī, -cessum:** to go away; to die

**decēns, -tis:** suitable, appropriate

**deceō, -ēre, decuī:** to befit, become, suit

**dēcurrō, -ere, -currī, -cursum:** to hasten; to have recourse to

**dēdō, -ere, -didī, -ditum:** to surrender, dedicate

**dēdūcō, -ere, -duxī, -ductum:** to lead forth

**dēfectiō, -ōnis (f.):** weakness, exhaustion

**dēfensiō, -ōnis (f.):** defense

**dēferō, -ferre, -tulī, -lātum:** to carry, convey, bring; to report, accuse

**dēficiō, -ere, -fēcī, -fectum:** to become weak; to be in eclipse

**dēflectō, -ere, -flexī, -flexum:** to turn aside

**dēfleō, -ēre, -ēvī, -ētum:** to weep

**dēfodiō, -ere, -fōdī, -fossum:** to bury

**dēfungor, -ī, -functus sum (dep. verb):** to die

**dehiscō, -ere:** to part, split

**dein, deinde (adv.):** then

**dēmittō, -ere, -mīsī, -missum:** to send down, lower down

**dēmum (adv.):** at last; then

**dēnique (adv.):** in short, certainly

**densus, -a, -um:** thick, dense

**dēposcō, -ere, -poposcī:** to demand

**dēpositum, -ī (n.):** deposit

**dēprecor, -ārī, -ātus sum (dep. verb):** to plead, beg

**dēprendō, -ere, -ndī, -nsum:** to perceive

**dēscendō, -ere, -endī, -ensum:** to descend, climb down

**dēserō, -ere, -seruī, -sertum:** to abandon

**dēsīderium, -ī (n.):** longing, sorrow, aching

**dēsīderō, -āre, -āvī, -ātum:** to desire

**dēsīdō, -ere, -sēdī:** to sit, sink

**dēsinō, -ere, -siī, -situm:** to cease, desist

**dēsōlō, -āre, -āvī, -ātum:** to forsake, abandon

**dēstinō, -āre, -āvī, -ātum:** to choose; to betroth

**dēstituō, -ere, -tuī, -tūtum:** to abandon; to deprive of (+ abl.)

**dēsum, -esse, -fuī, -futūrus:** to be absent, lacking

**dētineō, -ēre, -tinuī, -tentum:** to hold, hold back, detain

**deus, -ī (m.):** god

**diaeta, -ae (f.):** apartment

**dīcō, -ere, dixī, dictum:** to say, proclaim, pronounce; **male dīcere:** (+ dat.) to curse

**dictitō, -āre, -āvī, -ātum:** to say often, keep saying

**dictō, -āre, -āvī, -ātum:** to dictate

**dictum, -ī (n.):** word

**diēs, -ēī (m.):** day; daylight; **in diēs:** day by day

**differō, differre, distulī, dilātum:** to differ; to postpone

**difficile (adv.):** with difficulty

**difficilis, -e:** difficult

**diffugiō, -ere, -fūgī:** to flee in different directions

**diffundō, -ere, -fūdī, -fūsum:** to spread in all directions

**dignus, -a, -um:** (+ abl.) worthy, deserving

**dīgredior, -gredī, -gressus sum (dep. verb):** to leave, depart

**dīligens, -ntis:** careful, diligent

**dīligō, -ere, dilexī, dilectum:** to love, esteem

**dīmensus, -a, -um:** measured out

**dīmittō, -ere, -mīsī, -missum:** to dismiss

**dirimō, -ere, -ēmī, -emptum:** to separate

**discēdō, -ere, -cessī, -cessum:** to depart

**discernō, -ere, -crēvī, -crētum:** to separate, set apart

**discō, -ere, didicī:** to learn

**discrīmen, -inis (n.):** peril, danger; distinction, dividing line

**discursus, -ūs (m.):** flash

**dispiciō, -ere, -spexī, -spectum:** to discover, consider

**dispōnō, -ere, -posuī, -positum:** to put in place, post; arrange, spend (time)

**diū (adv.):** for a long time

**dīum (= dīvum), -ī (n.):** sky

**dīversus, -a, -um:** different

**dīvidō, -ere, -vīsī, -vīsum:** to divide, separate; to distribute

**dīvīnus, -a, -um:** divine

**dō, dare, dedī, dātum:** to give, grant; **dare operam:** to take care

**doceō, -ēre, -uī, doctum:** to teach, show, prove

**documentum, -ī (n.):** lesson

**doleō, -ēre, -luī:** to hurt (someone), cause pain; to feel pain, grieve, be hurting

**dolor, -ōris (m.):** grief, sorrow

**dominus, -ī (m.):** master, slave owner; absolute ruler; my lord (form of address to the emperor); owner of property

**domus, -ūs (f.):** family, family line; household; house, home. **Domi** is the locative: at home.

**dōnec (conj.):** until

**dōnō, -āre, -āvī, -ātum:** to grant, confer, bestow

**dubitō, -āre, -āvī, -ātum:** to doubt; to be uncertain

**dubius, -a, -um:** uncertain, ambiguous

**dūcō, -ere, duxī, ductum:** to lead, conduct

**dum (conj.):** while; until. When meaning *while*, the verb uses a present indicative tense where English uses a past tense. When meaning *until*, it uses a subjunctive mood.

**dumtaxat (adv.):** but only

**duo, -ae, -o:** two

**duodēvīcensimus, -a, -um:** eighteenth

**dūre (adv.):** rudely, harshly

**dūrō, -āre, -āvī, -ātum:** to continue, remain

**dūrus, -a, -um:** harsh, hard; rude, cruel

## E

**ē, ex:** (+ abl.) from, in consequence of, according to; for; out of

**ecce:** lo and behold!

**echīnus, -ī (m.):** sea urchin

**ecquid:** whether at all

**ēdictum, -ī (n.):** decree, edict

**ēdiscō, -ere, edidicī:** to learn by heart, memorize

**ēdō, -ere, edidī, editum:** to furnish, provide funds

**ēducō, -āre, -āvī, -ātum:** to educate

**efferō, eferre, extulī, ēlātum:** to carry out; to raise up, elevate

**efficiō, -ere, -fēcī, -fectum:** to cause, bring about

**effugiō, -ere, -fūgī:** to escape, avoid

**effulgeō, -ēre, -fulsī:** to shine forth

**effūsus, -a, -um:** unrestrained

**egeō, -ēre, -uī:** (+ abl.) to need

**ego (pers. pron.):** I

**ēgredior, -ī, egressus sum (dep. verb):** to go out, leave

**egregiē (adv.):** admirably

**egregius, -a, -um:** outstanding, excellent, admirable

**ēiusmodī (ēius modī):** of this kind, of this sort

**ēligō, -ere, -lēgī, -lectum:** to choose, select

**ēmendō, -āre, -āvī, -ātum:** to correct, amend

**ēmittō, -ere, -mīsī, -missum:** to send forth, utter

**emō, -ere, ēmī, emptum:** to buy, purchase

**ēmoveō, -ēre, -mōvī, -mōtum:** to remove, move

**emptor, -ōris (m.):** buyer, purchaser

**enim (conj.):** for

**ēnotō, -āre, -āvī, -ātum:** to make notes, to note down

**eō:** for this (reason), therefore

**eō, īre, īvī, ītum:** to go

**epistula, -ae (f.):** letter

**eques, -itis (m.):** literally horseman, equestrian; but also the designation for a member of a social class that consisted of people who were wealthy, but usually less wealthy and less politically connected than members of the senatorial class. **Eques** is often translated as *knight.*

**equidem (adv.):** of course, certainly

**equus, -ī (m.):** horse

**ergō (adv.):** therefore, accordingly

**ēripiō, -ere, -ripuī, -reptum:** to snatch away, rescue

**ērogō, -āre, -āvī, -ātum:** to pay out, expend

**error, -ōris (m.):** fault, error, mistake

**ērudītus, -a, -um:** erudite, learned, educated

**et (conj.):** and; also; and yet

**et . . . et:** both . . . and

**etiam:** also, even, likewise; yes; **verum etiam:** but even

**ēvādō, -ere, -vāsī, -vāsum:** to turn out, become; to leave, escape

**ēvehō, -ere, -vexī, -vectum:** to carry up, lift up

**ēventus, -ūs (m.):** outcome, result

**ēvigilō, -āre, -āvī, -ātum:** to wake up

**ex:** See ē.

**exacerbō, -āre, -āvī, -ātum:** to hurt, devastate

**exanimis, -e:** lifeless, dead

**excēdō, -ere, -cessī, -cessum:** to exceed, go beyond; to leave

**excerpō, -ere, -psī, -ptum:** to pick; to select and copy literary passages

**excĭdō, -ere, -cĭdī:** to fall from, to slip out

**excipiō, -ere, -cēpī, -ceptum:** to take, receive

**excitō, -āre, -āvī, -ātum:** to arouse, stimulate; to revive; to accentuate, intensify

**exclūdō, -ere, -sī, -sum:** to shut out, exclude

**excolō, -ere, -coluī, -cultum:** to cultivate

**excūsō, -āre, -āvī, -ātum:** to apologize, make an excuse

**excutiō, -ere, -cussī, -cussum:** to strike down; to shake; to examine, investigate

**exemplum, -ī (n.):** example, model

**exerceō, -ēre, -uī, -itum:** to exercise, train

**exēsus, -a, -um:** porous

**exhibeō, -ēre, -uī, -itum:** to exhibit, produce a display

**exigō, -ere, -ēgī, -actum:** to ask, request; to pass, spend

**exilium (= exsilium), -ī (n.):** exile

**eximius, -a, -um:** extraordinary, outstanding

**existimō, -āre, -āvī, -ātum:** to think, suppose

**exitium, -ī (n.):** fate, destruction; death

**exitus, -ūs (m.):** outcome, death; exit, egress

**expellō, -ere, -pulī, -pulsum:** to thrust aside, repudiate

**experior, -īrī, -pertus sum (dep. verb):** to learn, find out; to try; to experience, undergo

**expiō, -āre, -āvī, -ātum:** to atone for

**explōrō, -āre, -āvī, -ātum:** to ascertain, prove

**exprimō, -ere, -pressī, -pressum:** to express, describe, represent

**exscrībō, -ere, -psī, -ptum:** to copy

**exsequiae, -ārum (f. pl.):** funeral rites

**exsiliō, -ere, -luī:** to leap up

**exsilium, -ī (n.):** See **exilium**.

**exsolvō, -ere, -solvī, -solūtum:** to untie, release; to pay off, settle

**exspectō, -āre, -āvī, -ātum:** to expect, anticipate

**extendō, -ere, -tendī, -tentum:** to stretch out

**exterreō, -ēre, -uī, -itum:** to frighten, terrify

**extinguō, -ere, -inxī, -inctum:** to put out, extinguish

**extollō, -ere:** to extol, praise, exalt

**extrahō, -ere, -traxī, -tractum:** to pull out, withdraw

**extrēmum, -ī (n.):** end

### F

**faber, -rī (m.):** workman, laborer

**facile (adv.):** easily, with ease

**facilis, -e:** easy; willing

**facilitās, -ātis (f.):** ease; willingness

**faciō, -ere, fēcī, factum:** to make; to do; to bring about; to see that; to perform; **facere acceptum:** to make note as paid; to give credit

**factiō, -ōnis (f.):** chariot-racing company or stable; faction, group factum, -ī (n.): deed

fallō, -ere, fefellī, falsum: to
violate, break

falsō (adv.): falsely

fāma, -ae (f.): fame

familiāritās, -ātis (f.): friendship

fateor, -ērī, fassus sum (dep.
verb): to acknowledge, admit

faucēs, -ium (f. pl.): throat
(sing.)

faveō, -ēre, fāvī, fautum: (+ dat.)
to support, applaud

favor, -ōris (m.): applause,
support

fax, facis (f.): torch

febricula, -ae (f.): slight fever

febris, -is (f.): fever

fēcunditās, -ātis (f.): fertility

fēmina, -ae (f.): woman

fenestra, -ae (f.): window

ferculum, -ī (n.): dish

ferē (adv.): about, almost

fēriātus, -a, -um: of leisure,
holiday

ferō, ferre, tulī, lātum: to carry,
take; to bear, endure

ferrum, -ī (n.): knife, blade

fervens, -entis: hot, burning

festīnātiō, -ōnis (f.): haste,
urgency

festīvus, -a, -um: cheerful,
pleasant, good-natured

fictus, -a, -um: false

fidēlis, -e: loyal, trustworthy

fidēs, -ēī (f.): faith, belief,
confidence; promise

fīdō, -ere, fīsus sum (semi-
dep. verb): (+ dat.) to have
confidence in

fīdūcia, -ae (f.): confidence,
assurance

figūra, -ae (f.): shape, form

fīlia, -ae (f.): daughter

fīlius, -ī (m.): son

fingō, -ere, finxī, fictum: to
invent, imagine

fīnis, -is (m.): end, finish

fīnitimus, -a, -um: neighboring

fīō, fierī, factus sum: to happen,
come to pass; to become; used
as the passive of faciō, facere

firmō, -āre, -āvī, -ātum: to
strengthen, make strong

flāgitium, -ī (n.): shame, disgrace;
crime

flamma, -ae (f.): flame

flectō, -ere, flexī, flectum: to
turn

fōcilō, -āre, -āvī, -ātum: to warm;
to resuscitate

foedus, -a, -um: repulsive,
horrible

fons, -tis (f.): source, beginning

forīs (adv.): outside

forma, -ae (f.): form, shape

Formiānus, -a, -um: Formian,
that is, at or from Formiae, a
town on the west coast of Italy,
about halfway between Rome
and Naples.

formīdō, -inis (f.): fear, terror

formīdolōsus, -a, -um: alarming,
frightening

formō, -āre, -āvī, -ātum: to shape,
arrange, fashion

fortasse (adv.): perhaps

forte (adv.): by chance, as it
happened

**fortis, -e:** strong; brave
**fortitūdō, -inis (f.):** courage
**fortūna, -ae (f.):** fortune
**forum, -ī (n.):** open area for public activities, forum
**fractus, -a, -um:** broken
**frangō, -ere, frēgī, fractum:** to break, shatter
**frāter, -tris (m.):** brother
**frequens, -entis:** crowded, heavily populated
**frequenter (adv.):** frequently
**frequentissimē (adv.):** most frequently, very frequently
**frequentō, -āre, -āvī, -ātum:** to spend much time in
**frīgidus, -a, -um:** cold; dull
**frīgus, -oris (n.):** cold
**fructuōsus, -a, -um:** productive, profitable
**frūgālitās, -ātis (f.):** thriftiness
**frūgī:** useful, honest. The form is the dative of **frux**, but the word is treated as an indeclinable adjective.
**fruor, fruī, fructus sum (dep. verb):** (+ abl.) to enjoy
**fuga, -ae (f.):** flight, escape
**fugiō, -ere, fūgī, fugitum:** to flee, escape
**fulciō, -īre, fulsī, fultum:** to support, wedge
**fulgor, -ōris (m.):** flashing, brightness
**fulgur, -uris (n.):** lightning, lightning flash
**fulmen, -inis (n.):** lightning bolt, thunderbolt
**fūmus, -ī (m.):** smoke

**fungor, -ī, functus sum (dep. verb):** (+ abl.) to perform, discharge, be engaged in
**fūnus, -eris (n.):** funeral; death
**furtum, -ī (n.):** theft

## G

**Gaditanus, -a, -um:** a person from Gades, a town in southwestern Spain (modern Cadiz)
**gaudeō, -ēre:** to rejoice, be glad
**gaudium, -ī (n.):** joy, delight
**gemitus, -ūs (m.):** sigh, groan
**gemma, -ae (f.):** gemstone
**gener, -erī (m.):** son-in-law
**genus, -eris (n.):** kind, type
**Gerusia, -ae (f.):** a building in which members of the city's elite met
**gestō, -āre, -āvī, -ātum:** to carry, bear
**gladiātōrius, -a, -um:** gladiatorial
**glōria, -ae (f.):** glory, renown
**glōrior, -ārī, -ātus sum (dep. verb):** to boast
**gradus, -ūs (m.):** step, degree; **addere gradum:** to hurry
**grandis, -e:** great
**grandō, -inis (f.):** hail
**Graecus, -a, -um:** Greek
**grātia, -ae (f.):** gratitude, favor; popularity; **grātiās agere:** to give thanks
**grātuitus, -a, -um:** free
**grātus, -a, -um:** pleasing
**gravis, -e:** grave, grievous, distressful; heavy, labored; heavy, weighed down; serious, responsible

**gravitās, -ātis (f.):** dignity, seriousness; harshness, severity

**graviter (adv.):** strenuously, violently; reluctantly, with difficulty

**gremium, -ī (n.):** lap

**gubernāculum, -ī (n.):** rudder, helm

**gubernātor, -ōris (m.):** helmsman

**gustō, -āre, -āvī, -ātum:** to taste, have a bite to eat

## H

**habeō, -ēre, -uī, -itum:** to have

**habitātiō, -ōnis (f.):** lodging, rent

**habitus, -ūs (m.):** condition, appearance

**hāctenus (adv.):** to this extent, so far

**haereō, -ēre, haesī, haesum:** to stick, catch

**haesitō, -āre, -āvī, -ātum:** to hesitate, be in doubt

**hama, -ae (f.):** water bucket

**harēna, -ae (f.):** sand

**hauriō, -īre, hausī, haustum:** to swallow, drink

**hesternus, -a, -um:** of yesterday, yesterday's

**hetaeria, -ae (f.):** association, club

**heus (exclamation):** hey!

**hīc (adv.):** here, in this place

**hīc (or hic), haec, hōc (demon. pron.):** this; he she, it

**hiems (= hiemps), -emis (f.):** winter, winter cold

**hilaris, -e (= hilarus, -a, -um):** cheerful

**hinc (adv.):** from here, from this place; for this reason

**historia, -ae (f.):** history

**homō, -inis (m.):** man

**honestus, -a, -um:** honorable, honest

**honor, -ōris (m.):** public office

**hōra, -ae (f.):** hour

**horrendus, -a, -um:** dreadful

**horreō, -ēre, -uī:** to tremble, be afraid

**horreum, -ī (n.):** barn, granary

**hortor, -ārī, -ātus sum (dep. verb):** to urge, encourage

**hortus, -ī (m.):** garden

**hūc (adv.):** to here, here

**hūmānitās, -ātis (f.):** human sympathy

**hūmānus, -a, -um:** humane, kind

## I

**iaceō, -ēre, -uī:** to lie; to recline

**iaciō, -ěre, iēcī, iactum:** to throw, hurl

**iam (adv.):** indeed; now; already

**ibī (adv.):** there

**īdem, eadem, idem:** the same

**identidem (adv.):** again and again, repeatedly

**ideō (adv.):** on that account

**igitur (adv.):** therefore

**igneus, -a, -um:** burning, glowing

**ignis, -is (m.):** fire

**ignōrantia, -ae (f.):** ignorance

**ignōrō, -āre, -āvī, -ātum:** to be ignorant, not know

**ignoscō, -ere, -nōvī, -nōtum:** to pardon, excuse

**ille, illa, illud (demon. pron.):** that, that one; he, she it

**illic (adv.):** there, in that place

**illūc (adv.):** to that place, point; there

**imāginor, -ārī, -ātus sum (dep. verb):** to imagine

**imāgō, -inis (f.):** image, vision; statue

**immānitās, -ātis (f.):** savagery, brutality

**immātūrus, -a, -um:** premature, before one's time

**immineō, -ēre:** (+ dat.) to be imminent, threaten

**immō (adv.):** in fact, indeed; or rather

**immōbilis, -e:** motionless

**immodicus, -a, -um:** immoderate, excessive

**immortālis, -e:** immortal

**immortālitās, -ātis (f.):** immortality

**impellō, -ere, -pulī, -pulsum:** to push forward

**impendeō, -ēre:** (+ dat.) to hang over, threaten

**impendium, -ī (n.):** cost, expense; expenditure

**impendō, -ere, -endī, -ensum:** to spend; to devote

**impensus, -a, -um:** earnest, vehement

**imperātor, -ōris (m.):** emperor

**imperium, -ī (n.):** authority

**impetrō, -āre, -āvī, -ātum:** to obtain, succeed in a request

**impetus, -ūs (m.):** vehemence, violence

**impingō, -ere, -pēgī, -pactum:** to strike against, bang against

**impleō, -ēre, -ēvī, -ētum:** to fill, to satisfy

**implicō, -āre, -uī, -itum:** to envelop, ensnare

**impōnō, -ere, -posuī, -positum:** to put on board; (+ dat.) to place upon

**imprūdentia, -ae (f.):** foolishness, imprudence

**imputō, -āre, -āvī, -ātum:** (+ dat.) to blame

**in:** (+ abl.) in

**in:** (+ acc.) into; onto

**inānis, -e:** pointless

**inaudītus, -a, -um:** unheard

**incautus, -a, -um:** unguarded, without reserve, without anxiety

**incendium, -ī (n.):** fire, flame

**incertus, -a, -um:** uncertain, vague

**incestum, -ī (n.):** unchastity; incest

**incestus, -a, -um:** unchaste

**incĭdō, -ere, -cĭdī, -cāsum:** (+ dat.) to fall, fall upon; to occur

**incipiō, -ere, -cēpī, -ceptum:** to begin

**incitāmentum, -ī (n.):** incentive, inducement

**incohō, -āre, -āvī, -ātum:** to begin

**incrēdibilis, -e:** incredible, amazing

**increscō, -ere, -crēvī:** to grow, increase

incūsō, -āre, -āvī, -ātum: to accuse, blame

inde (adv.): thence, thus, for that reason; from there, from that place

index, -icis (m.): informer

indicium, -ī (n.): information; indication, evidence

indicō, -āre, -āvī, -ātum: to point out

indignus, -a, -um: undeserved, cruel

indolēs, -is (f.): inborn quality, good judgment

indūcō, -ere, -duxī, -ductum: to bring in; to cover over, erase; to induce, persuade

indulgeō, -ēre, -dulsī: (+ dat.) to indulge, gratify

induō, -ere, -uī, -ūtum: to dress

ineō, -īre, -īvī: to begin; **iniens aetās**: early age, youth

inerrō, -āre, -āvī, -ātum: to wander, roam

inertia, -ae (f.): idle leisure; inactivity, unresponsiveness

infans, -tis (m. and f.): infant, young child

infantia, -ae (f.): infancy

infirmitās, -ātis (f.): illness, weakness

inflexibilis, -e: inflexible, unyielding

infringō, -ere, -frēgī, -fractum: to break

infundō, -ere, -fūdī, -fūsum: to pour in. The perfect participle **infusus** + dat.: spread over.

ingenium, -ī (n.): talent, intellect

ingens, -gentis: huge, enormous

ingredior, -ī, -gressus sum (dep. verb): to begin, undertake

ingressus, -ūs (m.): beginning

inhaereō, -ēre, -sī, -sum: to cling

inhibeō, -ēre, -uī, -itum: to use

initium, -ī (n.): beginning

iniungō, -ere, -iunxī, -iunctum: to enjoin, urge

inlaesus, -a, -um: unharmed

inlūnis, -e: moonless

inlustris, -e: praiseworthy

inlustrō, -āre, -āvī, -ātum: to make bright, illustrious

innītor, -nītī, -nixus sum (dep. verb): to lean upon

innocens, -entis: innocent

innoxius, -a, -um: harmless, innocent

inoffensus, -a, -um: unharmed, without injury

inquam, inquis, inquit (defect. verb): I say; you say, you exclaim; s/he says, said

inquiētus, -a, -um: restless, fitful

inrīdeō, -ēre, -rīsī, -rīsum: to laugh at, mock

inrumpō, -ere, -rūpī, -ruptum: to burst in

insatiābiliter (adv.): insatiably

insideō, -ēre, -sēdī, -sessum: to settle in

insistō, -ere, institī: (+ dat.) to stand

instans, -tis: urgent, pressing

instituō, -ere, -uī, -ūtum: to instruct, raise, train; to establish

**instrūmentum, -ī (n.):** tool, instrument

**instruō, -ere, -uxī, -uctum:** to instruct

**integer, -gra, -grum:** whole, intact

**intellegenter (adv.):** intelligently

**intellegō, -ere, -exī, -ectum:** to understand, appreciate; to perceive, think

**intentiō, -ōnis (f.):** effort, concentration

**intentus, -a, -um:** intent, absorbed

**inter:** (+ acc.) among

**interdiū (adv.):** by day, during the day

**interdum (adv.):** sometimes

**interiaceō, -ēre:** to lie between

**interim (adv.):** meanwhile, however

**intermittō, -ere, -mīsī, -missum:** to suspend, interrupt

**interpellātiō, -ōnis (f.):** interruption

**interpretor, -ārī, -tātus sum (dep. verb):** to explain, interpret; to decide

**interrogō, -āre, -āvī, -ātum:** to ask

**intersum, -esse, -fuī:** (+ dat.) to be present, to take part in; **interest (impers. verb):** it concerns, is of importance

**interveniō, -īre, -vēnī, -ventum:** to come by, stop by

**intrā:** (+ acc.) within

**intrō, -āre, -āvī, -ātum:** to enter

**intueor, -ērī, -tuitus sum (dep. verb):** to look at, observe

**invādō, -ere, -vāsī, -vāsum:** to attack, rush upon

**invalescō, -ere, -luī:** to become stronger

**invalidus, -a, -um:** weak, not strong

**invehō, -ere, -vexī, -vectum:** to carry, bring

**inveniō, -īre, -vēnī, -ventum:** to find

**invicem (adv.):** mutually, in turn

**invideō, -ēre, -vīdī, -vīsum:** (+ dat.) to begrudge; to act hurtfully

**invīsitātus, -a, -um:** unseen before, strange

**iocus, -ī (m.):** joke

**ipse, -a, -um (demon. pron.):** self, (one)self; very (thing); of one's own accord

**is, ea, id (demon. pron.):** this (one), that (one)

**Īsēon, -ī (n.):** temple of Isis

**iste, ista, istud (demon. pron.):** that, those (pl.)

**ita (adv.):** thus, in this way

**ita ... ut:** in this way ... as; in such a way ... that

**itaque (adv.):** therefore

**iter, itineris (n.):** road, path; journey

**iterum:** again; a second time; **semel atque iterum:** again and again

**iubeō, -ēre, iussī, iussum:** to order

**iūcundus, -a, -um:** pleasant, enjoyable, delightful; good-natured

**iūdicium, -ī (n.):** judgment, discernment; court case, trial

**iūdicō, -āre, -āvī, -ātum:** to judge, pass judgment; to appraise

**iūrgium, -ī (n.):** quarrel

**iūs, iūris (n.):** law, justice; right, privilege

**iustus, -a, -um:** justified

**iuvenis, -is (m.):** young man

**iuvō, -āre, iūvī, iūtum:** help, assist

**iuxtā (adv.):** equally, in like manner

## K

**Kal.:** abbreviation for **Kalendae**

**Kalendae, -ārum (f. pl.):** Kalends, the first day of each month

## L

**lābor, -ī, lapsus sum (dep. verb):** to slip, sink, fail

**labor, -ōris (m.):** hardship, difficulty, toil

**lacrima, -ae (f.):** tear

**lactūca, -ae (f.):** lettuce

**laguncula, -ae (f.):** wine flask

**lancea, -ae (f.):** hunting lance

**languidus, -a, -um:** sluggish, sickly, faint

**lapis, -idis (m.):** stone, rock

**lassus, -a, -um:** weary, tired

**Latīnus, -a, -um:** Latin

**lātitūdō, -inis (f.):** breadth, width, extent

**latrōcinium, -ī (n.):** robbery

**lātus, -a, -um:** wide, widespread, extensive. The comparative adverb is **latius.**

**latus, -eris (n.):** side, direction

**laudō, -āre, -āvī, -ātum:** to praise

**laus, laudis (f.):** praise

**lautus, -a, -um:** sumptuous

**lavō, -āre, -āvī, lautum (or lōtum):** to bathe

**laxō, -āre, -āvī, -ātum:** to relax, ease

**lectiō, -ōnis (f.):** reading

**lectitō, -āre, -āvī, -ātum:** to read often, again and again

**lector, -ōris (m.):** reader, someone who reads aloud or recites to an audience

**legatus, -ī (m.):** a man of senatorial rank chosen to serve as governor of a Roman province

**lēgitimus, -a, -um:** legal, valid

**legō, -ere, lēgī, lectum:** to read; to recite

**lēniō, -īre, -īvī, -ītum:** to alleviate, calm

**levis, -e:** light, slight

**leviter (adv.):** lightly, gently

**lex, lēgis (f.):** agreement, law

**libellus, -ī (m.):** little book, small literary work; pamphlet

**libenter (adv.):** willingly, readily. The comparative degree adverb is **libentius.** The superlative is **libentissimē.**

**līber, lībera, līberum:** free, unrestricted

**liber, librī (m.):** book

**līberālis, -e:** generous

**līberālitās, -ātis (f.):** generosity

**līberī, -ōrum (m. pl.):** children

**libet, libuit (impers. verb):** it pleases, is agreeable

**Liburnica, -ae (f.):** a type of light, fast ship

**licentia, -ae (f.):** license, unrestrained power

**licet (impers. verb):** it is allowed (that), permitted (that); when used as a conjunction with the subjunctive: although

**licitus, -a, -um:** permitted, allowed

**līmen, -inis (n.):** threshold, doorway

**linteum, -ī (n.):** cloth

**līs, lītis (f.):** legal case

**littera, -ae (f.):** a letter of the alphabet; **litterae, -ārum (pl.):** literature; letter, epistle

**lītus, -oris (n.):** coastline, seashore

**locuplēs, -ētis:** wealthy, rich

**locus, -ī (m.):** place; opportunity

**longus, -a, -um:** long

**luctuōsus, -a, -um:** sorrowful, lamentable

**luctus, -ūs (m.):** grief, sorrow

**lūdibrium, -ī (n.):** derision, insult

**ludificor, -ārī, -ātus sum (dep. verb):** to deride, make a mockery of

**lūdō, -ere, lūsī, lūsum:** to joke; to amuse oneself; to play

**lūmen, -inis (n.):** light, lamp

**lūridus, -a, -um:** lurid, pale yellow

**lux, lūcis (f.):** light, daylight

**lymphātus, -a, -um:** frenzied, crazed

**lyristēs, -ae (m.):** lyre player. This word is a Greek word, and the declensional endings are therefore Greek, i.e., **-es** for the nominative singular, **-en** for the accusative singular.

## M

**maciēs, -ēī (f.):** thinness, wasting away, emaciation

**maculōsus, -a, -um:** stained, soiled

**maeror, -ōris (m.):** sadness, grief

**maestus, -a, -um:** sad, sorrowful

**magis (adv.):** more; **magis . . . quam:** more than

**magister, -trī (m.):** master, teacher

**magnitūdō, -inis (f.):** magnitude, importance

**magnus, -a, -um:** great

**māior, māius (comparative degree of magnus):** greater

**male (adv.):** badly; **male dīcere:** (+ dat.) to curse

**mālō, malle, māluī:** to prefer

**malus, -a, -um:** destructive; as a substantive: **malum, -ī (n.):** destructive thing, calamity, misfortune

**mandātum, -ī (n.):** order, mandate, instruction

**mandō, -āre, -āvī, -ātum:** to commit, entrust

**maneō, -ēre, mansī, mansum:** to remain, endure

**manifestus, -a, -um:** clear, plain

**manūmittō, -ere, -mīsī, -missum:** to liberate, set free

**manus, -ūs (f.):** hand
**mare, maris (n.):** sea
**margarīta, -ae (f.):** pearl
**marītus, -ī (m.):** husband
**māter, -tris (f.):** mother
**matrōna, -ae (f.):** a mature
  woman
**matrōnālis, -e:** matronly, of a
  mature woman
**maximē (adv.):** especially,
  particularly; **cum maximē:**
  when especially, precisely when
**maximus, -a, -um** (superlative
  degree of **magnus**): greatest,
  very great, most important
**mē (pers. pron.):** me; accusative
  or ablative singular case of **ego**;
  **mēcum = cum** (prep.) + **mē**
  (abl.)
**meātus, -ūs (m.):** movement,
  passage
**medeor, -ērī:** to heal, cure
**medicus, -ī (m.):** doctor
**mediocriter (adv.):** slightly, a
  little
**meditor, -ārī, meditātus sum**
  **(dep. verb):** to meditate about,
  think over
**medius, -a, -um:** middle; in the
  middle of; **medium tempus:**
  intervening time
**melius (adv.):** better. **Melius** is
  the comparative form of **bene**.
**—, —, meminī:** I remember. This
  defective verb has only perfect
  system forms, but its perfect
  tense forms have present tense
  meanings. **Mementō** is the
  imperative singular form.

**memorābilis, -e:** memorable
**memoria, -ae (f.):** memory
**memorō, -āre, -āvī, -ātum:** call to
  mind, recount
**mens, -tis (f.):** mind
**mentior, -īrī, -ītus sum (dep.**
  **verb):** to fabricate, invent.
  Although the verb is deponent,
  its perfect participle is often
  passive in meaning: **mentītus:**
  fabricated.
**mercēs, -ēdis (f.):** salary
**mereō, -ēre, -uī, -itum:** to
  deserve, earn
**mereor, -ērī, meritus sum (dep.**
  **verb):** to deserve, earn
**meritum, -ī (n.):** kindness, good
  deed
**metuō, -ere, metuī:** to fear,
  dread
**metus, -ūs (m.):** fear
**meus, -a, -um (poss. adj.):** my
**mihi (pers. pron.):** me; dative
  case of **ego**
**mīles, -itis (m.):** soldier
**militō, -āre, -āvī, -ātum:** to serve
  in the military
**mille (indecl.):** a thousand. The
  plural, **mīlia**, is declined.
**mināciter (adv.):** threateningly
**minimē (adv.):** minimally, not at
  all
**minimus, -a, -um** (superlative
  degree of **parvus**): very little,
  trivial
**ministra, -ae (f.):** female servant,
  attendant
**minor, -ārī, minātus sum (dep.**
  **verb):** to threaten

**minor, minus** (comparative
degree of **parvus**): lesser, less
significant; younger

**minus (adv.):** less; **quo minus
(quominus):** that . . . not

**mīrābilis, -e:** remarkable,
impressive

**mīrāculum, -ī (n.):** marvel,
remarkable phenomenon

**mīror, -ārī, -ātus sum (dep.
verb):** to wonder at; to
admire, revere; to be
astonished

**mīrus, -a, -um:** remarkable;
**mīrē (adv.):** remarkably

**misceō, -ēre, -cuī, mixtum:** to
mix; to blend, intermingle

**miser, -era, -erum:** wretched,
lamentable

**miseria, -ae (f.):** misery,
distress

**miseror, -ārī, -ātus sum (dep.
verb):** to lament

**mītis, -e:** kind, soft

**mittō, -ere, mīsī, missum:** to
send; to omit, say nothing
about

**modestē (adv.):** modestly

**modicus, -a, -um:** trivial,
insignificant; small

**modo (adv.):** only

**modus, -ī (m.):** moderation,
limit, boundary; manner,
way; kind, type; method

**mollis, -e:** soft, gentle

**moneō, -ēre, -uī, -itum:** to warn,
advise

**mons, -tis (m.):** mountain

**mora, -ae (f.):** delay

**morbus, -ī (m.):** illness

**morior, morī, mortuus sum
(dep. verb):** to die

**moror, -ārī, morātus sum (dep.
verb):** to stay, reside; to delay,
hinder

**mors, -tis (f.):** death

**mortālitās, -ātis (f.):** mortality

**mortiferē (adv.):** mortally,
deathly

**mōs, mōris (m.):** habit, custom;
**(pl.):** character, behavior

**mōtus, -ūs (m.):** motion,
movement

**moveō, -ēre, mōvī, mōtum:** to
move; to take up (arms)

**mox (adv.):** soon; then, after
that

**mulsum, -ī (n.):** honey-wine,
mead

**multum (adv.):** much

**multus, -a, -um:** many, much

**mundus, -ī (m.):** the world

**mūniceps, -cipis (m. and f.):**
citizen, fellow citizen

**mūnīmentum, -ī (n.):** defense,
protection

**mūnus, -eris (n.):** gift; public
show, exhibition; duty,
responsibility

**mussō, -āre, -āvī, -ātum:** to be
silent

**mūtātiō, -ōnis (f.):** change

**mūtō, -āre, -āvī, -ātum:** to
exchange; to change

**mūtuor, -ārī, -ātus sum (dep.
verb):** to borrow

**mūtuus, -a, -um:** mutual,
reciprocal

# N

**nam (conj.):** for

**nascor, -ī, nātus sum (dep. verb):** to be born

**nātālis, -e:** native, natal; as a substantive: birthday

**nātūra, -ae (f.):** nature, character

**nāvicula, -ae (f.):** little ship, boat

**nāvigātiō, -ōnis (f.):** sea voyage

**nāvigium, -ī (n.):** ship

**nāvis, -is (f.):** ship

**nē (conj.):** that not, so that not; introduces a negative subjunctive clause. When **nē** introduces a clause that follows a verb of fearing, it can be translated as *lest*.

**-nĕ:** an enclitic particle attached to the end of a word to indicate a question

**nē ... quidem:** not even

**nebula, -ae (f.):** mist

**nec (conj. adv.):** nor

**nec ... nec:** neither ... nor

**necessārius, -a, -um:** necessary

**necesse esse:** to be necessary. This construction is followed by a subjunctive.

**necessitās, -ātis (f.):** necessity, exigency, pressure

**necō, -āre, -āvī, -ātum:** to kill, put to death

**neglegens, -ntis:** careless, negligent

**neglegō, -ere, -lexī, -lectum:** to neglect, overlook

**negō, -āre, -āvī, -ātum:** to deny, refuse

**nēmō, neminis (or nullīus):** no one

**nempe (adv.):** surely, certainly

**neptis, -is (f.):** granddaughter

**nequāquam (adv.):** by no means

**neque (conj.):** not

**nesciō, -īre, -īvī, -ītum:** not to know, to be ignorant, unaware

**nesciō an:** I do not know whether; perhaps not

**nēve:** that not, so that not. Its meaning depends on the type of clause it is introducing; it is composed of the enclitic **-ve** (*and*) with a **ne** introducing the negative purpose clause (**ne -ve**).

**Nīcomēdēnsēs, -ium (m. and f. pl.):** residents of Nicomedia

**niger, -gra, -grum:** black

**nihil:** nothing; (adv.) not at all

**nihilum, -ī (n.):** nothing; ablative of degree of difference: **nihilō:** by nothing, not at all

**nimis (adv.):** too much, excessively

**nimium (adv.):** too much

**nisi:** if ... not; unless; except

**nix, nivis (f.):** snow

**nomen, -inis (n.):** name

**nōminō, -āre, -āvī, -ātum:** to name, accuse

**nōn (adv.):** not; **nōn sōlum:** not only

**nōndum (adv.):** not yet

**nōnus, -a, -um:** ninth

**nōs (pers. pron.):** we; nominative or accusative plural

**noscitō, -āre, -āvī, -ātum:** to identify, recognize

**noscō, -ere, nōvī, nōtum:** present tense: to learn (about); perfect tense: to have learned (about) and therefore: to know

**noster, -tra, -trum (poss. adj.):** our, our friend; my (= **meus**)

**nota, -ae (f.):** sign, indication

**notābilis, -e:** conspicuous, attracting attention; remarkable, noteworthy

**notārius, -ī (m.):** secretary, shorthand writer

**novem (indecl.):** nine

**novus, -a, -um:** new; recent. The superlative, **novissimus**, can mean *most recent* in the sense of *last, final*.

**nox, noctis (f.):** night

**nūbēs, -is (f.):** cloud

**nūbilus, -a, -um:** cloudy

**nullus, -a, -um:** no, not any

**nūmen, -inis (n.):** divinity, god

**numerus, -ī (m.):** number

**numquam (adv.):** never

**nunc (adv.):** now

**nuntiō, -āre, -āvī, -ātum:** to report, announce

**nuntius, -ī (m.):** messenger

**nūper (adv.):** recently, not long ago

**nuptiae, -ārum (f. pl.):** nuptials, wedding

**nusquam:** nowhere

**nūtō, -āre, -āvī, -ātum:** to sway, totter

**nutrix, -īcis (f.):** nurse, nanny

## O

**ō (interjection):** oh! For the exclamation, compare **heus**.

**ob:** (+ acc.) on account of, because of

**obdūcō, -ere, -duxī, -ductum:** to cover

**obeō, -īre, -īvī, -itum:** to take on, carry out

**oblīdō, -ere, -sī, -sum:** to compress, crush

**obnoxius, -a, -um:** (+ dat.) subject to, exposed to

**obscūrus, -a, -um:** obscure, unknown

**obsequium, -ī (n.):** compliance, obedience

**obsequor, -ī, -cūtus sum (dep. verb):** (+ dat.) to obey

**obstinātiō, -ōnis (f.):** obstinacy

**obstō, -stāre, -stitī:** to stand in the way, block

**obstringō, -ere, -strinxī, -strinctum:** to bind

**obstruō, -ere, -uxī, -uctum:** to block, impede

**obterō, -ere, -trīvī, -trītum:** to trample

**obversor, -ārī, -ātus sum (dep. verb):** (+ dat.) to hover

**occĭdō, -ere, -ĭdī:** to fall, perish

**occīdō, -ere, -īdī, -īsum:** to kill

**occupātiō, -ōnis (f.):** professional duty; activity

**occurrō, -ere, -currī, -cursum:** to meet, resist, prevent; to arrive

**occursō, -āre, -āvī, -ātum:** (+ dat.) to meet

**October, -bris, -bre:** belonging to the month of October

**oculus, -ī (m.):** eye

**odor, -ōris (m.):** perfume; smell, odor

**offensa, -ae (f.):** displeasure, annoyance

**officium, -ī (n.):** service, good deed

**ōlim (adv.):** for some time; in earlier times

**olīva, -ae (f.):** olive

**ōminor, -ārī, ominātus sum (dep. verb):** to predict

**ōminōsus, -a, -um:** ominous

**omittō, -ere, -mīsī, -missum:** to omit, leave out, leave aside

**omnīnō (adv.):** totally, completely; to be sure, certainly

**omnis, -e:** all; every

**opera, -ae (f.):** effort; **operam dare:** (+ dat.) to take care

**operiō, -īre, -uī, -ertum:** to cover, conceal

**opīniō, -ōnis (f.):** opinion, conjecture

**opīnor, -ārī, -ātus sum (dep. verb):** to conjecture, suppose

**oppidum, -ī (n.):** town

**oppleō, -ēre, -ēvī, -ētum:** to fill

**opportūnē (adv.):** opportunely

**opportūnus, -a, -um:** opportune, useful, welcome

**optimus, -a, -um:** excellent, best; superlative of **bonus**

**opus, -eris (n.):** work; literary composition; public building; activity, pastime

**opus est (impers. verb):** there is need; used with ablative of thing needed and dative of person needing

**opusculum, -ī (n.):** little, small work

**ōra, -ae (f.):** shore

**ōrārius, -a, -um:** coastal

**ōrātiō, -ōnis (f.):** speech, oration

**orbitās, -ātis (f.):** loss, bereavement

**ōrdō, -dinis (m.):** order, sequence; rank, social class

**orior, orīrī, ortus sum (dep. verb):** to rise

**ornō, -āre, -āvī, -ātum:** to praise, honor

**orō, -āre, -āvī, -ātum:** ask, beg

**ōs, ōris (n.):** mouth, face

**ostendō, -ere, -tendī, -tentum:** to show, make known

**ostentō, -āre, -āvī, -ātum:** to display, hold out as a model

**ostreum, -ī (n.):** oyster

**ōtiōsus, -a, -um:** idle

**ōtium, -ī (n.):** leisure, idle time

**ōvum, -ī (n.):** egg

### P

**paedagōgus, -ī (m.):** attendant for a child

**paene (adv.):** almost

**paenitentia, -ae (f.):** repentance

**paenitet (impers. verb):** it grieves, makes sorry; uses the accusative of the person regretting and genitive of the thing regretted

**palma, -ae (f.):** palm of the hand

**pānārium, -ī (n.):** food basket

**pannus, -ī (m.):** a piece of cloth

**pār, paris:** equal, corresponding

**parcē (adv.):** sparingly

**parens, -tis (m. and f.):** parent

**pareō, -ēre, -uī:** to obey

**pariēs, -etis (m.):** wall

**pariter (adv.):** at the same time, equally

**parō, -āre, -āvī, -ātum:** to
prepare, furnish; to buy

**pars, -tis (f.):** part; division,
faction; direction

**parum:** too little, not sufficiently

**passim (adv.):** everywhere, far
and wide

**pater, patris (m.):** father

**paternus, -a, -um:** paternal, of
one's father

**patientia, -ae (f.):** patience,
endurance

**patior, -ī, passus sum (dep. verb):**
to suffer, endure; to allow; to
experience

**patria, -ae (f.):** native land,
homeland

**pauculus, -a, -um:** a very few

**paucus, -a, -um:** few

**paulātim (adv.):** gradually, little
by little

**paulō (adv.):** a little, somewhat

**paulum, -ī (n.):** a little bit, slightly;
a little while. It is used in the
accusative as an adverb (an
adverbial accusative) to express
length of time or to define an
amount or degree.

**pavīmentum, -ī (n.):** floor

**pavor, -ōris (m.):** dread, fear

**pectus, -oris (n.):** chest

**pecūnia, -ae (f.):** money;
**pecūniae (pl.):** sums of money

**per:** (+ acc.) on account of; within,
in the course of; at

**peragō, -ere, -ēgī, -actum:** to
accomplish, achieve

**percutiō, -ere, -cussī, -cussum:**
to strike, hit

**perdō, -ere, -didī, -ditum:** to
lose; to squander

**peregrē (adv.):** away from home

**pereō, -īre, -iī, -itum:** to perish,
disappear, melt; to die; to be
lost

**perferō, -ferre, -tulī, -lātum:** to
endure, suffer

**perfodiō, -ere, -fōdī, -fossum:** to
pierce

**pergō, -ere, perrexī, perrectum:**
to undertake, endeavor,
attempt

**perīclitor, -ārī, perīclitātus sum
(dep. verb):** to be in danger, at
risk

**perīculōsus, -a, -um:** dangerous,
perilous

**perīculum, -ī (n.):** danger

**perimō, -ere, -ēmī, -emptum:** to
destroy, kill

**permaneō, -ēre, -mansī,
-mansum:** to remain, persist

**permittō, -ere, -mīsī, -missum:**
to permit, allow

**perpetuitās, -ātis (f.):** perpetuity,
immortality, permanence

**perpetuus, -a, -um:** permanent,
lasting

**persaepe (adv.):** very often

**persequor, -sequī, -secūtus sum
(dep. verb):** to record,
describe

**persevērō, -āre, -āvī, -ātum:** to
remain, persist

**perstō, -stāre, -stitī:** to stand
around

**pertinācia, -ae (f.):** stubbornness

**pertineō, -ēre, -tinuī:** to pertain

pervagor, -ārī, -vagātus sum
(dep. verb): (+ acc.) to spread
to, extend to

perveniō, -īre, -vēnī, -ventum:
to reach, arrive

pervigilō, -āre, -āvī, -ātum: to
remain awake

pēs, pedis (m.): foot

pessimus, -a, -um: worst;
superlative of malus, -a, -um

petō, -ere, -īvī, -ītum: to seek,
ask, request; head for, go to

philosophus, -ī (m.):
philosopher

pietās, -ātis (f.): family devotion

pīnus, -ī (f.): pine tree

piscātōrius, -a, -um: for fishing,
belonging to fishermen

placeō, -ēre, -uī: to please, be
pleasing. The person who is
pleased is put in the dative case.
When used reflexively, it can
mean *to flatter oneself*; when
used impersonally, *to seem good,
to be resolved.*

plānē (adv.): clearly, plainly,
certainly

plānus, -a, -um: flat, level

plēnus, -a, -um: full

plērīque, -aeque, -aque (pl.):
very many

plērumque (adv.): mostly,
generally

plūrimus, -a, -um: very many,
very much; superlative of
multus. The accusative neuter
singular, plūrimum, may be
used as an adverb (an adverbial
accusative).

plūs, plūris (comparative degree
of multus): more; plūrēs,
plūra (pl.): several; more

poena, -ae (f.): penalty,
punishment

polliceor, -ērī, pollicitus sum
(dep. verb): to offer, promise

polluō, -ere, -uī, -ūtum: defile,
pollute

pondus, -eris (n.): weight

pontifex, -icis (m.): priest

pontifex maximus, pontificis
maximī (m.): the highest
priest, the head of the Roman
religious clergy

populus, -ī (m.): people

porrigō, -ere, -rexī, -rectum: to
stretch out, hold out

poscō, -ere, poposcī: to demand,
request

possideō, -ēre, -sēdī, -sessum:
to own

possum, posse, potuī: to be able

post: (+ acc.) after; as an adverb:
afterward, subsequently

posteā (adv.): after that,
afterward

posterus, -a, -um: following,
future; posterī, -ōrum (pl.):
descendants, posterity

postquam (temp. conj.): after

postrēmō (adv.): finally, in the
end

potissimus, -a, -um: principal,
most important; potissimum
(adv.): especially

potius (adv.): more, preferably,
rather

pōtus, -ūs (m.): drink

**praecēdō, -ere, -cessī, -cessum:** to precede, come before

**praeceptor, -ōris (m.):** teacher

**praeceptum, -ī (n.):** rule, instruction

**praecipiō, -ere, -cēpī, -ceptum:** to give instructions

**praecipuē (adv.):** especially

**praeclārus, -a, -um:** very famous, celebrated

**praecursōrius, -a, -um:** running ahead, sent in advance

**praedicātiō, -ōnis (f.):** praise

**praedicō, -āre, -āvī, -ātum:** to proclaim, declare publicly

**praedium, -ī (n.):** estate, property

**praeeō, -īre, -īvī:** to lead the way

**praefectus, -ī (m.):** a Roman administrative official who had been appointed to his position by the emperor, rather than elected

**praeferō, -ferre, -tulī, -lātum:** to prefer

**praefīniō, -īre, -īvī, -ītum:** to determine beforehand, appoint

**praegnans, -ntis:** pregnant

**praemium, -ī (n.):** prize, reward

**praenuntius, -ī (m.):** harbinger, precursor

**praesens, -entis:** being present, in person

**praesentia, -ium (n. pl.):** present time, circumstances

**praesertim (adv.):** especially

**praestō, -stāre, -stitī, -stitum:** to furnish, be responsible for; to give, offer

**praeter:** (+ acc.) except

**praetereā (adv.):** besides, beyond this; moreover

**praeteritus, -a, -um:** gone by, past. The neuter accusative singular may be used as a substantive: the past.

**praetextātus, -a, -um:** wearing a **toga praetexta**

**praetor, -ōris (m.):** a high-ranking Roman magistrate whose duties were mainly judicial

**praetōrius, -a, -um:** of praetorian rank, an ex-praetor

**praevaleō, -ēre, -uī:** to be stronger, prevail

**prāvus, -a, -um:** perverse

**precor, -ārī, -ātus sum (dep. verb):** to pray for

**premō, -ere, pressī, pressum:** to press

**prīmum (adv.):** first

**prīmus, -a, -um:** first

**princeps, -cipis (m.):** the **princeps**, the emperor

**priōrēs, -um (m. pl.):** those prior to us, our forefathers, ancestors

**prius (adv.):** first, before then

**prīvātus, -ī (m.):** a private individual

**prō:** (+ abl.) on behalf of, for the benefit of; according to, in accordance with

**probātus, -a, -um:** excellent

**prōcēdō, -ere, -cessī -cessum:** to advance, go forward

**procul (adv.):** from afar

**prōcurrō, -ere, -(cu)currī, -cursum:** to project, jut out prōdūcō, -ere, -duxī, -ductum: to bring out

proficiscor, -ī, -fectus sum (dep. verb): to set out, depart, travel

profiteor, -ērī, -fessus sum (dep. verb): to declare publicly; to offer, volunteer

proinde (adv.): therefore

prōmiscuus, -a, -um: common, ordinary

prōmittō, -ere, -mīsī, -missum: to promise

pronepōs, -ōtis (m.): great-grandchild

prōnus, -a, -um: sloping downward, easy

prope (adv.): almost

properō, -āre, -āvī, -ātum: to hurry, hasten

propius (adv.): more closely; the comparative form of prope

prōpōnō, -ere, -posuī, -positum: to promise; to publish, circulate

propter: (+ acc.) on account of, because of

prōripiō, -ere, -ripuī, -reptum: to snatch; sē prōripere: to snatch oneself, hurry away

prōrumpō, -ere, -rūpī, -ruptum: to burst forth

prōsequor, -ī, -secūtus sum (dep. verb): to accompany

prosocer, -cerī (m.): the grandfather of a spouse

prosperē (adv.): favorably, happily

prōsum, prōdesse, prōfuī: (+ dat.) to be of use, to benefit

prout: according to whether, depending on whether

prōvincia, -ae (f.): an area incorporated into the Roman Empire

proximē (adv.): very recently

proximus, -a, -um: nearest, very near

prūdens, -entis: wise, discreet

prūdentia, -ae (f.): wisdom, judgment

Prūsēnsēs, -ium (m. and f. pl.): residents of Prusa

publicē (adv.): publicly, with community funds

publicō, -āre, -āvī, -ātum: to publish, make public; to confiscate (for the public treasury)

publicus, -a, -um: public

pudīcus, -a, -um: virtuous

puella, -ae (f.): girl

puellāris, -e: girlish

puellāriter (adv.): girlishly, not as an adult

puer, -ī (m.): boy

pueriliter (adv.): childishly

pueritia, -ae (f.): boyhood, childhood

pugillārēs, -ium (m. pl.): writing tablets

pūgiō, -ōnis (m.): dagger, blade

pulcher, -chra, -chrum: beautiful; fine, honorable

pulchritūdō, -inis (f.): beauty, good looks

pūmex, -icis (m.): pumice stone

pūniō, -īre, -īvī, -ītum: to punish

pūrus, -a, -um: pure

putō, -āre, -āvī, -ātum: to think; to consider

# Q

**quadrirēmis, -is (f.):** a large ship
with four banks of oars

**quaerō, -ere, -sīvī, -sītum:**
to inquire, ask; to examine
judicially

**quaestor, -ōris (m.):** a Roman
magistrate who was a financial
and administrative assistant to
a higher-ranking magistrate

**quālis, -e:** such as, of the kind;
**tālis ... quālis:** such ... as

**quāliscumque, quālecumque:**
whatever

**quam (exclam.):** how

**quam (relat.):** than; **magis ...
quam:** more than; **tam ...
quam:** as ... as. **Quam** with a
superlative, for example, **quam
cārissimum** = as dear as
possible.

**quamlibet (adv.):** however much,
however

**quamquam (conj.):** although

**quamvīs (conj. + subj.):** although

**quandō (adv.):** ever

**quandōque (adv.):** at some time

**quantulus, -a, -um:** how little,
how small

**quantus, -a, -um:** how much,
how great. The word can be
interrogatory or exclamatory.

**quārē (interr. adv.):** why?

**quartus, -a, -um:** fourth

**quasi:** as it were, as if; already

**quātenus (adv.):** to what extent

**quatiō, -ere, —, quassum:** to
shake (This verb does not have
perfect active forms.)

**quattuordecim:** fourteen

**-que:** and; an enclitic particle
attached to the end of a word

**quem ad modum (=
quemadmodum):** in what
manner, how?

**querella, -ae (f.):** complaint

**queror, -ī, questus sum (dep.
verb):** to complain

**quī, qua, quod (indef. adj.):**
some, any

**quī, quae, quod (rel. pron.):** who,
which

**quī, quae, quod (interr. adj.):**
what?, what kind of?

**quia (conj. + indic.):** because

**quīcumque, quaecumque,
quodcumque:** whoever,
whatever, whichever

**quīdam, quaedam, quiddam:**
certain, a certain one; so to
speak; some

**quidem (adv.):** indeed, certainly;
**nē ... quidem:** not even

**quiēs, -ētis (f.):** tranquillity,
restfulness

**quiescō, -ere, -ēvī, -ētum:** to rest,
sleep; remain motionless

**quīn etiam:** yes even, also,
moreover

**quīn immō:** yes indeed, and in fact

**quintus, -a, -um:** fifth

**quirītātus, -ūs (m.):** scream, wail

**quis, quid (interr. pron.):** who?,
what?; for what reason? why?

**quis, quid (indef. pron.):**
anything, something; used
instead of **aliquis, aliquid** after
the conjunctions **sī, nisi,** and **nē.**

**quisquam, quidquam:** anyone

**quisque, quaeque, quidque:** each one

**quisquis, quidquid:** whoever, whatever. Both parts of this word are declined.

**quō (adv.):** to which place

**quō:** wherefore, for which reason; for this reason; introducing a purpose or result clause that contains a comparative degree adjective or adverb; **quō ... eō** (or **hōc**): by what amount ... by this amount; the more ... the more

**quō minus** (= **quōminus**): that ... not

**quod (conj.):** because; that; as to the fact that

**quoque (adv.):** also

**quot (indecl.):** how many

**quotiens (adv.):** as often as

## R

**rāmus, -ī (m.):** branch

**rārō (adv.):** rarely

**rārus, -a, -um:** infrequent, sparse

**ratiō, -ōnis (f.):** reckoning, consideration; rational consideration; rational explanation

**recēdō, -ere, -cessī, -cessum:** to withdraw, retreat

**recens, -entis:** recent, fresh, newly formed, sudden

**recipiō, -ere, -cēpī, -ceptum:** to admit, accept

**recitō, -āre, -āvī, -ātum:** to read aloud

**recolligō, -ere, -lēgī, -lectum:** to gather up again

**recordor, -ārī, -ātus sum (dep. verb):** to remember, call to mind

**recreō, -āre, -āvī, -ātum:** restore, revive

**rectē (adv.):** correctly

**rectus, -a, -um:** straight

**recubō, -āre:** to lie (This verb does not have a perfect system.)

**reddō, -ere, reddidī, redditum:** to repay, pay as a debt; to return; to restore; to give

**redeō, -īre, -īvī, -itum:** to return, go back

**reditus, -ūs (m.):** income, revenue

**redormiō, -īre, -īvī:** to go back to sleep

**referō, -ferre, rettulī, -lātum:** to relate, tell; give back, reproduce, mirror; to bring back

**reficiō, -ere, -fēcī, -fectum:** to revive, refresh

**reformīdō, -āre, -āvī, -ātum:** to shrink from, dread

**refugiō, -ere, -fūgī, -fugitum:** to flee, run from

**Regia, -ae (f.):** the office of the Pontifex Maximus in the Roman Forum

**regiō, -ōnis (f.):** region

**regō, -ere, rēxī, rectum:** to command; to guide, direct

**regredior, -ī, -gressus sum (dep. verb):** to return

**rēiciō, -ere, -iēcī, -iectum:** to refuse, reject

**relēgō, -āre, -āvī, -ātum:** to banish, send into exile

**religiō, -ōnis (f.):** scrupulousness

**relinquō, -ere, -līquī, -lictum:** to leave behind, abandon, desert; to bequeath

**reliquus, -a, -um:** remaining; as a neuter plural substantive, **reliqua:** the things remaining

**relūceō, -ere, -lūxī:** to shine back, blaze

**relūcescō, -ere, -lūxī:** to become bright again

**remaneō, -ēre, -mansī, -mansum:** to stay behind

**remedium, -ī (n.):** remedy

**remissus, -a, -um:** indulgent, gentle

**remittō, -ere, -mīsī, -missum:** to send, remand

**repellō, -ere, reppulī, repulsum:** to drive back

**repente (adv.):** suddenly

**reperiō, -īre, repperī, repertum:** to find

**repetō, -ere, -īvī, -ītum:** to trace, recount; to seek again

**reportō, -āre, -āvī, -ātum:** to bring back, carry home

**repraesentō, -āre, -āvī, -ātum:** to show, display

**reprehendō, -ere, -endī, -ensum:** to censure, reprove

**requiēs, -ētis (f.):** rest, respite

**requīrō, -ere, -quīsīvī, -quīsītum:** to search for; to request, seek

**rēs, rēī (f.):** thing, matter, affair; **rē vērā:** truly

**rēs publica, rēī publicae (f.):** state, community; commonwealth, state; city, town

**rescindō, -ere, -scidī, -scissum:** to tear open again

**residō, -ere, -sēdī, -sessum:** to settle down, abate; to sit down

**resiliō, -īre, resiluī:** to shrink from

**resistō, -ere, -stitī:** to resist

**resorbeō, -ēre:** to suck back

**respiciō, -ere, -spexī, -spectum:** to look back

**respondeō, -dēre, -dī, -sum:** to reply

**resūmō, -ere, -mpsī, -mptum:** to resume, take up again

**rēte, -is (n.):** hunting net

**retineō, -ēre, -tinuī, -tentum:** to detain

**retrō (adv.):** back

**reus, -ī (m.):** a defendant in a criminal trial

**reverentia, -ae (f.):** respect

**revertor, -vertī, -versus sum (dep. verb):** to turn back, return

**revocō, -āre, -āvī, -ātum:** to recall, call back

**rideō, -ēre, rīsī, rīsum:** to laugh

**rōbustus, -a, -um:** strong, mature

**rogō, -āre, -āvī, -ātum:** to ask, ask for, request

**Rōmānus, -a, -um:** Roman

**ruīna, -ae (f.):** collapse, debris

**rumpō, -ere, rūpī, ruptum:** to break, tear

**ruō, ruere, ruī, rutum:** to fall, fall down, collapse

**rursus (adv.):** again

## S

**S.:** The abbreviation **S.** when used in the salutation of a letter stands for **salūtem dat.**

**sacrāmentum, -ī (n.):** oath

**sacrum, -ī (n.):** sacred rite

**saeculum, -ī (n.):** century; period of rule, time period

**saepe (adv.):** often

**saevus, -a, -um:** cruel

**salūbris, -e:** healthy

**salūs, -ūtis (f.):** well-being, health; greeting, salutation; **salūtem dat:** (he) gives greeting, (he) greets. Pliny uses this form of salutation for all the letters of Books 1 to 9.

**salūtō, -āre, -āvī, -ātum:** to greet, pay respects

**salvus, -a, -um:** safe

**sanctitās, -ātis (f.):** purity, sanctity

**sanctus, -a, -um:** pure, innocent

**sapiens, -entis:** (as an adjective) wise; (as a substantive) wise man, philosopher

**sapiō, -īre, -iī:** to understand; to know; to be wise

**sarcina, -ae (f.):** load, baggage

**satietās, -ātis (f.):** sufficiency, satiety

**satiō, -āre, -āvī, -ātum:** to fill, satisfy

**satis:** as a substantive, enough; often followed by a partitive genitive; adverbial: sufficiently, well enough; comparative **satius:** better, preferable

**scelus, -eris (n.):** wickedness

**scīlicet (adv.):** of course, certainly

**sciō, scīre, scīvī, scītum:** to know

**scrībō, -ere, scrīpsī, scriptum:** to write

**scrīnium, -ī (n.):** writing box, cylindrical box in which papyrus rolls were kept

**scriptum, -ī (n.):** something written, literary composition

**sē (reflex. pron.):** himself, herself, itself, themselves

**sēcessus, -ūs (m.):** seclusion, solitude

**secundum:** (+ acc.) in accordance with

**secundus, -a, -um:** following, favorable

**sēcūritās, -ātis (f.):** confidence, composure

**sēcūrus, -a, -um:** safe, secure; free of anxiety

**sed (conj.):** but

**sedeō, -ēre, sēdī, sessum:** to sit

**sēdēs, -is (f.):** foundation

**sēdulō (adv.):** diligently

**segnis, -e:** lazy, unfocused, inattentive

**semel (adv.):** once; **semel atque iterum:** again and again

**semper (adv.):** always

**senātus, -ūs (m.):** Senate. For **senātūs consultum**, see **consultum.**

**senectūs, -ūtis (f.):** old age

**senescō, -ere, senuī:** to grow old, decay; to decrease in strength

**sensim (adv.):** gradually, gently

**sentiō, -īre, sensī, sensum:** to feel, to be conscious; to be aware

**septem (indecl.):** seven
**September, -bris, -bre:** belonging
   to the month of September
**septimus, -a, -um:** seventh
**sequor, sequī, secūtus sum (dep.
   verb):** to follow, accompany
**sēriō (adv.):** seriously, in earnest
**sermō, -ōnis (m.):** conversation,
   communication
**serviō, -īre, -īvī, -ītum:** to be a
   slave
**servō, -āre, -āvī, -ātum:** to
   preserve, maintain, save
**servulus, -ī (m.):** diminutive of
   **servus:** little slave, young slave
**servus, -ī (m.):** slave
**seu (conj.):** or
**sevēritās, -ātis (f.):** severity,
   strictness
**sexus, -ūs (m.):** sex, sexual identity
**sī (conj.):** if
**sīc (adv.):** thus, so
**siccus, -a, -um:** dry
**sīcut (adv.):** as it were
**silentium, -ī (n.):** silence
**silva, -ae (f.):** woodland, forest
**similis, -e:** (+ dat.) similar;
   resembling
**similitūdō, -inis (f.):** likeness,
   resemblance
**simplex, -icis:** sincere, artless,
   guileless
**simul (adv.):** at the same time;
   together
**simulācrum, -ī (n.):** image, statue
**simulō, -āre, -āvī, -ātum:** to
   pretend, feign
**sincēritās, -ātis (f.):** integrity
**sine:** (+ abl.) without

**singulāris, -e:** exceptional, unique
**singulī, -ae, -a (pl.):** one each;
   one at a time
**sinus, -ūs (m.):** bay (of a body of
   water); lap, embrace
**sīpō, -ōnis (m.):** a siphoning tube
   or pump to draw up water
**sistō, -ere, stitī, statum:** to make
   stand; to stop, check
**sīve ... sīve:** whether ... or
**socer (= socerus), -ī (m.):**
   father-in-law
**sōl, sōlis (m.):** sun
**sōlācium, -ī (n.):** consolation,
   comfort, solace
**solea, -ae (f.):** sandal
**soleō, -ēre, solitus sum (semi-
   dep. verb):** to be accustomed
**sōlitūdō, -inis (f.):** solitude;
   wilderness
**solitus, -a, -um:** usual, common,
   frequent
**sollemnis, -e:** customary
**sollicitō, -āre, -āvī, -ātum:** to
   attract
**sollicitūdō, -inis (f.):** anxiety,
   concern
**sōlor, -ārī, -ātus sum (dep.
   verb):** to comfort, relieve,
   lessen
**solum, -ī (n.):** soil, land
**sōlus, -a, -um:** single, one; alone;
   **nōn sōlum:** not only
**solvō, -ere, solvī, solūtum:** to
   loosen, untie; to free; to pay (a
   debt), pay back
**somnus, -ī (m.):** sleep
**sonans, -tis:** noisy, loud
**sordidus, -a, -um:** dirty

**soror, -ōris (f.):** sister

**spargō, -ere, -rsī, -rsum:** to scatter, spread

**spatium, -ī (n.):** space, extent, length

**speciēs, -ēī (f.):** appearance, form

**specimen, -inis (n.):** proof, evidence

**spectāculum, -ī (n.):** show, spectacle

**spectātor, -ōris (m.):** spectator

**spectō, -āre, -āvī, -ātum:** to look at, watch, see

**spērō, -āre, -āvī, -ātum:** to hope, expect

**spēs, -ēī (f.):** hope

**spīritus, -ūs (m.):** blast of air; breath, breathing; spirit

**sponte (adv.):** of one's own accord, voluntarily

**statim (adv.):** immediately

**sternō, -ere, strāvī, strātum:** to throw down, knock down

**stilus, -ī (m.):** an instrument for writing

**stō, stāre, stetī:** to stand

**stola, -ae (f.):** female garment, dress

**stomachus, -ī (m.):** windpipe, trachea; esophagus; digestive system

**stringō, -ere, strinxī, strictum:** to draw out, pull out

**studeō, -ēre, -uī:** to pursue, be busy with, apply oneself to; to learn; to study, be a student

**studiōsē (adv.):** studiously, diligently

**studiōsus, -ī (m.):** (as a substantive) studious person, student; (as an adjective) studious, scholarly

**studium , -ī (n.):** study, literary pursuit; enthusiasm

**suādeō, -ēre, suāsī, suāsum:** to persuade, recommend

**suāvitās, -ātis (f.):** sweetness, charm

**sub:** (+ abl.) under

**subiaceō, -ēre, -uī:** (+ dat.) to lie below

**subitus, -a, -um:** sudden

**subiungō, -ere, -iunxī, -iunctum:** to add, to join

**subsequor, -ī, -secūtus sum (dep. verb):** to follow

**subsistō, -ere, -stitī:** to remain, stay, stop, halt

**subterrāneus, -a, -um:** underground

**suburbānum, -ī (n.):** in an area just outside Rome, in the suburbs

**subveniō, -īre, -vēnī, -ventum:** (+ dat.) to assist, help

**succurrō, -ere -currī, -cursum:** to occur to, come into one's mind

**sufficiō, -ere, -fēcī, -fectum:** to be sufficient, adequate

**sulpur, -uris (n.):** sulfur

**sum, esse, fuī, futūrus:** to be

**summa, -ae (f.):** sum

**summoveō, -ēre, -mōvī, -mōtum:** to remove, expel, banish

**summus, -a, -um:** highest, extreme, very high, very great

**sumō, -ere, sumpsī, sumptum:** to take; to take on, assume

**sumptuōsus, -a, -um:** extravagant

**sumptus, -ūs (m.):** expense

**super:** (+ acc.) on

**superbus, -a, -um:** arrogant

**superstes, -stitis:** surviving

**superstitiō, -ōnis (f.):** superstition

**supersum, -esse, -fuī, -futūrus:** to remain, be left

**supplicium, -ī (n.):** punishment, execution

**supplicō, -āre, -āvī, -ātum:** (+ dat.) to kneel down before, pray to

**supprimō, -ere, -pressī, -pressum:** to suppress

**suprā (adv.):** over, from on high

**suprā:** (+ acc.) above, beyond, more than

**surgō, -ere, surrexī, surrectum:** to rise up

**suscipiō, -ere, -cēpī, -ceptum:** to undertake

**suspensus, -a, -um:** uncertain, suspenseful, anxious

**suspiciō, -ere, -exī, -ectum:** to look up to, admire; to suspect

**sustineō, -ēre, -nuī:** to sustain, maintain

**suus, -a, -um (poss. adj.):** his, her, its, their; *in salutations:* his dear friend

**T**

**tālis, -e:** such; **tālis ... quālis:** such ... as

**tam (adv.):** so, to such a degree; **tam ... quam:** as ... as; so much ... as

**tamen (adv.):** nevertheless

**tamquam (conj.):** as if, as though

**tandem (adv.):** finally, at last

**tangō, -ere, tetigī, tactum:** to touch

**tantum (adv.):** only; **nec tantum ... sed etiam:** not only ... but also

**tantus, -a, -um:** so much, so great

**tantus ... quantus:** as much as, as great as

**tardus, -a, -um:** late

**tē (pers. pron.):** you; accusative or ablative singular case of **tū**

**tectum, -ī (n.):** roof; house. The plural **tecta** sometimes means just one house.

**temperantia, -ae (f.):** restraint

**tempestās, -ātis (f.):** storm

**templum, -ī (n.):** temple

**tempus, -oris (n.):** time; temporal opportunity; **medium tempus:** intervening time

**tendō, -ere, tetendī, tentum:** to stretch out

**tenebrae, -ārum (f. pl.):** darkness

**teneō, -ēre, tenuī, tentum:** to hold, maintain, preserve

**tener, -era, -erum:** young, tender

**tenuō, -āre, -āvī, -ātum:** to diminish; passive: to become less dense

**tergum, -ī (n.):** back

**ternī, -ae, -a (pl.):** three each

**terra, -ae (f.):** land, region; earth, soil

**terrificus, -a, -um:** frightful, alarming

**terror, -ōris (m.):** terror
**tertiō (adv.):** third time
**tertius, -a, -um:** third
**testāmentum, -ī (n.):** will (legal
  document)
**tibi (pers. pron.):** you; dative case
  of **tū**
**timeō, -ēre, timuī:** to fear
**timor, -ōris (m.):** fear,
  apprehension
**tollō, -ere, sustulī, sublātum:** to
  raise, take up
**tormentum, -ī (n.):** torment;
  torture
**torqueō, -ēre, torsī, tortum:** to
  torture
**torrens, -entis (m.):** torrent, flood
**tortus, -a, -um:** twisted
**tot (indecl.):** so many
**tōtus, -a, -um:** all; as a substantive:
  **tōtum, -ī (n.):** the whole
**tractātus, -ūs (m.):** process,
  procedure
**tractō, -āre, -āvī, -ātum:** to treat
**trādō, -ere, -didī, -ditum:**
  transmit, hand down
**trahō, -ere, traxī, tractum:** to
  pull, drag; to attract, draw
**transeō, -īre, -īvī, -itum:** to pass,
  cross over
**transferō, -ferre, -tulī, -lātum:** to
  transfer, move
**transitus, -ūs (m.):** passage
**transmittō, -ere, -mīsī, -missum:**
  to experience; to spend (time)
**Transpadānus, -a, -um:**
  Transpadane, on or from the
  other side (north) of the Po
  (Padus) River

**tremor, -ōris (m.):** tremor, shock;
  trembling
**trepidātiō, -ōnis (f.):** panic, fear
**trepidō, -āre, -āvī, -ātum:** to
  tremble, be agitated; to be
  confused
**trēs, tria:** three
**tribūnus, -ī (m.):** a person holding
  a public office or performing
  official duties
**tribūnus mīlitum:** military
  tribune; a young man posted
  with a Roman army unit as an
  assistant to the commander
**tribūnus plēbis:** plebeian tribune.
  This position, with a term of
  one year, originated in the very
  early republican period as a
  protector of the interests of
  the plebeians. In the imperial
  period, its powers became very
  limited.
**tribuō, -ere, -uī, -ūtum:** to
  attribute, yield, grant, concede.
  The verb can take both a direct
  (accusative) and indirect
  (dative) object.
**triennium, -ī (n.):** three years, a
  period of three years
**trīgintā (indecl.):** thirty
**tristis, -e:** sad
**triumphō, -āre, -āvī, -ātum:** to
  celebrate a triumph
**truncus, -ī (m.):** trunk of a tree
**tū (pers. pron.):** you; accusative
  and ablative cases are **tē**
**tum (adv.):** then
**tunc (adv.):** at that time, then
**tunica, -ae (f.):** tunic

**turba, -ae (f.):** crowd, mob

**tūs, tūris (n.):** incense

**Tusculānus, -a, -um:** Tusculan; of the area near the town of Tusculum, about sixteen miles southeast of Rome in the Alban Hills

**Tuscus, -a, -um:** Tuscan, of Tuscany (Etruria)

**tussis, -is (f.):** cough

**tūtus, -a, -um:** safe

**tuus, -a, -um (poss. adj.):** your (singular)

**tyrannus, -ī (m.):** tyrant

### U

**ubī (interr. adv.):** where?

**ubī (conj. + indic.):** when

**ulciscor, ulciscī, ultus sum (dep. verb):** to punish, avenge

**ullus, -a, -um:** any

**ultiō, -ōnis (f.):** revenge

**ultor, -ōris (m.):** avenger

**ultrā (adv.):** further

**ultrō (adv.):** of its own accord, voluntarily

**ululātus, -ūs (m.):** wailing

**umquam (adv.):** ever, at any time

**ūnā (adv.):** along, alongside; together

**unde:** from which, from where, whence

**undique (adv.):** on all sides, everywhere

**ungō, -ere, unxī, unctum:** to apply oil

**unguentum, -ī (n.):** scented oil

**ūniversus, -a, -um:** whole, entire

**ūnus, -a, -um:** one

**urbānus, -a, -um:** urban; refined

**urbs, urbis (f.):** city

**usquam (adv.):** anywhere

**usque:** (+ **ad** + acc.) right up to

**ut (correlative):** just as, like

**ut (conj. with subj.):** that, so that, in order that; how

**ut (conj. with indic.):** as; when

**ut (exclam. adv.):** how

**ut ... ita:** certainly, indeed ... but, although

**ut quī:** inasmuch as he, as being one who, because. In this type of relative causal clause, **ut quī** requires the subjunctive mood.

**ut ... sīc:** not only ... but even; even as ... so also; while ... yet

**utcumque (adv.):** as best we could

**uter, utra, utrum:** which of the two

**uterque, utraque, utrumque:** each (of two); both

**utinam:** would that; introduces an optative subjunctive

**ūtor, ūtī, ūsus sum (dep. verb):** (+ abl.) to use, enjoy; to take advantage of, be mindful of

**uxor, -ōris (f.):** wife

### V

**vacuus, -a, -um:** empty

**vadum, -ī (n.):** shallow water, shoal

**vagor, -ārī, -ātus sum (dep. verb):** to wander

**valeō, -ēre, -uī:** to fare well, be well, be strong

**valētūdō, -inis (f.):** ill health, illness

vanescō, -ere: to fade away

varius, -a, -um: varied, manifold; different

vastus, -a, -um: empty, devastated; rough, wild

vāticinātiō, -ōnis (f.): prediction, prophecy

-ve: or; an enclitic particle attached to the end of a word

vehementer (adv.): exceedingly, strongly

vehiculum, -ī (n.): vehicle, carriage, wagon

vel: or; vel ... vel: either ... or

vēlōcitās, -ātis (f.): speed, swiftness

vēlox, -ōcis: fast, quick

vēlum, -ī (n.): curtain

velut: just as, as if

vēnābulum, -ī (n.): hunting spear

vēnālis, -is (m. and f.): slave

vēnātiō, -ōnis (f.): hunting

vēneō, -īre, -iī, -itum: to be for sale; to be sold

venerandus, -a, -um: worthy of respect, inspiring admiration

veneror, -ārī, -ātus sum (dep. verb): to revere, venerate

venia, -ae (f.): pardon, indulgence

veniō, -īre, vēnī, ventum: to come

vēnor, -ārī, -ātus sum (dep. verb): to hunt

venter, -tris (m.): belly, stomach

ventus, -ī (m.): wind

verberō, -āre, -āvī, -ātum: to beat, strike

verbum, -ī (n.): word

verēcundia, -ae (f.): modesty

verenda, -ōrum (n. pl.): genital area, private parts

vereor, -ērī, veritus sum (dep. verb): to fear; to respect, revere

vēritās, -ātis (f.): honesty

vērō (adv.): certainly, truly; but

Vērōnēnsēs, -ium (m. and f. pl.): the people of the city of Verona

versor, -ārī, -ātus sum (dep. verb): to be engaged; to engage in

versus, -ūs (m.): verse, poetry

vertō, -ere, vertī, versum: to turn; to change; to overturn

vērum, -ī (n.): truth

vērum (adv.): but; vērum etiam: but even

vērus, -a, -um: true, valid; accurate; rē vērā: truly

vespera, -ae (f.): evening

Vestālis (virgō), -is (f.): Vestal Virgin, priestess of Vesta. The Vestalis Maxima was the senior or chief Vestal Virgin.

vester, -tra, -trum (poss. adj.): your (pl.)

vestīgium, -ī (n.): footstep; track; ē vestīgiō: immediately

vestiō, -īre, -īvī, -ītum: to dress

vestis, -is (f.): clothing, clothes

vetō, -āre, vetuī, vetitum: to prohibit, forbid

vexō, -āre, -āvī, -ātum: to trouble, disturb

via, -ae (f.): route, way, road

viāticum, -ī (n.): travel expense

vibrātus, -a, -um: quivering

victima, -ae (f.): sacrificial animal

vīcus, -ī (m.): village

**videō, -ēre, vīdī, vīsum:** to see. The passive voice can mean *to seem,* or *to seem best.*

**vidua, -ae (f.):** widow

**vigeō, -ēre, -uī:** to be strong

**vigil, -ilis:** awake

**vīgintī (indecl.):** twenty

**vigor, -ōris (m.):** vigor, strength

**vīlis, -e:** worthless, cheap

**vīlitās, -ātis (f.):** cheapness, low price

**villa, -ae (f.):** home outside the city; farm

**vincō, -ere, vīcī, victum:** to overcome, overwhelm; to be victorious; to prevail over

**vindicō, -āre, -āvī, -ātum:** to avenge; to claim

**vīnum, -ī (n.):** wine

**violentia, -ae (f.):** force, ferocity

**vir, -ī (m.):** man

**vīrēs, -ium (f. pl.):** See **vīs** below.

**virginālis, -e:** maidenly

**virgō, -inis (f.):** virgin; Vestal Virgin

**virtūs, -ūtis (f.):** virtue

**vīs (abl. vī) (f.):** attack, severity, force. The plural, **vīrēs, -ium (f. pl.),** means bodily strength.

**vīsō, -ere, vīsī:** to see, spend time with

**vīta, -ae (f.):** life

**vitium, -ī (n.):** fault, flaw

**vīvō, -ere, vīxī:** to live, to be alive

**vīvus, -a, -um:** alive

**vix (adv.):** scarcely

**vocō, -āre, -āvī, -ātum:** to call, summon; to invite; to use the word

**volō, velle, voluī:** to wish; to be willing

**voluptās, -ātis (f.):** pleasure

**vōs (pers. pron.):** you; nominative or accusative plural

**vox, vōcis (f.):** voice

**vulgus, -ī (n.):** crowd, mass of people; rabble

**vulnus, -eris (n.):** wound, injury

**vultus, -ūs (m.):** face; appearance, expression

**vulva, -ae (f.):** udder, womb

## X

**xystus, -ī (m.):** a terrace with flower beds

# Index I

## Grammar and Syntax

# Index 2

## Subject Index

Page numbers given in italics indicate that the name or term appears only or primarily in the Latin text.

# Annotated Latin Collection

Read Catullus, Cicero, Horace, and Ovid with these well-annotated texts designed for intermediate to advanced students. With same-page notes and vocabulary, introductory essays on each author and work, full glossaries, and helpful appendices, reading unadapted Latin has never been more rewarding.

## Cicero: *PRO ARCHIA POETA ORATIO*, 3rd Edition
Steven M. Cerutti; Teacher's Guide by Linda A. Fabrizio

*Student Text:* xxxi + 157 pp. (2014) 6" x 9" Paperback, ISBN 978-0-86516-805-3
*Teacher's Guide:* xii + 152 pp. (2014) 6" x 9" Paperback, ISBN 978-0-86516-806-0

## Horace: *Selected ODES and SATIRE 1.9*
## 2nd Edition Revised
Ronnie Ancona

*Student Text:* xxxix + 171 pp., 4 maps (2014, 2nd edition revised)
   6" x 9" Paperback, ISBN 978-0-86516-608-0
*Teacher's Guide:* xiii + 95 pp. (2014) 6" x 9" Paperback, ISBN 978-0-86516-612-7

## Writing Passion, *A Catullus Reader, 2nd Edition*
Ronnie Ancona

*Student Text:* xl + 264 pp. 2 illustrations & 4 maps (2013) 6" x 9" Paperback, ISBN 978-0-86516-786-5
*Teacher's Guide:* xi + 138 pp. (2014) 6" x 9" Paperback, ISBN 978-0-86516-787-2

## Writing Passion Plus
## A Catullus Reader Supplement
Ronnie Ancona

ix + 22 pp. (2013) 6" x 9" Paperback, ISBN 978-0-86516-788-9

## Ovid: *AMORES, METAMORPHOSES Selections*
## 3rd Edition
Phyllis B. Katz and Charbra Adams Jestin

*Student Text:* xxx + 212 pp., 6 maps (2013) 6" x 9" Paperback, ISBN 978-0-86516-784-1
*Teacher's Guide:* xi + 124 pp. (2013) 6" x 9" Paperback, ISBN 978-0-86516-785-8

**BOLCHAZY-CARDUCCI PUBLISHERS, INC.**
**WWW.BOLCHAZY.COM**

# Selections to Fit a Variety of Classrooms

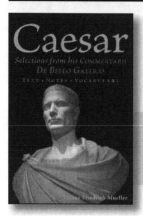

## Caesar
### Selections from his COMMENTARII DE BELLO GALLICO
Hans-Friedrich Mueller

*Student Text:* xli + 372 pp. (2012) 6" x 9"
Paperback, ISBN 978-0-86516-752-0
Hardbound, ISBN 978-0-86516-778-0
*Teacher's Guide:* viii + 283 pp. (2012) 6" x 9"
Paperback, ISBN 978-0-86516-754-4

This intermediate text features the Pharr format of same-page notes and vocabulary and a pullout vocabulary. The introduction provides a lively and in-depth discussion of Caesar's life and an overview of the Roman army. The text (**825 lines**) includes unadapted Latin passages from Caesar's *De Bello Gallico*: Book 1.1–7; Book 4.24–35 and the first sentence of Chapter 36; Book 5.24–48; Book 6.13–20; and the English of Books 1, 6, and 7.

## Vergil's Aeneid
### Selected Readings from Books 1, 2, 4, and 6
Barbara Weiden Boyd

*Student Text:* xxxiv + 164 pp. (2012) 6" x 9"
Paperback, ISBN 978-0-86516-764-3
Hardbound, ISBN 978-0-86516-765-0
*Teacher's Guide:* vi + 93 pp. (2012) 6" x 9"
Paperback, ISBN 978-0-86516-766-7

This Pharr-format text features passages (**844 lines**) including Book 1.1–209, 418–40, 494–578; 2.40–56, 201–49, 268–97, 559–620; 4.160–218, 259–361, 659–705; and 6.295–332, 384–425, 450–76, 847–99.

BOLCHAZY-CARDUCCI PUBLISHERS, INC.
WWW.BOLCHAZY.COM